Acclaim for John McGahern's

ALL WILL BE WELL

"Extraordinary, spellbinding, spiritual."
—*The Irish Independent*

"Magnificent. . . . Stand[s] supreme in the Irish canon."
—Declan Kiberd, *The Irish Times*

"McGahern's writing has endured."   —*Los Angeles Times*

"This book is a story about a lost country, for McGahern's Ireland is not found on a map; and a story about innocence and grace, power and the abuse of power. It illuminates his work—six novels, four story collections—and confirms his status. Simply, McGahern is the best writer; this is his best book."
—*The Sunday Telegraph* (London)

"John McGahern writes with pastoral passion and a painter's eye about the fields, flowers, hedges, waters and gentle sweep of hills in County Leitrim. [He is] a master of contemporary Irish fiction."   —*The New York Times*

"[A] complex and beautiful book."
—*The Sunday Times* (London)

John McGahern

ALL WILL BE WELL

John McGahern wrote six highly acclaimed novels and four collections of short stories and was
the recipient of many awards and honors, including an award from the Society of Authors, the
American Ireland Fund Literary Awards, the Prix
Ecureuil de Littérature Étrangère and the Cheva-
lier de l'Ordre des Arts et des Lettres. *Amongst
Women*, which won both the GPA Book Award
and the *Irish Times* Award, was short-listed for
the Booker Prize. He died in 2006.

INTERNATIONAL

ALL WILL BE WELL

ALL WILL BE WELL

A Memoir

John McGahern

Vintage International
Vintage Books
A Division of Random House, Inc.
New York

146122990

I want to thank my editors, Sonny Mehta for his support over many years, and Neil Belton for his painstaking reading of the manuscript. Ian Jack first read the manuscript in a very rough draft, and his suggestions were invaluable.

I want especially to thank my sisters, Rosaleen, Margaret, Monica, Dympna, for their careful readings, corrections, their help with letters, and for bringing back into the light two important scenes that had slipped my memory.

I owe Madeline McGahern debts of advice and help stretching back over many books.

ALL WILL BE WELL

THE SOIL IN LEITRIM IS POOR, in places no more than an inch deep. Underneath is daub, a blue-grey modelling clay, or channel, a compacted gravel. Neither can absorb the heavy rainfall. Rich crops of rushes and wiry grasses keep the thin clay from being washed away.

The fields between the lakes are small, separated by thick hedges of whitethorn, ash, blackthorn, alder, sally, rowan, wild cherry, green oak, sycamore, and the lanes that link them under the Iron Mountains are narrow, often with high banks. The hedges are the glory of these small fields, especially when the hawthorn foams into streams of blossom each May and June. The sally is the first tree to green and the first to wither, and the rowan berries are an astonishing orange in the light from the lakes every September. These hedges are full of mice and insects and small birds, and sparrowhawks can be seen hunting all through the day. In their branches the wild woodbine and dog rose give off a deep fragrance in summer evenings, and on their banks grow the foxglove, the wild strawberry, primrose and fern and vetch among the crawling briars. The beaten pass the otter takes between the lakes can be traced along these banks and hedges, and in quiet places on the edge of the lakes are the little lawns speckled with fish bones and blue crayfish shells where the otter feeds and trains her young. Here and there surprising islands of rich green limestone are to be found. Among the rushes and wiry grasses also grow the wild orchid and the windflower. The very poorness of the soil saved these fields when old hedges and great trees were being levelled throughout Europe for factory farming, and, amazingly, amid unrelenting change, these fields have hardly changed at all since I ran and played and worked in them as a boy.

A maze of lanes link the houses that are scattered sparsely about these fields, and the lanes wander into one another like streams until they reach some main road. These narrow lanes are still in use. In places, the hedges that grow on the high banks along the lanes are so wild that the trees join and tangle above them to form a roof, and in the full leaf of summer it is like walking through a green tunnel pierced by vivid pinpoints of light.

I came back to live among these lanes thirty years ago. My wife and I were beginning our life together, and we thought we could make a bare living on these small fields and I would write. It was a time when we could have settled almost anywhere, and if she had not liked the place and the people we would have moved elsewhere. I, too, liked the place, but I was from these fields and my preference was less important.

A different view of these lanes and fields is stated by my father: "My eldest son has bought a snipe run in behind the Ivy Leaf Ballroom," he wrote. In some ways, his description is accurate. The farm is small, a low hill between two lakes, and the soil is poor. My father would have seen it as a step down from the world of civil servants, teachers, doctors, nurses, policemen, tillage inspectors to which he belonged. Also, it was too close to where my mother's relatives lived and where I had grown up with my mother. The very name of the Ivy Leaf Ballroom would have earned his disapproval.

A local man, Patsy Conboy, built it with money he made in America. He first called it Fenaghville—it was the forerunner of the Cloudlands and the Roselands—and later it became, more appropriately, the Ivy Leaf. All through the 1950s and into the 1960s he hired famous dance bands. In spite of being denounced from several pulpits, the ballroom prospered and Patsy Conboy became a local hero, dispensing much employment. People came by bus, by lorry, hackney car, horse trap, on bicycle and on foot to dance the night away. Couples met amid the spangled lights on the dusty dance floor and invited one another out to view the moon and take the beneficial air: "There wasn't a haycock safe for a mile around in the month of July." All the money Patsy Conboy made on the dancehall was lost in two less rooted ventures: a motorcycle track that turned into a quagmire as soon as it was used and an outdoor, unheated swimming pool amid the hundreds of small lakes and the uncertain weather. They were not rooted in the permanent need that made the ballroom such a success.

Patsy was more than able to hold his ground against the pulpits. When he was losing money digging the unheated swimming pool out of daub and channel, men turned up for work with letters from their priests stating that they had large families to support and should be employed. Patsy was unmoved: "My advice to you, Buster, is to dump the priest and put a cap on that oil well of yours. They have been capping such oil wells for years in America. Families are smaller and everybody is better off."

He was living close by when we bought the snipe run. The Ivy Leaf was then a ruin, its curved iron roof rusted, its walls unpainted, and Patsy had gone blind. Nothing about Patsy or his ballroom or the snipe zigzagging above the rushes would have commended themselves to my father. We settled there and were happy. My relationship with these lanes and fields extended back to the very beginning of my life.

———————

When I was three years old I used to walk a lane like these lanes to Lisacarn School with my mother. We lived with her and our grandmother, our father's mother, in a small bungalow a mile outside the town of Ballinamore. Our father lived in the barracks twenty miles away in Cootehall, where he was sergeant. We spent the long school holidays with him in the barracks, and he came and went to the bungalow in his blue Baby Ford on annual holidays and the two days he had off in every month. Behind the bungalow was a steep rushy hill, and beside it a blacksmith's forge. The bungalow which we rented must have been built for the blacksmith and was a little way up from the main road that ran to Swanlinbar and Enniskillen and the North. The short pass from the road was covered with clinkers from the forge. They crunched like grated teeth beneath the traffic of hoofs and wheels that came and went throughout the day. Hidden in trees and bushes on the other side of the main road was the lane that led to Lisacarn where my mother taught with Master Foran. Lisacarn had only a single room and the teachers faced one another when they taught their classes, the long benches arranged so that their pupils sat back to back, a clear space between the two sets of benches on the boarded floor. On the windowsill glowed the blue Mercator globe, and wild flowers were scattered in jamjars on the sills and all about the room. Unusual for the time, Master Foran, whose wife was also a teacher, owned a car, a big Model-T Ford, and in wet weather my mother and I waited under trees on the corner of the lane to be carried to the school. In good weather we always walked. There was a drinking pool for horses along the way, gates to houses, and the banks were covered with all kinds of wild flowers and vetches and wild strawberries. My mother named these flowers for me as we walked, and sometimes we stopped and picked them for the jamjars. I must have been extraordinarily happy walking that lane to school. There are many such lanes all around where I live, and in certain rare moments over the years while walking in these lanes I have come into an extraordinary sense of security, a deep peace, in which I feel that I can live forever. I suspect it is no more than the actual lane and the lost lane becoming one for a moment in an intensity of feeling, but without the usual attendants of pain and loss. These moments disappear as suddenly and as inexplicably as they come, and long before they can be recognized and placed.

I don't think I learned anything at school in Lisacarn, though I had a copybook I was proud of. I was too young and spoiled, and spoiled further by the older girls who competed in mothering me during the school breaks. I remember the shame and rage when they carried me, kicking and crying, into the empty schoolroom to my mother. Everybody was laughing: I had sat on a nest of pismires on the bank until most of the nest was crawling inside my short trousers.

I am sure my mother took me with her because she loved me and because I had become a nuisance in the house. I had three sisters already, the twins Breedge and Rosaleen and the infant Margaret, not much more than three years spanning all four of us. Our grandmother had been a dressmaker and stood arrow-straight in her black dresses. My handsome father, who stood arrow-straight as well until he was old, was her only child. She had been a local beauty and was vain and boastful. She was forever running down the poor land of Leitrim and its poor-looking inhabitants, which must have done nothing for her popularity. It was true that my father's relatives were tall and many were handsome: "When we went to your mother's wedding and saw all those *whoosins* from Cavan—Smiths and Leddys and Bradys and McGaherns—we felt like scrunties off the mountain," my Aunt Maggie told me once laughingly. The McGaherns set great store on looks and maleness and position. There was a threat of vio-lence in them all, and some were not a little mad and none had tact. There was a wonderful-looking first cousin of my father's, Tom Leddy, a guard like my father, who had also married a teacher. He was stationed at Glenfarne on the shores of Lough Melvin. Years later, out of the blue, he called soon after my father had remarried to find my stepmother alone in the house, a clever, plain-looking woman who adored my father and was both his slave and master. Having introduced himself forthrightly, he demanded, "Who are you? Are you the new housekeeper?" "I'm Frank's wife," she responded. "Frank's wife," he looked at her in amazement and broke into such uncontrollable laughter that he had to sit down. "Frank's wife. That's the best one I've heard in years. The whole country must be going bananas." When he rose, he repeated, "Frank's wife. You have made my day. Well, whoever you are, tell Frank that his cousin Tom Leddy called and that I'll call soon again one of these years," and left as abruptly as he came.

Whether my grandmother was a little mad as well, I was too young to know. She either had a great influence on my father or their temperaments were similar. Who can tell whether certain temperaments are ever influenced by nurture? They were both violent and wilful. Once, when she caught me burning bits of paper in the open grate of the small range to watch them blaze in the fascination children have with flame, she caught and thrust my finger between the glowing bars. She disregarded both my cries and my mother's horrified protestations. "You have the child half ruined already. There's only one way he'll learn." Neither she nor my father had any sense of humour, and they hardly ever smiled or laughed, and they looked on any manifestation of enjoyment in others as a symptom of irresponsibility. They also saw it as diverting attention from themselves. The difference between them was great as well. My father was intelligent and could be charming, even gallant, when he wanted. Though he was as vain and proud as she, he was never boastful: "Nobody blows themselves up other than fools. If you need praise, get others to do it for you."

I was a single star until the twins arrived, and I became insanely jealous of the natural transfer of attention. On dry days, when my mother was at school, my grandmother often left the twins out in the sun between the house and the forge, high on the sloping pass of clinkers that ran to the open gate on the road. I was forever around the forge, and she would warn me to mind them before going back into the house, having locked the brake on their big pram. I must have been planning how to get them out of my life for some time. I learned to unlock the brake, and one day, after careful checking that nobody was watching either from the forge or the house or the road, I pushed the pram down the slope. The pass wasn't steep and the wheels would have bumped and slowed on the clinkers, but before it came to a stop the pram wheeled off the pass and overturned. The twins weren't hurt, but all this time my grandmother had been observing me from behind a curtain, and made not the slightest attempt—she had only to tap the window—to protect the twins, though she was out of the house and able to seize me as I was watching the pram overturn in terrified dismay.

I saw this same calculating coldness in my father many times. When he retired and was living on a small farm in Grevisk, he saw two boys on their way from school leave their bicycles on the side of the road to cross the fields into his orchard. Instead of confronting them there or giving them a few apples, as many would have done, he walked out to the road and wheeled their bicycles into the house. When they returned from the orchard, they found their bicycles gone. That night he telephoned the parents.

As well as becoming troublesome in the house, I was also beginning to cause trouble around the forge, haunting the place, persecuting the men with questions, wanting to swing from the bellows. I was fascinated by all that went on in that dark cave, the huge horses arriving, the carts, the traps, the mules, the jennets, the donkeys. At the very back of the shed glowed the coal fire on the raised hearth, regularly doused with more coal and blown into a white heat. The red smouldering iron was taken with tongs from the fire. The hard, metal sparks flew in an arc as the iron was battered into shape on the anvil. An acrid smell of burning rose as the hot shoe sizzled on the lifted hoof. Outside the forge was a large stone circle on which the iron shoeing for cartwheels was beaten into shape. Watching all this battering and hammering, I was driven to furious imitation. I had a little red car with a steering wheel and pedals and a seat that was already too small. The big toy could be propelled slowly along with pedalling, more speedily and dangerously on a steep hill. From somewhere I borrowed a hammer—possibly from the forge—and spent the whole morning working on the car. The result was a wreck. Instead of having an enlarged car that travelled at speed, it now would not move. In tears, I took it to the forge. They must have been amused and beat it gently back into something close to its original shape, but I never felt that the car was the same again. Soon afterwards I was found in the forge underneath a horse, gravely looking up at the blacksmith burning the track of the new shoe on the pared hoof, and was carried in to my grandmother. I was scolded and beaten and wasn't allowed outside the house for days, and when I eventually was, the forge was forbidden. The men often talked to me and answered my questions and were kind, but I did not enter the forge. I had learned that you crossed my father's mother at your peril. Though I was not yet school-going age, my mother decided to take me out of harm's way and my grandmother's rule.

Along the high hedges, the banks of flowers that we walked, there was a meadow that was to acquire a darker history. John Gilchrist killed Bernie McManus with a hedge knife because of what went on in this meadow. Gilchrist, Giolla Iosa, the Servant of Christ, was a homeless labourer who lived with the Galligans. One of John Gilchrist's tasks was to draw water from a spring well in a corner of Bernie McManus's meadow. There was a right of way through the meadow to the spring. Bernie McManus used to tie the gates and stand in the middle of the right of way after rain to force Gilchrist off the path into the long wet grass of the meadow. This had apparently gone on to everybody's amusement for a long time, and there were other petty persecutions, until one evening Gilchrist went to Bernie McManus's house with a hedge knife and killed him in the cowhouse with a number of blows to the head and neck. The guards said that Gilchrist was very quiet when they came to arrest him: "He was trying to drive me from the place. He made my life not worth living," was all he would say. At his trial he was found to be insane. Vincie McManus, a big, quiet, gentle boy, who lived to see his father's murder, often walked that lane with us to Lisacarn.

My mother was unusual in that she disliked using any form of physical punishment when it was routine and widespread and savage beatings were a commonplace in schools, but she had trouble with the inspectors over the lack of strict discipline in her classes. In those remote schools the teachers were expected to serve the inspector lunch, and I remember her anxiety as she prepared the lunch the night before, having bought rare delicacies such as ham and tomatoes. The demand that all the children of the State should be able to speak and write in Irish had been raised to a punitive level. If the classes were found to be less than proficient in Irish, the teacher could lose salary increments. This brought an added tension to the inspections and insured that a great many school hours were wasted on the teaching of Irish, to the neglect of other subjects, at a time when most of the children would have to emigrate to Britain or America to find work in factories or on building sites or as domestics. Such was her nature that she tried to put a good face on everything and to keep us from her own anxiety.

I haven't a single memory of my father staying in the bungalow, though he must have come many times in the blue Baby Ford he owned. On the dashboard of the small car was a glass jar filled with long sugarsticks wrapped in cellophane. Most were yellow but some were green and red and black. I thought they were beautiful as well as desirable, but they were never unwrapped or given around and seemed to serve the same function as permanent flowers.

That I have not a single memory of my father in the house and that the lane to Lisacarn was walked alone with my mother conforms to a certain primal pattern of the father and the son. The first memory I have of him in all that time seems to reinforce this further. The memory is of a summer in the barracks in Cootehall. My grandmother, my mother, the twins and I must have gone there during the long school holidays.

I had a head of curls like a girl. My father decided to remove them in spite of my frightened protests, made worse by my mother's and grandmother's obvious distress, which served only to strengthen his resolve. In his uniform with the three silver stripes of his rank on the blue sleeve, he took me out into the long hallway that ran along the stairs to the door of the dayroom. He took a chair and newspaper and the small silver shears from the green box and locked the two women into the living room.

This hallway was always dark, but there must have been light enough from the small window beneath the stairs. The chair was set down on the newspaper and it did not take long to remove the curls. Exultant, he brought me back into the living room, where my outraged cries must have added to the distress of the two women. He carried the curls in the folds of the newspaper. "Weep not for me, O women of Jerusalem, but for yourselves and for your children," he quoted triumphantly.

In trying to explain that open or latent sense of conflict that always lay between us at even the best of times, my sisters, who remained close to my father, used to say that after my birth he felt displaced in my mother's affections and was never able to forgive or come to terms with that hurt; but I am certain if that hadn't been present, something else would have been found. In turn, those brown curls in the folds of the newspaper came to resemble for me John the Baptist's severed head borne into the room on a silver plate. Religion and religious imagery were part of the air we breathed.

Prayers were said each morning. Work and talk stopped in fields and houses and school and shop and the busy street at the first sound of the Angelus bell each day at noon. Every day was closed with the Rosary at night. The worlds to come, hell and heaven and purgatory and limbo, were closer and far more real than America or Australia and talked about almost daily as our future reality.

Heaven was in the sky. My mother spoke to me of heaven as concretely and with as much love as she named the wild flowers. Above us the sun of heaven shone. Beyond the sun was the gate of heaven. Within the gates were the thrones and mansions, the Three Persons in the One God, the Blessed Virgin, the angels and saints, and beyond those mansions were the gardens of paradise where time ceased and everything entered an instant of joy that lasted for all eternity at one with the mind of God. It was her prayer and fervent hope that we would all live there together in happiness with God for all eternity.

Heaven was in the sky. Hell was in the bowels of the earth. There, eternal fire raged. The souls of the damned had to dwell in hell through all eternity, deprived forever of the sight of the face of God. At its entrance was a great river. Across a wide plain, naked and weeping, came the souls of the damned from the Judgment Seat, bearing only a single coin to give to the boatman to take them across the river into eternal fire.

Between this hell and heaven, purgatory was placed. Descriptions of it were vague, probably because all of us expected to spend time there. The saints alone went straight to heaven. In purgatory, we would have to be purified in flame to a whiteness like that of snow before we could join the saints in the blessedness of heaven.

Away in a silent corner was limbo, where grave-faced children who hadn't received baptism slept, without consciousness or pain, throughout all eternity. Limbo was closed to us because of our baptism. In those young years, contemplating a future hell, or at best the long purifications of purgatory, it did not seem a bad place at all, and there were times when I hoped that some essential rite had been overlooked during my baptism; but I could not communicate this to my mother.

At Easter my mother always showed us the sun. "Look how the molten globe and all the glittering rays are dancing! The whole of heaven is dancing in its joy that Christ has risen." When Easter arrived with overcast skies and we asked for the sun, she assured us it was dancing behind the clouds. Blessed are those who have not seen but have believed.

At times in the evening the sun appeared within reach, when it stood in the whitethorns high on the hill behind the house before disappearing. I began to watch it as I had earlier eyed the bright battering at the forge. If I could climb the hill while it rested in the whitethorns, I could walk through the sun to the gate of heaven. Once I started to climb, it was like climbing a terrible stairs, having to claw and drag my way up through the rushes; but with every step the sun grew closer, and it was still there when I got to the whitethorns. I pushed through a hole in the hedge and rolled down into a dry drain. I intended to walk into the sun when I rose from the drain, but what confronted me was a mocking mirage: the sun was miles away, on the top of another hill. A long, flat plain of wheaten sedge lay between the two hills that would take days and hours to cross. I must have crawled or fallen back into the drain in a sleep of pure exhaustion.

It was dark when I woke to hear voices calling my name and saw stars bright in the sky. I was scolded and carried down to the house. Their anxiety changed to amusement and laughter and some wonder when they learned my story. I had tried to climb to the sun to get to the gate of heaven. I had not understood that you have to pass through death to reach that gate.

My grandmother had grown very possessive, and this must have been one of the reasons my mother took me with her on that lane to Lisacarn before I was of school-going age. When I went down with whooping cough my grandmother had her revenge. She shut me up in her own room and locked the door when she left the room. My mother did not see me for weeks. She had to go to school, my grandmother argued, and she and the twins and the infant Margaret couldn't be let run the risk of infection. As soon as the first wave of the illness passed, I became very distressed that I couldn't get to my mother nor she to me. I shouted and called out to her through the locked door. Even the Rosary was said with the door locked. My mother counselled me to be patient and to pray that soon I'd be better and able to walk the lane to school again. In those weeks only once was I taken from the room.

There was a cure for the whooping cough that involved a mule or jennet or a donkey. A neighbour of ours, Tommy Quinn, who spent any money he got on drink and was thought to be a little simple, lived with his brother Jim in a black house across the road in a rookery of trees. He came with the animal very late one night to the back door. I am sure the idea of the cure came from my grandmother and that Tommy came late at night so that the ritual could not be observed. The night was very cold. In a bundle of blankets I was taken out and passed beneath the jennet or mule or donkey three times in the name of the Father and the Son and the Holy Ghost. I remember the frost glistening on the hard ground and the sky was full of stars as I was handed back and forth. My happiness was intense when I was restored to my mother and we were walking the lane to Lisacarn together again.

Troubles with my grandmother did not cease; I was now her undisputed favourite, albeit a wary and unwilling one. She took to boasting about me in the same way she did about Cavan and the *whoosins* from there who were her relatives, the McGaherns and the Bradys and the Smiths and the Leddys. Though I was never to be handsome or tall, she would say, "Sean has the brains of the world and can do anything." My mother would have disliked this boasting and done everything she could to temper it.

One Saturday my grandmother decided to send me all the way into town to Aunt Maggie's shop for a packet of cornflakes. My mother protested that I was too young for such a long journey and offered to accompany me. My grandmother would have none of it: "He's well able. He's far too mollycoddled. It's time he learned to strike out on his own."

The town was a little less than a mile from the bungalow, and my aunt's shop was beside the railway station. Her brother, my Uncle Pat, who owned a hackney car, lived with her and met the trains with his car. She also kept lodgers, men who worked on the railway, firemen, drivers, repair linesmen, nearly all of them from Dublin. The shop sold sweets, chocolate, fruit, cigarettes, toys, groceries, schoolbooks and stationery. I was delighted at the prospect of getting away into the town on my own.

There was no rain, and I arrived at the shop with the coins and a note from my mother. The errand was probably greeted with derision as soon as its source was discovered. I was fussed over, given biscuits and tea in the delicious heat and comfort of the kitchen, before being sent on my way home with the packet of cornflakes. At Lisacarn I had watched enviously from the bank as the older boys played football, and my dream was to learn to play. Once I was clear of the town, I had a free road. There was no traffic, no carts, no bicycles, only a few people walking. As soon as they passed, I put the packet down and kicked it the whole way home—free kicks, kicks from the hand, kicks at goal. By the time I reached the bungalow, the packet wasn't recognizable. As soon as my grandmother saw it, she was beside herself. The beating would have been much worse but for my mother's intervention.

Suddenly, my grandmother disappeared. She was there one day and gone the next. I must have accepted whatever explanation was given. She was there and then she was gone, and the days continued without her disappearance making any difference to our lives.

I was to see her a last time. One Sunday my father came for us in the Ford, the jar of wrapped sugarsticks on the dashboard like permanent flowers. He was in the brown suit that had been tailored for his wedding day, which he wore for years afterwards. My mother was dressed in a long pleated woollen dress. Not only was this Sunday outing unusual but even more so was the shining care with which they were both dressed. We were told that the twins and I were going to Carrick-on-Shannon to visit our grandmother. Rosaleen and Breedge were dressed identically in cotton dresses of the same flowery material; even their hair was parted and combed in the same fashion and tied with the same colour of ribbon. When the twins were dressed like this, hardly anybody outside the family was able to tell them apart. I was in my summer Mass clothes—white shirt, short blue trousers, white ankle socks, polished black shoes. The car stopped at Aunt Maggie's shop, and Mother got out to buy grapes and sweets. My father must have felt she was spending too much time with her sister in the shop because soon he was muttering and complaining aloud to us, and then he blew the horn. She was full of apologies when she came out, but he continued muttering to himself, driving away in an angry silence. There were many times, then and later, when Aunt Maggie and my father weren't speaking, and this must have been one of those times, for otherwise she would have come out to the car to greet us.

We drove through the town in silence, passing the big stone barracks by the bridge to which our father had come as a young sergeant when the Civil War was ending. By the canal on the outskirts of the town was the convent with the blue-and-white grotto of the Blessed Virgin that had been our mother's first school. The punishing silence was broken only when the spires of the churches came into view above the low roofs of Carrick. On a higher isolated hill stood a water tower, like a huge concrete mushroom, beside a grey stone building that was once the poorhouse and was now the hospital we were going to visit.

We walked down a long corridor before pausing outside a numbered door. My mother and father whispered together. They must have been afraid to face my grandmother. My father put the grapes into my hands. "Sean, you go and see Granny first."

The door opened. I saw her head on pillows and went towards her with the black grapes. She was glad to see me, and we kissed. The twins came next with the chocolates, and, a long time afterwards, my father and mother. All I remember of the rest of the visit was my grandmother's bitter complaints that they had put her in the poorhouse and left her to die. She wouldn't concede that it was a hospital or that she needed care. As we were leaving, she wanted to give back the grapes and chocolates, but my father insisted that they had been bought specially for her. He scolded her that she should make more of an effort to like the place, as she was being given great care. This was the only time I ever saw her cry. My mother took us out into the corridor and my father remained behind with her a long time.

Some time afterwards, a Hail Mary for the repose of her soul was added to the prayers we said each night at the end of the Rosary. We said the prayer mechanically, as we said all prayers, without the words having any import or meaning.

For all her boasting, my grandmother never once mentioned her husband. Neither did I ever hear her son make any reference to his father, though later he was always pontificating on the filial respect and duty sons owed their fathers. There were rumours that my father was illegitimate, that his father was a bar owner in New York who had come home to marry the local beauty and returned to New York with the intention of selling the bar. The more probable history is that he was a small farmer or labourer who died soon after marrying my grandmother. Except for my father's physical presence in the world, by this time it was as if he had never lived.

———————

A greater change now happened. The number of pupils fell in Lisacarn. At a time of harsh government cutbacks no new teachers were being employed. My mother was placed on the "Panel." All vacancies had to be filled from these panels, and the teachers had no choice but to move. The school was Beaghmore, close to Carrigallen, ten or eleven miles away. Unusual for the time, it had a woman principal, a large, pleasant woman who had married into a prosperous farm beside the school. We left the bungalow and moved into a stark two-storeyed house overlooking a bog near Cloone.

There was no running water then, other than in streams or rivers, no electricity, no TV, very few radios, and when newspapers were bought they were shared between houses. Each locality lived within its own small world, and moving to the house overlooking the bog was like moving to a different country. The war that was now all over Europe was a distant rumour. I remember vividly an excited man coming into the house and waving his arms around as he declared, "German planes are manuring bombs down on England!"

My mother walked the two miles from the house to Beaghmore in all weathers with the twins. Margaret and our baby sister Monica were minded by the new maid. I walked in the opposite direction to Augharan School, no more than a half-mile away on the road to Newtowngore. There were mornings I wished it was a hundred miles away.

For long, my father had been complaining that my mother spoiled me—that she spoiled us all—and he saw the closeness of Augharan as an opportunity for correction: I would be torn from my mother's petticoats and be made into a man in the natural harshness of the world. At Augharan he got his wish.

Mrs. McCann was the junior teacher in Augharan. She was married to a tailor in Carrigallen and cycled to and from the town each day. She kept a supply of bright yellow bamboo canes in the press, and when they splintered she used ash and sally and hazel from the hedges and plied them with zeal all through the day, for errors and mistakes, oral or written, for any straying of attention or the slightest indiscipline. The worst punishments were administered out in the corridor, away from the classroom.

I probably wasn't beaten any more than the other children, but I wasn't used to being beaten, and after my mother's gentleness it was a descent into hell. I tried fiercely to leave Augharan and go with her and the twins to Beaghmore, but to no avail.

My father stood behind the decision. Whether it was because we were older and more aware, he seemed to be coming more often to the house. Talk of the war in Britain and Europe was now constant, and I made a silent, fervent prayer of my own each night after the Rosary that God in His mercy would send one of the German planes over England astray in the night to manure a bomb down on Augharan School while we slept.

I doubt if Mrs. McCann was unusually violent for that time. I have seen men my own age grow strange with anger when recalling their schooling: "Often we wouldn't be able to hold tools in the evenings, our hands would be that black and swollen. They'd often pull across the legs or the arms and shoulders. How we learned anything was a mystery. Heading out to school each day was pure misery."

I am sure there were exceptions, but once anything is licensed it can grow monstrous and be scarcely noticed. The only recourse for parents then was to come to the school to complain or go to the priest, or threaten law, but that was rare. Authority's writ ran from God the Father down and could not be questioned. Violence reigned as often as not in the homes as well. One of the compounds at its base was sexual sickness and frustration, as sex was seen, officially, as unclean and sinful, allowable only when it too was licensed. Doctrine separated body and soul. The soul was eternal and belonged to God. The body that carried it was unclean, prone to sin and disease, and would die, though I doubt if Mrs. McCann was concerned with this duality as she plied her canes and hazels.

Since all my attempts to get away had come to nothing, I turned now to see if I could chance on anything that might woo her to my side. On the way to school was a little garden by an abandoned cottage. Someone had enriched and cultivated it once, but it was neglected now and wild, rank with thistle and nettle and briar and dock. I developed the habit of looking at the wild flowers along the way on my own, as we had once named them together on the lane to Lisacarn. It might also have been a way of delaying my arrival at Augharan, but I thought the purple thistle blossoms were especially beautiful, lovely as roses. A small wooden gate opened into the garden, and I thought that if I could beat my way into the tall growth I would be able to gather a big bunch of the purple blossoms to take to Mrs. McCann. By the time I had a small bunch picked, I was stung with nettles and my hands and legs were bloodied from the crawling briars. Perhaps not recognizing the thistles immediately, Mrs. McCann took the bunch of purple blossoms in amazement, but as soon as she felt the thorns and recognized the despised weed, she grew enraged. What did I think I was doing bringing thistles to the school? Who did I think *she* was? Was I making fun of her and the school? She had never seen the like. She ordered me to throw the thistles out before she lost control of herself. I returned to the classroom humiliated, knowing that my attempt at ingratiation had only worsened my position. If I wasn't able to find knowledge of this shameful abasement within myself, I had only to look around at the sly, knowing smiles of my classmates.

My humiliation was further deepened when I told my mother

what had happened. I showed her my torn legs and wrists, the nettle stings, but when I finished she was unable to stop laughing and was joined by my sisters. I was about to run from the house when she drew me to her. I had only another month to go till my first communion, she told me. If I learned my catechism well and received my First Confession and communion, I could then leave Augharan and go with her and the twins to Beaghmore. I was barely able to believe my good fortune.

Mrs. McCann's husband made the blue suit for my first communion. The evening before, my mother had taken me to the dark church of Aughavas where my First Confession was heard. That night Mr. McCann came on a motorbike to our house above the bog with the tailored blue suit. I wore it the next morning with a white shirt and white ankle socks in new shoes. The farm next to the house where we bought milk had a big sidecar. There wasn't place for my mother, but I was given a seat in front with the driver. My mother cycled to the church. I had never felt so high up before and was too terrified to look down at the road or the horses' hoofs as the hedges flew past. Mrs. McCann was in the church, and she shepherded the class to our seats and then to the altar rail, where, with closed eyes, we received from the priest the white wafer that was the Body of Christ. I was made much of afterwards. People gave me coins that were heavy and jingled when I shook the pockets of my new blue suit. As we came home on the sidecar, I was less afraid and began to enjoy the height and wide view in my newfound grace. If I fell now and died, I would go straight to heaven. I had been fasting from the night before and was starving. A royal feast waited in the house: a mug of steaming tea, a plate of buttered toast, a fried egg, pork sausage, two slices of grilled bacon and a piece of black pudding. "Daddy wrote that he'd love to be here but wasn't able to get off," our mother said.

The next morning I did not have to turn away and face for Augharan when we got to the road. In pure relief and happiness, I reached out and took my mother's hand as she and I and the twins set out for Beaghmore.

All these roads were dirt roads that ran between wild hedges studded with mature trees—ash or oak or sycamore—and high grass margins. The road from the house reached the wider road to Carrigallen. We crossed a stone bridge and then turned up the short lane to the school.

Beaghmore had two classrooms but no porch and was on the lane; it had no playground, just space for the two dry lavatories beneath the tall boundary hedge at the back. The playground was a field on the other side of the lane where we played ball and ran and jumped amid the grazing, incurious cattle.

The woman principal became very friendly with my mother. I remember her comfortable pleasantness but not her name, while I can never forget Mrs. McCann. Her house was close to the school and we were often invited there, and on many Friday evenings we stayed for tea. When we left, we were often given pots of jam or preserves or eggs and fresh vegetables or material that could be made into children's clothes. The two women would sit and chat while we listened without understanding or wandered out into the farmyard. There were many sheds full of pigs and cattle, a house for fowl, a stable with three horses, ploughs and harrows, mowing machines, mangles, tedders, rakers. What I came away with was a sense of plenty, warmth and ease and comfort, even luxury set against the bareness of our rented rooms. I took this same sense away from most of the houses we visited, together with a vague troubled feeling of shame and diminishment.

"Why can't we have a house like those houses, Mammy?"

"Maybe one day we will—but money and comfort isn't everything. When people are rich it is often harder for them to leave the world."

"Does it mean it is harder for them to get to heaven?"

"If they come to love the world too much it is harder. God is more important than the world and He sees all."

On occasional Sundays we also visited the Cooneys, who had a roadside shop on the main road to Carrigallen and a travelling shop. This was a horse-drawn van Mr. Cooney took round different roads on set days each week, selling goods and groceries, buying fowl and rabbits, eggs and butter. The Cooneys had a boy and a girl in my mother's classes in Beaghmore. I remember a Sunday when the air was full of swallows, swooping and darting low around the windowsills. Mr. Cooney told us that if we could place a grain of salt on a swallow's tail the bird would freeze in the air and we could take it in our hand. We spent frustrating hours while a full packet of salt was wasted and Mr. Cooney grew sore with laughter. As recompense, he gave us pocketfuls of sweets. Like many people, Mrs. Cooney was very drawn to my mother, but the Cooneys never visited our house. I have no idea what excuses were made, what inadequacies were pleaded, if any. The explanation may have been simply that Mrs. Cooney, like many women of the time, never liked leaving her own house.

On rare Saturdays Mr. and Mrs. King cycled to us across the bog. They were both teachers and talked with Mother. To us they were kindly but distant, and belonged much more to their class and profession than our mother did. Years afterwards their daughter told me that Mrs. King and my mother had spent five years together in the Marist Convent in Carrick-on-Shannon and were the outstanding students in their year, both of them winning scholarships to Trinity College. Because of the ban on Trinity, they couldn't be employed in the National Schools when they graduated, but as the nuns had educated them and found a way round the ban to allow them to avail of the scholarships, they now disregarded the Church edict further by employing them in their own convent schools. Once established in the system, they were then able to move out to the schools the priests managed.

Our close neighbours were our most constant visitors, dropping in at all sorts of times throughout the day, as was usual then—to be passing the house was reason enough—and they sometimes came at night to sit around the fire. In good weather Aunt Maggie cycled out to us on Wednesdays, which was the half-day closing in the town. We looked towards Wednesdays with excitement, as she always brought sweets and biscuits from the shop, and were disappointed when it rained, and Uncle Pat sometimes came unexpectedly in his big car when he had a hackney run near Carrigallen.

The other visitors we had were all relatives of my father's. His home place near Gowna was not far from Carrigallen, and he encouraged them to visit us, though he'd be far from happy if they took to visiting him. I suspect that he viewed them as a counterweight to my mother's relatives, whom he resented. They were, for the most part, young women who would cycle over to us from Gowna in the evening, stay the night and leave with us when we set out for school in the morning. Secretly, my mother did not welcome these visits, but neither did she stand in their way, and when they came she put them at their ease and made them welcome. After a succession of maids, we now had Bridgie McGovern, a handsome, temperamental girl, who was to stay with us for some time.

Of the young girls and women who cycled over to us from Gowna, I remember a close cousin of my father's, perhaps because of her beauty—she had very pale skin and black hair—but it is more likely that the memory is fixed by an incident on the way to school. As we walked to school in the morning, the girl wheeling her bicycle on her way home after staying the night, my mother quietly excused herself and turned aside. A grey stream poured from her mouth into the long grass and nettles growing on the margins of the road.

"It's only early morning sickness," she explained to the girl when she had composed herself and resumed the walk. The girl nodded and asked some further question, and the walk and conversation continued normally as if nothing had happened. In spite of this, I was touched by a strange foreboding, but was too fearful to ask anything.

I felt the same fear when my father was in the house. I knew he resented that I had been given my way over Augharan and Mrs. McCann. There was always tension when he was in the house, scolding about how money was being wasted, or the poor way the house was being run, or my mother's relatives. In certain moods he did not need a reason to fall into a passion of complaint, which then fed off its own anger. A child can become infected with unhappiness. This was further worsened by a scene that reached back to the shearing of my head of curls beneath the stairs in the barrack hallway. Late at night the small blue car arrived with my father in one of his black moods. This focused instantly on my face, which was covered with scabs from a childhood disease, probably impetigo. In the morning he kept me from school and drove me to the doctor in Carrigallen. He had a love/hate relationship with doctors, and though we spent a long time in the surgery and there was much argument, I was too afraid and confused to know what was happening. From the surgery we went straight to the chemist's, probably for an antiseptic lotion or ointment. When he got home he ordered Bridgie McGovern to boil water, got a basin and mirror and towel and sharp knife, and disinfected the water and knife. Then he proceeded to remove all the scabs with the knife. I was terrified of him—the knife, the ceremony that was as fixed as an execution.

The treatment worked, the sores healed, and the knife left no scars, but the next time I saw the blue Baby Ford arrive I ran to a big chestnut tree we were used to climbing near the house, and I hid there. I was able to observe the house and the car, and though I heard my name called out, I remained in the tree. Towards evening the car left, and the calling became more anxious and constant, and I went into the house.

The next time he came to the house he was at his most charming. He had a physical attractiveness that practically glowed when he was in this humour, but seldom was he able to sustain it: he demanded that the whole outside world should reflect it perfectly back. Once this mirror dimmed or failed, his mood would turn. On this day in the stark house above the bog, we must have responded perfectly because the house was filled with contentment and peace all through the day and into the night and morning, until we gathered outside the house to wave to the car as he drove away.

While he was with us I was given the special task of introducing him to the house of two children who attended Beaghmore, a boy and a girl, a few years older than I was, whose parents were both dumb. One of the wonders of the school was that, while neither the father nor the mother could utter a word, both children could speak perfectly and were bright. The father was a skilled watchmaker, repairing clocks and watches and various sorts of light machinery; it was said he could fix anything that ran. They lived in an iron-roofed cottage behind tall hedges, and they had a little land. They kept one cow, and gardened, growing flowers and many varieties of vegetables, and the place was beautifully tended. Their industry was such that it was often remarked how much time so-called normal people wasted on talk. Close to the houses the father had built and erected a tall wind-charger that he used to light the house, and this is what attracted my father.

After we went through the gate in the tall hedge, the daughter met us at the door. Over her shoulder we could see her father with his eyeglass in place working at his watchmaker's bench. Proudly, I introduced my father and explained the reason for our visit. She went back into the house and brought the father out. With rapid hand signals they communicated, she rotating her arm in imitation of the movement of the blades and pointing to my father. Her father then nodded his understanding and agreement, and gestured to my father to follow him to the windmill and the small house at its foot where the wet batteries were stored. They spent a long time together. The boy now joined his sister and they both showed me the gardens, the white-washed cowhouse and their brindled cow, the ducks and geese and hens they kept. I thought I glimpsed the mother within the house, but she didn't appear. My father remained in the same good humour as we drove away. He talked of erecting a similar wind-charger alongside the sycamore tree at the barracks that would not only light the rooms but work the big Cossor radio he kept on the shelf beside the curtained medicine press.

—————

A few weeks later the world of Beaghmore was ended. Mother suddenly had to go away. For what or why we were not told. "You all have to be good now and cause no trouble and pray for Mammy." Faces were grave and anxious and closed against questioning. The house above the bog was closed. All five of us and Bridgie McGovern were moved to the barracks in Cootehall. The rooms in the living quarters had been uninhabited for so long, other than by my single father and a maid, that they gave back our voices when we shouted out. This shouting soon got on his nerves down in the dayroom: he opened the dayroom door and roared up at us to have manners, to be quiet and remember that we were no longer living in a field.

The village of Cootehall was scattered randomly about a big triangular field, Henry's field. No two shops or houses adjoined one another, and they were set down as haphazardly as if they had been carried there on various breezes. There was a church, a post office, the barracks, a presbytery, two shops, three bars, a few houses. A row of buildings, all owned by Michael Henry—

stables, cowhouses, a granary, a bar, a dwelling house, a grocery store—stood across a narrow lane from the church wall.

Michael Henry had bought the grocery and farm with money he made in America, and added a low building to the two-storeyed row of buildings already there to serve as a grocery store. It stood directly across from the church gates and was designed to attract worshippers who would not want to be seen entering a bar. A few yards further down the road at McDermott's Cross was Cassidy's shop. The Cassidys were said to have old money from the time Granny McDermott ran dances and concerts in the wooden hall that still stood in their yard. This was no longer in use as the priests now ran all these events in the new parochial hall built well beyond the village, presumably to keep it as far away as possible from the bars. Mrs. Cassidy, Granny McDermott's daughter, was married to Guard Cassidy, a handsome, melancholy man, and they had two girls and a boy, all good-looking. The children lived in the shop with their mother and grandmother and a maid, as we had lived, and only saw their father when he came on his holidays a few weeks every year from his Monaghan barracks. Directly across from the main door of the church stood Henry's Bar, where Michael Henry was fond of moralizing as he served drink, often after hours: "I guess, Mr. Langan, that I will serve you a pint since that is what you have requested but I advise you at the same time that in my opinion a loaf of bread is more in your line." Another long separate building was Doyle's. Once it had been the most prosperous business for miles around, with many shop attendants, the road outside crowded with people and carts, but now all that was left was the bar, selling only whiskey and bottles of stout. John Doyle was married to the district nurse, and only for her it was said he would have been out on the road.

At Lavin's Cross stood John Lavin's thatched cottage, the roof of the one room fallen, green oats and weeds sprouting from what remained of the other two rooms. On good days he could be seen shaping wood into cartwheels or chairs outside the cottage. The rich fields behind the cottage he had once owned had been lost to Charlie Reagan, who had the bar and grocery across from the post office. Behind Charlie's Bar and sheds was the football field where cattle could be seen scratching themselves against the goal-posts. Below the bridge was the barracks and the large barrack garden. An avenue with a single line of sycamores ran from the road to the barracks and continued under the high stone archway before climbing between thick banks of laurel to Lenihan's Bawn. All that remained of Chidley Coote's old castle was a corner tower where the Cannons lived between the Finans and the Lenihans. There were many stories about the Cootes, who once owned everything around Cootehall. "I cannot get my two sons to come to you to work," said a tenant to Chidley Coote. "They pay no heed to anything I say."

"Bring them to me and I'll make them see sense."

In the morning the man forced his sons to go with him to the Bawn and left them with Coote. When night came and they didn't return home, he went back to the Bawn.

"You passed them in the dark," Chidley Coote told him. "They are obedient now."

They were both hanging from the archway beside the barracks. We passed under it every day by the back entrance to the barrack living quarters.

The gates had gone and the small shiny leaves and red berries of the cotoneaster now covered much of the stone. Beside Moran's well, on the shore of Cootehall Lake, where we went in the boat for spring water in dry summers, a strip of rock was pointed out where another of the Cootes was thrown from his horse and killed when hunting a priest. Around this rock the grass was said to turn red in summer.

Along Lenihan's high orchard wall ran Gilligan's field where they grazed their cow and the small horse that drew their travelling shop around the roads. Their small thatched cottage faced

Henry's street and the back of Jimmy Shivnan's forge. Like the Cassidys and Henrys, the Gilligans had three children and they often walked with us to Cootehall School.

The school stood just outside the village and was relatively new, with concrete shelters in the playground. Mrs. Finan and Mrs. Mullaney shared the junior classroom. They were severe and of their time, but neither was as violent as Mrs. McCann. We learned to dread Mrs. Finan's wedding and engagement rings when she used her fist. They were handsome women, Mrs. Finan some years the younger. Mrs. Mullaney was a junior assistant— she had never been formally trained—and thus wasn't as secure either professionally or socially as Mrs. Finan, who was married to a teacher and had two brothers who were priests. Mrs. Mullaney made up for this with a will of iron. She had a boy and a girl by her first husband. Under her fierce tutelage, they had both won scholarships and were now in college. Her second husband, Mr. Mullaney, was old, but fame of sorts clung to him as a horseman—he was said to have cleared dangerous and almost impossible gates and ditches when young. Once they married, he sold his farm and built her a bungalow beside the church. Each day he brought her a hot lunch to the school, traces of his early horsemanship showing in his walk as he made his slow way with the dishes between the bungalow and the school. Mrs. Mullaney was prominent in all things connected with the church, and it was assumed that both her son and daughter were being driven towards the priesthood and the convent.

The principal was Master Glynn, a gentle, easygoing alcoholic. The two women teachers both protected and managed him. He had entered teaching as a monitor in the British system, but had never managed to learn any Irish after Independence, when even the letterboxes acquired a coat of green paint. When Irish had to be taught to his classes, he and Mrs. Finan swapped rooms. Those were very pleasant times when he came to our room, as he generally gave Mrs. Finan's classes copying work and passed the time chatting with Mrs. Mullaney. Most teachers used their foothold in education to better their children in the world, getting them into the church or the professions or the civil service through their knowledge of the examination system, but Master Glynn's large family had all returned to the land in much the same way as uncultivated fields return to the wilderness. Now they were no different in ambition or interests or social standing than most of the parents of the children he taught. His easygoing nature combined with heavy drinking had become a disability. Shortly before, a gang of older boys, who were out of control and did more or less whatever they wanted, locked him in one of the cloakrooms. When released by the women teachers, who caned the ringleaders within an inch of their lives, he foolishly sent to the barracks for the guards to come to the school and restore order. My father would have nothing but contempt for the weakness of such a man. He went down to the trees growing on the river bank, cut an ash plant and sent it back to the Master with a note giving detailed, ironic instructions for its use.

Every night Master Glynn went to Henry's Bar, where he was popular with his old pupils. If he had never taught them much, neither had he ever abused them, and many of them were still able to quote reams of Goldsmith from his tutelage. As the drinks flew round, he assured them of the great intelligences they all possessed, and they in their turn told him that he was the best teacher any class of scholars ever had and how they remembered as if it was yesterday everything he had ever taught them. Their voices brimming with emotion, another round of drinks was called and, "A large brandy for the Master!"

Cootehall was my fourth school in as many years. We were new and stood out, but we were also from the barracks. In the Ireland of that time the law was still looked upon as alien, to be feared and avoided, and kept as far away from as possible. This conferred on us an ambiguous protection that was paper thin.

Up to now our mother had always been with us at home and

in school. Now that she was gone we were at the mercy of our father—the scoldings, his sudden rages, the beatings he administered. In their surviving letters my father often complains to my mother that she is turning us against him, when it was he himself who was turning us away from him. While, in fits, he could charm and seduce us, when we did go towards him he found us tiresome and could not sustain what he had brought about. The protection our mother gave had not always been without danger to herself.

There were two entrances to the living quarters: through the long hallway from the stairs and dayroom or by the back door through the scullery. The back door opened on a small concrete yard. Across the yard was a small slated house my father used as a workshop. There was a water barrel under the eve pipe and an open turf shed beyond; across from the turf shed was a slated lavatory. It was dark within, and instinctively we ran to its darkness after beatings. Between the shed and the lavatory was a rough lawn with a rhubarb bed in its centre. In the summer, butterflies, especially white butterflies, seemed endlessly to flicker and flit and toss in the light above this bed, sometimes alighting and taking off from the great rhubarb leaves. Often we tried to close our hands on these flickering lights.

Margaret was the most wilful of the girls, with a stubborn energy, and was then, and later, always the one most likely to cross my father. She ran from the house, pursued by my father in full uniform. The day was heavy and hot and still. Beyond the netting wire, where the tarred boat was moored below the barracks, the river did not seem to move. All the doors were open. We were gathered at the back around our mother. Margaret could not have been much more than three at the time. My mother did not so much move as just stand in his way as the child went past. He was in such a passion that he didn't pause, but drew out to send her spinning into the rhubarb beds. She did not fall but reached down into the rhubarb stalks for support before getting to her feet. My father caught the child before she reached the lavatory and lifted and shook her violently. She was too paralysed to kick or cry out, and eventually he put her down without further chastisement.

"God. O God, O God," he began. "You'd think those children were brought up in a field!"

He seemed to have no sense of what he had done or that our mother might be hurt.

"They are very young," she said.

"There's no peace since they came. You'd hear them in Boyle, never mind down in the barracks. No peace or work can get done with their constant racket."

Now there was only Bridgie McGovern. She cooked and washed and sewed for my father and us and minded Monica when the rest of us were at school. She was now with us longer than any of the other maids. She was a young, attractive woman, flirtatious and egotistical, and my sisters say she used to flirt with my father. There is little doubt they got on well together.

The three men attached to the barracks were Guard Guider, Guard Murray and Guard Cannon. They were all married and lived in rented houses. The Guiders, who were from Tipperary, had the largest family, ten or twelve children, and they lived in a big slated house beside the quay that belonged to the Water Authority. One of the Guider children, Tom, had a heart condition, and rode to school on a donkey. His father was fond of saying that if Christ could ride into Jerusalem on an ass, it was no disgrace for a Guider to ride to school on the same animal. Later the Guiders were transferred and replaced by a newly married couple, the Walshes, who in turn were to have many children. The Murrays lived in a huge stone house that had once been a British military barracks and was later torn down for its stone and slates and lead. Guard Murray was from Virginia in Cavan. He was gentle and humorous, anxious to please. His sharp, ambitious wife from Mayo ran him and their five children. The Cannons, recently married, were both from Donegal, he from the Gaeltacht.

Teresa Cannon was often in the barracks. She was tall and hand-some and sweet on my father. The Cannons had rooms in Leni-han's Bawn, their living room the surviving corner tower of Coote's Castle, which was supposed to be haunted by, among other things, a turkey cock with spurs. Mrs. Cannon was afraid to sleep there alone when her husband was barrack orderly, and for years my sisters had to go to sleep with her on those nights in the Bawn. She was hypocritical and disliked, especially by women. "I am fluent in two languages and haven't a word to say in either," her husband was fond of boasting; "while my wife doesn't even know her own language and has enough to say for six people." He had worked as a shoemaker and then as a bus conductor in Glasgow before joining the guards. He was older than his wife, bald and very gentle when he wasn't on the tear. When he was barrack orderly and my father wasn't in the house, he would often leave the dayroom door open and sit with us in the big living room, chatting away as if his world and ours were the very same. Whenever there was a soccer match on the BBC, he stood for hours with his ear glued to the Cossor, trying to pick up the faint, crackling sounds as they came over the air from Scotland or England.

The barracks itself was a strange place, like most of the coun-try at the time. Though the Free State had been wrested in armed conflict from Britain, it was like an inheritance that nobody quite understood or knew how to manage. The Catholic Church was dominant and in control of almost everything, directly or indi-rectly. In a climate of suppression and poverty and fear, there was hardly any crime and little need of a barracks in a place like Cootehall, other than as a symbol.

The place was run on lines that were no longer connected to any reality, if indeed they ever were. Though my father slept every night in the barracks, the guards in their turn had to leave their own families and sleep the night beside the telephone that hardly ever rang, even in the daytime. I cannot remember anybody coming to the barracks at night. If there was a sudden death or illness, people went to the priest, or to the doctor if they weren't poor.

The familiar sounds each night were the heavy boots of the barrack orderly taking down the bedclothes from the upstairs room to make up his bed for the night beside the phone. We'd hear the sounds of raking and blowing as he started the fire in the morning and then the unlocking of the back door when he went down to empty his chamber pot and bucket of ashes into the ash pit over the river. We were able to tell the different guards by their sounds and footsteps. Sometimes in the mornings they hummed or whistled, which always set my father muttering.

My father would come down the stairs in his shirt and trousers and unlaced boots. The fire had to be going by then, the kettle boiling. We went through these mornings on tiptoe. While he sharpened his open razor on a leather strap that hung from the wall, we'd pour the shaving water into a basin that stood in a tall, rusted, iron stand in front of the scullery window. Then he would lather his face with a small brush and shave in the mirror that stood in a brown wooden stand in the window. Outside were the beds of rhubarb, and beyond the low wall the shapes of Lenihan's fields.

The house went completely still while he shaved. Sometimes he would nick himself with the razor and we'd bring him bits of newspaper to staunch the bleeding. A clean, dry towel had to be placed in his hands as soon as he washed. In the living room he would polish and lace up his boots, draw the silver buttons of his tunic together on a flat, brass comb while he wetted them with a white substance, and brushed them till they shone. As soon as he buttoned his tunic, he would comb his hair in the big sideboard mirror. The signal that he was completely dressed was when he picked up his new handkerchief from the table and placed it inside the cuff that wore the three silver stripes of his rank. Then he would sit down to breakfast, facing the big sideboard mirror. At this time Bridgie McGovern would have served him, later my sisters. He never acknowledged the server or any of the small acts of service, but would erupt into complaint if there was a fault—a knife or dish or fork or spoon missing, or something accidentally spilled or dropped. When he wasn't eating from his plate, he stared straight ahead into the big mirror, chewing very slowly. At exactly nine he would go down to the dayroom, and the whole of the living room relaxed as soon as the dayroom door slammed shut.

The morning inspection took place in the dayroom, the three policemen lined up in front of my father on the far side of the long wooden table. Occasionally voices were raised and we would go silent to try to listen. The patrols for the day were assigned and written into one of the big ledgers on the table. The new orderly took over from the old, who was then free to go home to his own house and breakfast.

The new orderly's first task was to take the bottle from the copper rain gauge in the garden, measure the rainfall in a long glass vial, and write the measurement on a chart that was sent at the end of each month to the meteorological office in Dublin. As soon as the green mail van crossed the bridge, a guard went to collect the mail, if there was any, and the *Irish Independent* from Charlie Reagan's. At that time the *Independent* printed the death notices on the front page. They were read out aloud. In a small country, with all the guards coming from different parts, on most mornings they would have some connection with one or more of the deceased, and the person or persons and their localities would be discussed. Then the headlines and any interesting news would be gone over while the newspaper was passed around. When all that was achieved, they scattered out on their different patrols, leaving the barrack orderly in charge in the dayroom. If there was wind and rain or heavy rain, they would hang about the dayroom looking out at the rain, and after a few hours they'd sign themselves back in and write up a fictitious account of the patrol without having left the dayroom.

Most of the accounts that were written into the big ledgers, in good weather and in bad, were fictitious, and were referred to laughingly as Patrols of the Imagination, but never by my father. Many of the patrols they cycled out on were spent working in their gardens or conacre or on their plots of turf on Gloria Bog. Only when the monthly inspection from the superintendent was due or a surprise inspection feared were the patrols observed and reported properly. Even then some invention was probably needed, as hardly anything ever happened on those potholed roads.

As I grew older I sometimes helped with the writing of the reports while hanging about the dayroom when my father was away.

"Would you ever put your head out the door, Sean, and see what way the wind is blowing?"

"It is from the priest's boathouse, Guard Cannon, with bits of rain."

"Wind from the south-west, and beginning to rain. Everything quiet," Guard Cannon would call out as he wrote in the big ledger. "Everything still quiet until I reached Knockvicar," he'd continue. "There I found a cow grazing along the road as soon as I turned for Cootehall. I made enquiries and discovered that the said animal belonged to Patrick McLoughlin. The owner denied any knowledge of the cow and said that if it was his it must have broken through a fence. I warned him as to the dangers of having an animal trespassing on the public highway and that I'd be forced to take further measures if the trespass was to occur again. Paper never refuses ink, Sean," Guard Cannon would shout out as he concluded with a flourish: "What is a masterpiece, Sean? A masterpiece is the correct distribution of ink on the correct number of white pages!"

What work did they do? Occasionally they summonsed people for not having lights on their bicycles at night, for after-hours drinking, for assault, or trespass, owning unlicensed dogs, possessing fields of thistle, ragwort or dock. This came under the Noxious Weeds Act, which was printed on a framed poster that sometimes stood outside the porch on good days. There was a small bounty for dead foxes, and they cut the tongues out of the foxes brought to the barracks so that they couldn't be returned for further bounty. Occasionally, old and starving animals, donkeys and the occasional horse, were found abandoned on the roads, and they were brought in shivering to lie among the three circular flowerbeds on the barrack lawn until they were collected by the Burnhouse lorry. When the lorry arrived, they were pushed/carried on to the lorry, where they were shot with a humane killer. Once the shot rang out, the horses fell with a heavy thud, but the donkeys were so light that the creatures crumpled to the floor of the lorry as silently as leaves.

I was seven years old during this first long stay in the barracks, and my whole childish world had been overturned. We didn't know where our mother was or what had happened to her and we were under our father's direct rule for the first time. When we asked about her we were warned not to ask but to pray to God. To veil everything in secrecy and darkness was natural to my father, and it turned out that my mother was far from happy with this secrecy. She wrote him from the Mater Hospital, "Sean is beginning to have more sense and will not be put off as easily as the others about my whereabouts. Well, thank God I will soon be home with you all again, looking forward to that is making me better."

She had been diagnosed with breast cancer and was kept some weeks in the hospital for tests and treatment. Briefly she came back to us in the barracks for the new birth. It must have been a balm to have her home, but I have hardly any memory of that brief stay other than a vague, delirious happiness. My one sharp memory is going in Packie McCabe's car with my father to the nursing home in Boyle to bring her and the baby girl home. She must have asked for me to go. All private cars had been taken off the roads because of the war. Our father's small Ford rested on blocks in one of the barrack sheds. I remember vividly the journey home, my mother carrying Dympna in a white shawl. Both the baby girl and Packie McCabe had red hair and there was laughter about this on the journey home that I couldn't understand. Packie was unmarried at this time and his face turned a deeper red than his hair. Mother must have spent a week or so in the barracks. Then she was gone from us again, leaving the baby with Bridgie McGovern. Where she had gone to we still did not know.

We come from darkness into light and grow in the light until at death we return to that original darkness. Those early years of the light are also a partial darkness because we have no power or understanding and are helpless in the face of the world. This is one of the great miseries of childhood. Mercifully, it is quickly absorbed by the boundless faith and energy and the length of the endlessly changing day of the child. Not even the greatest catastrophe can last the whole length of that long day.

We grow into an understanding of the world gradually. Much of what we come to know is far from comforting, that each day brings us closer to the inevitable hour when all will be darkness again, but even that knowledge is power and all understanding is joy, even in the face of dread, and cannot be taken from us until everything is. We grow into a love of the world, a love that is all the more precious and poignant because the great glory of which we are but a particle is lost almost as soon as it is gathered.

We were many years from that knowledge as we moved between Mrs. Mullaney's classroom and the church and the barracks. We had no power and no knowledge. Even as we went about our endless days we did not know that our overturned world was being rearranged once more. Maggie and Pat had been setting about finding our mother a school closer to the town where they could help her. Beaghmore and the bog of Cloone and Carrigallen were too far away. She and they were well liked and they had many contacts. There was now the urgency of serious illness which overcame a characteristic reluctance to push their own needs. While she was still in hospital, through their offices she was offered a permanent position in Aughawillan, a two-teacher school on a hill three miles from Ballinamore. There was also a house and farm for sale at Corramahon, which was no more than a ten-minute walk from the school. Between Corramahon and the school was the small railway station of Garradice Halt, with trains to Ballinamore. The priest agreed to hold the position for her until she came out of hospital. Pat and Maggie and the people they enlisted must have been very active on her behalf because soon afterwards she was offered her old position in Lisacarn as well, but she kept to Aughawillan. "It never rains but it pours," she wrote on being offered the second school.

Many of the letters she wrote to my father from hospital, in which this and other matters between them are played out, have survived. My father would have preferred her to stay on in Beaghmore, probably because it was farther from her relatives. Her tone throughout the letters is conciliatory and submissive, but on this point she is surprisingly blunt. "*No,*" she underlined. "I do not need a sub in Beaghmore. Aughawillan is what concerns me now." As soon as she was allowed out of hospital she would teach in Aughawillan for a day in order to secure the position, put in a sub, and return to the Mater Hospital for the rest of her treatment. About the purchase or not of the farm and house in Corramahon she is deferential and careful.

He was against it at first because it involved the spending of money, and because he saw her own family's hand in the move; but he was also drawn to the purchase as an investment. Briefly the idea was floated that she should retire from teaching on the grounds of her illness—she would receive a small pension—and come with us to live in the barracks. She appeared to consider this. We would all be together as a normal family for the first time, something she had longed for, but then questioned what kind of a housekeeper would she make. What she concealed was that her own family was adamantly against the move. Her schooling and training had been hard won. They knew his character. She would be giving up her independence and placing herself and the children in his volatile care. She is almost carelessly non-committal about the purchase of the house and farm. In her first weeks back in hospital she had certainly more immediate concerns: "No. I never saw Mahon's house—it happens to be the one bit of that country I do not know. I hope you didn't invest as yet anyway—until we see further," she wrote him from the hospital.

He writes about selling the house and small farm he owned at McGahern's Cross, a mile outside Gowna, which was then rented, but he worries that he will not get a fair price, as no one will bid against the family in possession. She advises him not to sell if he cannot obtain a fair price. What emerges is that she is more interested in divining his wishes and agreeing with them than in offering any opinion of her own. She also has to face his anxiety over her medical bills, and assures him she has taken an ordinary ward because it is less expensive.

She had to be extraordinarily careful. Though my father was often coldly calculating, his general moods were so changeable that, apart from a passion for contrariness, he never knew his mind from one minute to the next. All decisions had to be seen as his or he would fly against them, and he saw hands plotting against him in the most innocuous of moves. Even when the decision was his alone he would try to turn it round in blame on someone else once it started to go wrong.

After she recovered from surgery she moved to a boarding house in Dún Laoghaire and went into the Mater by tram for treatment. This appears to have been less expensive and more pleasant than staying in a ward, and again in the letters she assures him that she knows he has big expenses and that she is spending nothing in the city other than on her tram fare. She looks in shop windows when she has time to while away in the city and finds it tiring. Once she went to a cinema to see *Gone with the Wind,* and while she admired the vividness of the cinematic technique, she disliked the vision of life it portrayed. She thought it shallow.

Amidst his constant worries and anxieties about money, her decision against giving up teaching appears to harden. After discussing the doctors' and surgeon's fees, she writes:

> *I think fees here are two guineas a week, just an ordinary ward as I did not want to be running up the bill. It will be enough in any case but please God we wouldn't be so long paying up afterwards. I talked of resigning in my last letter. Well I don't know if the doctor would give me a cert to that effect and perhaps it is best to continue until we see further. I just don't like to see you unhappy and I think we would be happier together. That is why I mentioned doing so.*

My father must have become more demanding. In her next letter she has decided definitely. She will not give up teaching. She will take up the position in Aughawillan. She then reverses their positions. Would he consider getting out of the guards and coming to live with us?

> *I got your letter today and I don't really know what to say, so God direct me now. Well, I expect with God's help I will get alright. Would I not be better able for teaching than housework? If I gave up teaching would I*

be much of an asset at home—would I be able to cope with the work singly? I am afraid not. Perhaps in the name of God we should buy Mahons [the Aughawillan house and farm], and I suppose it could always be resold if necessary. If you could get out on a small pension we could live better there than in the barracks. I suppose it would be a safe investment. I can't think rightly. Do as you think best.

That he should retire and come to live with us and work the farm would have appeared preposterous to him while she continued to teach, and was never mentioned again.

At the same time, he was writing to the consultant in charge of her case in the Mater. Unusually, the letter is typed. He must have typed it on the typewriter that sat in the middle of the deal trestle table upstairs in the big room where the office supplies and the bedclothes were kept that the barrack orderly took down each night:

> *Garda Siochana*
> *Cootehall*
> *Boyle*
> *Co. Roscommon*
> *21/11/42*

Mr. John Corcoran, M. Ch. M. B.
64 Harcourt Street
Dublin

Dear Sir,

I hoped to see you when I was in Dublin but was disappointed owing to you being on holiday. I had hoped that it would not be necessary to communicate with you and cause you further annoyance. I find however that it is the family interests that I should try and ascertain the medical outlook on my wife's case. Would you, therefore be good enough to advise me on the following:

1. Should my wife give up teaching?
2. What is your opinion of her chances of recovery?
3. What roughly are the percentages of recovery from her disease taken at this stage she was operated on?

On second thought perhaps I should give you more clearly why I want to know these things. I am very pessimistic in her case. Her relatives are anxious she should remain teaching and while I am quite indifferent as to whether she should remain teaching in normal health, I am anxious she should do what is best in her illness. Her relatives are urging me to financial liabilities which if she remained teaching and enjoyed reasonable health or if there was likelihood of she recovering would be worth chancing and might easily be a boon to herself and the family, but if otherwise might easily prove a disaster. Trusting I am not asking the impossible, I remain, dear sir,

> *Yours sincerely,*
> *Francis McGahern (Sgt.)*

He had already written at the very beginning of her illness and received a detailed report, which may account for the defensive, slightly bullying tone, but it is also in character. The reply came within a few weeks:

30 Fitzwilliam Square
Dublin
8.12.42

Dear Mr. McGahern,

Re your letter of 21st. I would not advise that your wife give up teaching as long as she continued in good health and then only on medical advice. She will probably be happier at her work than otherwise.

She had a highly malignant type of growth in which the outlook is, in general, very bad. Without treatment she would have had no chance of survival beyond a year from the time I saw her first. She has had the most radical operative treatment possible and thorough deep X-ray treatment afterwards which gives her the maximum hope of recovery. She probably has a 30% chance of complete recovery. I would not advise you to undertake any financial liabilities on the hope of her complete recovery. She is obviously a bad risk, everything possible has been done for her, you can now only hope for the best.

Yours,
John Corcoran

He communicated neither this nor the previous report to my mother or to anybody else but went ahead and bought Corrama-hon. When he sold his homeplace at Gowna, it went most of the way to paying for the new house and farm. My mother saw her new home for the first time that September when she was allowed out of hospital for a few days. She travelled alone by train to Dromod. Pat met the train and she stayed with him and Maggie in the shop in Ballinamore. Her time was too short to visit the barracks; she said she would find it too hard to leave once she was there.

What is amazing is that my father did not go to see her even for a few hours while she was in Ballinamore. Cootehall was only eighteen miles away. She wrote him a long account of the visit when she returned to Dublin and the hospital.

At eight o'clock on the morning the school reopened after the summer holidays, Pat drove her to the priest's house in Aughawillan. The priest, Father McEntee, was glad to see her. Here, Maggie's and Pat's part in securing the school becomes clear, as "Pat insisted it was most necessary to give him (Father McEntee) an offering of five pounds." This was the fee the surgeon had been paid for her operation. My father, despite his religiosity, would never have agreed to pay such a sum. At the time, teachers paid fixed dues to the priests at Christmas and Easter and on being appointed to schools. The fact that this tax was unofficial made it no less mandatory. She and Maggie and Pat understood this. After my mother signed the necessary forms, she joked that she had better be leaving if Mr. McMurrough was keeping new time or she'd be late for school. "You are in plenty of time, Mistress Susan. You don't have to worry," the priest's good will can be glimpsed in the answer. "He's an oddity who keeps neither new or old, just McMurrough's time, any time he comes, Mistress Susan."

"In the school the children stared me out of a face for a few moments, and then Mr. McMurrough came and greeted me," she wrote of her first morning in the school.

She taught for the day. Arrangements had already been made for someone to take over from her until she was well. The system allowed the sick teacher to pay the sub and to keep the difference between her own salary and what she paid the substitute. When the school closed, she went to see Corramahon. What she saw dismayed her. The small, two-storey slated house had recently been thrown up in the middle of a field and was already deteriorating. A similarly built cowhouse with an asbestos roof stood in the same field close to a hedge. There was no gate or garden or footpath, or even a street in front of the house. "Firstly it is good to get a house so near the school," she wrote my father. "I admit I was disappointed with its appearance, but I expect a bit of plastering and painting will make it alright. I believe there will be no point doing this next year so we must do what we can this year. But in time we can improve things and I suppose we were lucky to get it. So thank God it is something to call our own at last."

He would have been furious when he received the letter, and he would have seen the hand of her relatives in the improvement plans as well as the expense. "I was not so disappointed in Mahons as you seem to think," she wrote back defensively. "On the contrary I am very glad to get it as what would we have done otherwise for a house. The only thing that annoyed me was the dampness in the rooms caused by the piping becoming loose etc. As far as I can remember you gave your opinion on it and it was quite favourable. Maybe you have changed." In her next letter, when she is back in treatment, the battle lines are clear and she appears to withdraw, but far from abjectly: "I have no notion of having repairs done without your advice. The only thing is that if the plastering was done before the winter the walls would be drier. In my opinion the most important repairs are the walls, windows and outside doors. Of course I am not much of a voice on these matters. You will know best yourself."

The family my father's suspicions and resentment had turned on were intelligent, hard-working, kind, humorous, sociable and disciplined. They were, above all, rooted in their own lives and helped one another in spite of the hostilities and irritations, competing self-interests and the differences of personality that come into play in all close relations. The small fields they had wrested a living from on the Iron Mountains above Corleehan Church were worse than poor. On the hill behind the house, where there was a trout stream with small pools, rock and bare gravel showed between the rushes. A few boggy meadows below the house gave them potatoes, turnips, cabbage and the winter's fodder. All the names on that part of the mountain were Northern—McManus,

McGovern, McGirl, Maguire—many of them related. Generations earlier, some had been weavers in the North who were
undercutting the established Protestant weavers. In organized violence, their looms were broken, their houses burned, and they fled
west and south. Before they settled on the mountain, these slopes
were thought too poor to support a people, though its thin seams
of coal and iron had been mined sporadically for generations. As
a people they were resourceful, thrifty, careful; they had to be.
Even when my aunt and uncles grew comfortable, and one
relatively rich, they abhorred any kind of extravagance or self-
indulgence. The single aberration seems to have been the girls'
choice of husbands. All three McManus girls married vain, self-
indulgent men who were essentially childish, as if the sexual
instinct craved a rougher cloth.

The road that climbed into the mountains from Corleehan
was often torn with floods. From this road a narrow lane between
low whitethorns ran to my grandmother's house. In its humble
way, this lane was beautiful. On its banks grew primroses, vetch,
blueberries and many wild strawberries. This must have been the
source of my mother's love of lanes. To the right of the lane was
Maguires, a big two-storeyed slated house—they had made
money from gravel pits and contracting, and priests were in the
family—and at the very end of the lane stood the three-roomed
cottage. My Uncle Jimmy thatched a seventh of the roof every
year, and each strip of thatch showed up in shades of black and
brown and recent gold. The thick walls below the thatch were
whitewashed, and at each end of the house were climbing roses.
The stones of the wall across from the house were also whitewashed, and a little iron gate underneath an arch made from
trained whitethorns led into a small herb and flower garden.
Above the house the byre and small stable and fowl house were
thatched and whitewashed, as was the turf shed and the cart
house. At the bottom of the meadows they kept a row of white
beehives. The heather honey was sold to the forerunner of health

shops in Dublin, and it was a useful supplement in good years, allowing the house luxuries they couldn't otherwise afford. The piece of bog they owned was so high up on the mountain that when drawing home the turf Uncle Jimmy had to leave with the horse and cart at five in the morning if he wanted to get a second load home by night.

Inside, the house was so clean and trim that it was like the inside of a small ship or boat. Beneath the deep window a folded table hung from a blacksmith's rail set in the wall. It was lifted out and set at mealtimes and folded back when the meal was finished. Pots hung from an iron rail that swivelled above the open hearth. There was a large brown flour bin and a neat open dresser against the wall, but very little else other than chairs and stools and some buckets. A few religious pictures and a shop calendar were on the whitewashed walls, and a small red lamp burned beneath a picture of the Sacred Heart on a narrow mantel above the hearth. The space above the lower room was open beneath the thatch and reached by a ladder. When I saw it as a child, the horse's harness hung there, and it was where my uncles slept when they were young. The three sisters slept in the room beneath the loft. The door to the upper room was always closed.

Jimmy and my mother were exceptionally bright. They both won the King's Scholarship in different years, around the time the First World War began, and they were the first to do so off the mountain. As this was a source of pride within the family, I often heard it discussed, and it was generally agreed that Jimmy was even better than Sue.

"To think that all my life I have lived among stupid people," Jimmy, who was wonderful company but who could be very sharp and unforgiving, complained to me when he was old. "Most of them do not even know where their own dead are buried. They have to come to me when they need to find the grave."

Their house was the one house my father could never enter.

Once, when he drove me to see my grandmother before she died, he had to wait by his car at the end of the lane. When the visit was over, my Uncle Jimmy walked me part of the way down the lane, but said goodbye to me before my father or his car came into view.

There was never much of a possibility of Jimmy being able to take up the scholarship: he was the older boy and his father was ailing. I learned later that when my mother took the scholarship and went as a boarder to the Marist Convent in Carrick-on-Shannon, it was far from easy for them to keep her there. They had to scrape to pay for the extras the scholarship didn't cover, but they would never complain or draw light to themselves for such sacrifices. They managed and were proud of her and that was all. She, in her turn when she began teaching, helped both Pat and Maggie to establish themselves in Ballinamore, and the three of them lived together for years at the shop on High Street by the railway station until my mother married. My father's constant suspicion that she was still giving them money at the time of Aughawillan was unfounded. If anybody was helping anybody, by then it was Maggie and Pat who were helping our mother.

The rooms behind and above the shop were comfortable, and they too had something of the neatness and spareness of a ship. A long, lino-covered table stood beneath the window on the yard. A smaller table, usually covered with a bright tablecloth, rested between the black-leaded range and the little curtained spy window on the shop. In the evenings the shop was often left untended, a bell above the door announcing the customers. There were customers my aunt disliked, and whenever one of them entered and was recognized through the spy window she would send out whichever girl was helping her at the time. "Go out, Mary, like a good girl and get rid of that dose as soon as you can." At the back of the room was a large sofa where visitors sat. Neat strips of old bicycle tyres protected the steps of the stairs. On a nail in the shining bathroom beside the toilet bowl were pink wrapping papers taken from the Jaffa oranges she sold. A roll of toilet paper was a luxury too far.

After her first home on the mountain and this comfortable house on High Street, my mother must have been a great deal more than "disappointed" at the first sight of the house that was now her own. Nothing could have looked more bare or unlived in than the house in the middle of the field. Standing alone in the field in the evening after teaching for the one day in Aughawillan School, it must have filled her with dismay; but in her practical way, and placing her trust in God to see her through, she would make of it what she could, in the same way as she faced back alone into her illness and its treatment the next day. Pat left her to the train at Dromod.

Behind her practicality and quiet cheerfulness, and the unusual gift of making people feel better about themselves, was deep religious belief: "God has given me near-perfect health for forty years," she wrote to my father, "and now that He has taken that health away, it must be for some inscrutable reason of His own to test my faith. In Him and by Him and for Him I live and place my trust, and to Him alone I pray." When life became too difficult, it was to this source she turned, and was unreachable there even to my father.

In nearly all things they were opposites. His upbringing was as an only child. He was religious too, but his religion was of outward show, of pomp and power, edicts and strictures, enforcements and observances and all the exactions they demanded. In his shining uniform he always walked with slow steps to the head of the church to kneel in the front seat. She would slip quietly into one of the seats at the back.

He was also extraordinarily secretive. Neither then nor later did I ever hear him speak of his early life, or the Latin school in Moyne which he had attended into the ninth or tenth grade, the equivalent of secondary schooling. His mother must have entertained hopes that he would become a priest. A number of his classmates went on to be ordained for the American mission. One, it was said, rose to be a bishop in Oregon. After my father died, the curator of the Garda Museum sent me his complete garda file. It detailed the outwardly honourable and undistinguished career of a garda sergeant who had been in the first intake of recruits on the foundation of the State. He won immediate promotion. The single document that interested me most was a copy of his application form filled out in his own hand. To "Previous Work Experience," he answered, "Three years in the IRA." I knew he had fought in the war, but none of the details, since he never spoke about either the war or his part in the war; but it meant that he had gone straight from the Latin School in Moyne into the IRA and from the IRA into the new garda force when the Civil War began.

When I was very young, I heard cousins of his describe one incident from that time. As he was in the IRA and on the run, the neighbours gathered to save the hay for his mother because it was too dangerous for him to be seen around the house. They were in the middle of the hay-saving on a hot day above Lough Gowna when, without warning, he appeared in the hayfield dressed in a tailored suit, white shirt, tie, new shoes. He took hold of a pitchfork and proceeded to work with his neighbours until nightfall, when he left as suddenly as he came. What amused and interested them was that never once, in spite of the heat, did he remove his jacket or loosen his collar and tie. They were plainly proud of his authority and striking good looks—"A young lord turning up at a barn dance"—but even more intrigued by his stance and vanity.

The other interesting detail on the application form was that his two sponsors were both parish priests. When Britain placed the Catholic Church on an equal footing with the Church of Ireland, they did so because they saw it as a tool of social order. The country I grew up in was a theocracy in all but name, but I had naively thought that in the early days of the State lip service at least would have to be paid to the Proclamation of the Republic in

1916 which guaranteed equal rights to all citizens irrespective of class or creed; but here it was, without a miss of a beat, still in charge, even as the old dispensation gave way to the new.

Hand in hand with my father's refusal of the past was the demand that his continuing physical presence be immediately responded to without regard to anything that went before or would come after, and that even his most mercurial moods should be reflected in his surroundings. As we grew up we knew hardly anything about him, other than this continuing physical presence. All his relatives were distant. He never sought them out and was generally unwelcoming when they visited. Soon they ceased to come at all, except the occasional cousin, like Tom Leddy, who was as unpredictable as he was. Even when he lived alone in the barracks he did not want them, but, perversely, would encourage them to visit my mother, who was ill prepared for guests and barely managing on her own. There were times when I was curious about his background and early life, and there did come a time when I could ask him without fear, but any enquiry was met with a low glare and silence, the thumbs rotating slowly around one another, and he would simply rise and leave.

Later on in my life, distant relatives of his did seek me out, and I could easily have discovered all that he had refused, but did not. This was not because I was no longer interested or curious—curiosity must be one of the last passions to leave us—but I had come to view the pursuit as idle and was content to leave that part of his life as he wished. Such are the many mysteries of personality that they can, at the very most, be only partially explained by nurture and background.

How did it come about that all three McManus girls, from a background of care and gentleness, good humour and discipline, chose self-centred, childish men? Katie was the oldest and the first to marry into a farm along the canal above a small lake a mile from Ballinamore. Close by was a rich planter's farm, Willow-field, that cousins of ours, the McGoverns, had bought with money Hugh McGovern had made in Alaska. It was through the five beautiful McGovern girls that Katie met Francie McGarry. He was tall and good-looking and had the need to shine even among children, and he drank. Like my father, he was a hypochondriac; when he wasn't drinking he was ailing. My father, too, had drunk to excess when he was young, and was so violent and accident prone in drink—he had a motorbike at the time—that his career was put at risk. Never a man to do anything by half, when he was forced into giving it up he joined the total abstinence movement, the Pioneers, and remained a prominent member of the association for the rest of his life. Katie was small and sharply humorous and hard-working. Francie was so fond of work he'd lie down beside it.

Francie McGarry had a better farm than the farm Katie had grown up on, and it should have been easier to make a living. One time he was in bed with some mysterious complaint for so long they had to send for the doctor. The doctor knew his patient, and after a straight-faced examination concluded that there was nothing wrong that a noggin of hot whiskey wouldn't cure. The doctor had another sick call to make on his way back, and as he returned to his car he was passed by his former patient of an hour earlier powdering towards town on a bicycle.

As Pat and Maggie disliked Francie, Katie turned to Jimmy and her mother for help with her husband's drinking. There was a priest in the Gran monastery near Enniskillen who had a great name for curing drunkards. After some careful diplomacy, it was agreed that Francie would cycle into the mountains, since it was nearer to Enniskillen, spend the night there, and then he and Jimmy would head for the Gran the next morning. To brace himself for his ordeal, Francie had a number of drinks in the town and was fairly tired by the time he reached Drumderg. He was welcomed and indulged, but not with alcohol, and after a pleasant evening he slept like a log in the lower room. Early in the morning the two men set out for the Gran. The priest received them agreeably. An offering was made. He then interviewed Francie privately, and the two men prayed together. His confession was heard. Francie made a solemn resolve to go from day to day without alcohol for the next three months when he'd return to the Gran, and the priest would review his progress. In the meantime, he should say certain prayers every day and the priest would pray that he be given the strength to keep his pledge. Francie was overjoyed. As they left, he suggested that they go into Enniskillen to celebrate the happy resolution. Jimmy resisted and managed to steer him towards the mountains and his home outside Ballinamore. Along the way his mood changed, and he launched into a bitter tirade against Katie and her children. It was they who were unsettling his nerves and driving him to drink. He hadn't slept as well in months as he had slept the night before. Nothing Jimmy was able to say could dissuade him from returning with him to Drumderg. He was going to live with them for ever in the mountains and be free of all stress and anxiety and drink. My grandmother's strong, humorous face must have been a study when she saw the two men returning together late in the evening and learned the outcome of their mission to the Gran. What reasoning or coercion they used the next morning to shift him back to his long-suffering wife and children, I do not know.

At this time, because of the power of the Church and the Church's teaching, many married without any sexual knowledge or knowledge of the person they were marrying. The men generally married for sex. There was no other way to have it. The result was usually the arrival of a large number of children in rapid succession. There were families in which the children were cherished, but many more where they were resented as unwanted mouths that had to be fed, the unpleasant and unavoidable results of desire. Some men and women observing this were determined not to marry. This was strengthened by economic necessity, as many did not come into the means or the freedom to provide for a wife and family until they were old. The ideal of the society was the celibate priest. The single state was thus elevated. The love of God was greater than the love of man or woman; the sexual was seen as sin-infected and unclean. As an altar boy in red and white with a lighted candle I took part in many ceremonies of "churching," when after Mass in the empty church women who had recently given birth would come to the altar rail to be cleansed and re-admitted into the full body of the faithful.

My father seems to have shared this reluctance to marry. When he came to Ballinamore as a young sergeant in the early 1920s, my mother had moved from her first position in the convent to the small school of Lisacarn a mile outside the town. Such were the puritanical constrictions of the time, there were not many places a young woman teacher and her suitor could meet without giving cause for scandal. One such respectable house was Kelly's, close to Lisacarn. They were cousins of my mother, with a tradition of priests in the family. Here the courting couple met on most Sunday evenings. My father always enjoyed such evenings, in which weighty events of the nation or locality were discussed solemnly between intervals for tea or cards. He usually dominated evenings like these by his physical presence. One Sunday when the evening was in progress within the house, his expensive black Crombie overcoat was stolen from the porch. Someone had entered the porch silently during the evening and left with nothing but the black Crombie. As such coats would stand out if worn or sold for gain, the only reason for taking the coat was to get even. "He was severe and very strict with everybody," Thomas Kelly explained. My father had the guards make extensive inquiries and searches, but the black Crombie was never found.

Part of this small society of young people in the town were two teachers, Madge and Tom Sharpley, a brother and sister, who were regular visitors at Maggie's shop on High Street. The Sharpleys came from a rich farm on the edge of the town, and their brother sold milk and cream from a horse and cart to the whole town. The milk was measured out from the creamery cans into whatever vessels the people brought to the cart as it drove slowly through the town. Tom was unsuccessfully in love for years with the beautiful Kathleen McGovern of Willowfield. Neither of them was ever to marry. He had a small car and would drive parties of young people to the sea at Strandhill or Bundoran in the summer. In his later years, I often found him sitting on the sofa in Maggie's, wearing his brown hat, recovering from a hangover.

Madge Sharpley was a ferocious snob, and when another brother married a Miss Delahoyde from a prosperous family which dealt in fowl and goats and rabbits, she remarked, "Won't the Sharpleys look nice down among the feathers?" She herself married Mulligan who owned the bakery in the town. He was tall and strong and as proud as Madge, but embarked from time to time on drunken sprees. On one such tear he got out of hand, and word was sent to the barracks. "There's no man in this town fit to take me to the barracks," Mulligan boasted when my father arrived. "I'll take you," my father responded, and drew his baton without making any attempt at persuasion. Not only did he take him to the barracks but he gave him such a beating that there was talk of civil action. Madge never spoke to him again, while remaining friendly with my mother and Pat and Maggie. Some time afterwards Mulligan ran away to England with another woman, leaving Madge high and dry in the big house across from the bakery, but she always spoke sentimentally about him, seeing his elopement as an aberration brought about by the beating he had received.

During my father's stay of duty, the bank in Ballinamore was robbed at gunpoint by the Doherty brothers who had been in the IRA and fought on the Republican side in the Civil War. This was private enterprise. When the IRA came looking for the proceeds of the robbery, the Dohertys disappeared to America and didn't return until the 1930s, when they invested in dancehalls and bars and large farms. Pat Doherty boasted that he never allowed a man into his dancehall that he wasn't able to throw out personally. Their younger brother Jimmy, too young for both the bank robberies and America, burned down his house a number of times for the insurance money and succeeded as a politician. This was an instance when my father broke his embargo on the past. I heard him remark casually while speaking about the Dohertys that if he had been armed on the day of the bank robbery not one of them would have left Ballinamore alive. I believed him.

Because of the political unrest, the young guards were never allowed to remain in any one station for long but were kept regularly on the move to different parts of the country. My father's next transfer was to Burtonport in Donegal, but before he left Ballinamore he and my mother became engaged to be married.

The engagement was to last many years. Over those years he was sent to different parts of the country and he had dalliances with many women. All that time, she remained in Ballinamore, teaching in Lisacarn, helping Maggie in the shop, and though she had admirers, she looked on the engagement ring she wore as being as binding as plain gold. In May of 1932, the year of the Eucharistic Congress, she returned his engagement ring. Whether this uncharacteristic assertiveness was brought about by rumours of other women or because she had found someone else she was interested in, or because of pressure from family and friends about the unseemly length of the engagement, I am uncertain. From the vague talk that swirls and vaporizes about such events in every family, I think that all three may have come into play. There was a young teacher in love with her, and there were rumours of other women, and the engagement had dragged on for seven years. What is certain is that the return of the ring was not done for effect, but the effect was instantaneous.

He, who had all kinds of excuses for postponing his visits over the years, was in Ballinamore the very next day and did not leave until she agreed to marry him in August. The only record of their relationship is the letters she wrote him from Ballinamore to where he was stationed in Shanaglish in Galway in the months leading up to the wedding. They are concerned for the most part with practical matters: the letters of freedom he needed to obtain, where the wedding should be held, the honeymoon spent, the clothes they'd wear, their wedding guests.

What shows throughout all the letters is that she was very happy. The nationalist flavour of the time can be glimpsed in the *cupla focail* that ends each letter, *Mo gradh siorrai* and *Mo gra go Daingin*. She writes of spending a whole day in the convent listening to a broadcast of the Eucharistic Congress on the Athlone station. A letter is written from St. Patrick's Purgatory on Lough Derg, where she had gone on pilgrimage to ask God's blessing on their marriage: "Came here yesterday and feeling a bit blue after the vigil last night. The tea is as black as ever and the water as brown but it is worth all. I feel very happy now."

My father was both incensed and shaken by the return of the engagement ring. When he writes her from Shanaglish, after securing her agreement to marry him in August, he wants to give the ring back immediately. This she refuses: "No need to talk of returning your ring. With God's help we will be married in August and then you will be giving me the one—just a plain gold band."

Whenever he was put on the defensive, as he would have been by the return of the ring, his immediate reaction was to switch his attack to something unconnected where he felt he held the advantage. Maggie and my mother shared the same bedroom on High Street, and during the time he was winning back my mother— declaring that he had tried to extinguish his love for her but wasn't able—he spotted a jar of expensive powder on her dressing table, and as soon as he was back in Shanaglish he wrote accusing her of this extravagance. He didn't choose well:

*Well, Frank, dearest, you will be glad to hear that I do
not use powder. That powder you saw on the dressing
table was given to Maggie last summer as a present from
Annie Reynolds. I sometimes shake it on my hands to
save them perspiring but never any further. You see it has
lasted a long time. So don't worry on that score. I never
use powder since the row we had a long time ago about
same and won't ever use it again unless you tell me I need
it. It is quite harmless in moderation, but I couldn't
afford it, and couldn't bother either, so now that's that.*

There is a faint hint of Maggie's mockery in the tone. In a happier letter she writes of meeting her old parish priest on her way to tell him of her impending marriage:

"I was going to see you, Father."

"What did you want with me, Susan?"

*"I'm getting married in early August and wanted to
tell you, Father."*

"Who are you getting married to?"

*"Sergeant McGahern who was stationed in the town
a while back."*

"The sergeant here, is it?" he said laughing.

"No," and this time I shouted.

*"Yes. I remember him. That's a good little while ago
since he was here."*

The priest gives her every offer of help, and she thanks him and he shakes her hand and gives her his blessing:

*"Goodbye now and God bless you and God's blessings
go with you."*

I had only gone a few steps when he called me back.

"Are you going with him or staying?"

"I am staying."
"That's right, stay."
Now that's my interview with Fr. McKiernan. He was
a very nice poor old man, nice with me always.

My father wanted the wedding to take place in Dublin. He feared she would invite too many of her friends if it was held in Ballinamore. She dissuaded him against Dublin, on the grounds that it would be too expensive—they'd have to pay for Father McKiernan's travel and hotel, as well as other expenses—and promised not to invite many people, adding that since it is August most of the local teachers she'd be expected to invite would be away on holidays.

She writes of helping Maggie in the shop on a Fair Day until late at night, and is glad the Fair is held only once a month. Maggie acquires a pup no bigger than a kitten, and she describes their delight in its play. Maggie goes for a week's holiday to the ocean at Bundoran, taking advantage of an excursion fare on the Aughawillan Pioneer Bus, and my mother takes over the shop from the stand-in girl when she comes from Lisacarn at the end of the school day.

Her love of Lisacarn and its summer lane of wild flowers appears in another letter: "I have not any news—doing my bit each day in Lisacarn, and so the time flies uneventfully, thank God for everything. I like Lisacarn in the summertime and enjoy getting out in the mornings to go there. All the teachers seem to like Lisacarn—casts a spell of its own—Mrs. Gannon is lonely for it still."

They were married in Ballinamore that August, and took a car from the wedding breakfast to catch a train to Dublin from Belturbet. At the end of the honeymoon they returned to Shanaglish in Galway. She spent the rest of the long school holidays in the barracks. When the holidays were over, she returned to Lisacarn and the shop by the railway station on High Street and he stayed on in Shanaglish.

Though my father's secrecy was practically pathological, he and I were to live at such close quarters over so many years that it became impossible to close every door, blind all the windows. I heard him one day in casual conversation with another man about how expensive oranges were when they were young. My father said he loved oranges then, and when he knew he was going to be married he bought two dozen oranges in Galway and went to sit on a park bench and ate them all. He felt he would never be able to afford oranges again once he was married. In those first years his fears couldn't have been much realized other than in his imagination. My mother's salary was higher than his.

They were married a year and a half before she was pregnant. Even when children did start coming year after year, he stayed relatively free. He was not stripped of his car and continued to live in the barracks with the big Cossor radio, a woman coming in each day to cook and clean for him, while my mother's salary kept us.

We spent the long holidays of the summer in the barracks, but outside of that he saw us only when he wanted to, visiting us in the blue Ford.

The day we all arrived at the barracks with Bridgie McGovern after our mother had entered hospital he must have felt that everything he feared when he bought and ate twenty-four oranges on the park bench had come home to roost and crow. The schooling that he had long advocated now came into full force. In silence we ate at the table under the window on Coote's Archway, while he ate in the middle of the room facing the big sideboard mirror. Any squabble or sound from us would bring a quelling look. Before he left to go down to the dayroom, we lined up for him to inspect our presentability before we'd head for school. Most mornings he'd check behind our ears. Each day was closed by the Rosary. He knelt at the same place as he ate, placing a newspaper on the cement and resting his elbows on the table as he faced the big sideboard mirror. We knelt at chairs around the room. There were many prayers after the Litany and always one for "the children's mother," though we had no idea where she was or for what we were praying. When all the prayers were ended, we went up to him one by one to where he sat on the chair and kissed him on the lips, "Goodnight, Daddy."

The best times were the days he took me on the river in the tarred boat. I'd hold the lines while he rowed. In the silence I'd hear my sisters' cries from the barracks, now uninhibited in their play. "I can hear a big pike on his motorbike coming up from Moran's Bay," he would say when he was in good humour. Often, the river seemed to liberate him from himself, but those moments were fragile. Tangled lines or a sudden slip of the tongue could cause the whole day to unravel; but fraught as they sometimes were, these outings were my introduction to the river, which became in the years ahead both an escape and a blessed need.

In her letters from the hospital at this time, my mother finds the treatment hard and unpleasant but does not complain. "Such is life." She makes friends with the nuns and other people in the wards, especially a Mrs. Flanagan, whose son Paddy was a newly ordained priest. She may have spoken of her hopes for me to Mrs. Flanagan. She borrows money from my father to pay the hospital bills and promises to pay back the loan and to clear off all the other expenses as soon as she gets back to teaching. When she moves from the hospital out to lodgings in Dún Laoghaire, she assures him that she spends nothing but her board and tram fare to and from the hospital. Eventually, he pushes her too far, and again it is over the children, as if he had no knowledge or care for the boundaries that exist between people. "God direct us," she writes. "He knows all. He can do all. In Him I trust." She places herself beyond any human jurisdiction, including his, before she continues to the heart of what she has to say:

*And the children. What shall I say? I can only ask God to
make them better children and give me His help to bring
them up in His fear and love. So I must pray hard and
that is all I can do while here. It is not fair though to
blame them for my illness. I only did for them what any
other mother would do, and I was happier doing so,
never the less I must try and mend my ways and theirs,
God helping us all.*

The tarred boat had been taken from the water and left upside-down on lengths of timber under the sycamore tree. Out from the tree my father started to erect a windmill that would bring electric light to the barracks. The days had turned golden. In fields along the roads corn was being reaped and tied into sheaves and stooked. All the turf was home and stacked. Soon the digging and pitting of the potatoes would begin.

I was seven years of age and would be eight by the time the potatoes were pitted. I must have written to my mother, though I had no idea where she was and I have no memory of writing. A letter from her to me survives, written in very large letters. She hopes that I am a good boy and catching big fish and helping Daddy. What must have been words from heaven end the letter: "I hope to be home soon and to see you all."

She did not come to the barracks but to the shop on High Street. She stayed there while Corramahon was being made habitable, and Pat drove her out to the school in Aughawillan each morning. When the school closed at three, she walked to the house to oversee the work and put down fires. Pat collected her there in his hackney car late in the evenings and brought her back to the shop. I don't know if my father visited her or not at this time, but it would appear from the letters that he didn't. When Corramahon was ready, she asked that I go and live with her for the first week before being joined by the other children and

Bridgie. The doctors had advised her to make her way gradually back into teaching and the full life of the house.

When I saw my mother again it was as if my lost world was restored and made whole and given back. Pat had come to the barracks for me in his car. We drove straight to Aughawillan. I hardly saw anything when we got out of the car at the little iron gate on the road, so great was my longing. It was half-day in the town, and Maggie had cycled out to be with my mother after school. They heard the car and came outside. I could hardly believe the joy that my eyes were seeing, and instinctively drew back and grew so self-conscious that I was barely able to walk beside my uncle down the new path of cinders. Not until I was nearer did I give way and run towards her until I was in her arms. Maggie teased me about my loss of words because of always talking too much and asking too many questions. I was ashamed that I was weeping.

Inside, a big fire of branches was blazing in the open hearth. Above it a kettle hung from a black iron rail that swung. Maggie had brought a sweet cake from the town and tea was made.

"They are all the best in the barracks," Pat said as we drank the tea and ate the sections of cake. "They'll be down next week."

I could taste nothing, neither tea nor cake, with the relief that she was back again and that I could touch her sleeve if I reached out. She was smiling and happy in her quiet way, while being attentive to everything, but there were times too when she looked close to tears.

"I heard you were a good boy and caught big fish with Daddy in the boat."

"We caught pike and perch and eels."

"And you had new teachers?"

"None of us liked the school. They were very hard. We did not know where you were. We were beginning to be afraid you might never come back."

"I was in hospital," she said quietly. "I was sick and had to be there on my own for them to make me better. I hope you prayed for me."

Maggie went outside and Pat climbed the short wooden stairs to look at the bedrooms.

"Every night we prayed for you at the Rosary, and I prayed for you on my own. For God to send you home to us again."

"It's not a mansion, this house, but it's our own," she said. "The land is good. There are fine meadows."

"We won't have to move and we'll be able to have animals?"

"Our moving is over. I'm permanent in Aughawillan."

When Maggie returned, she was unusually quiet. The bedroom floors were so thin that we could hear every sound Pat made in the bedrooms.

"They're drying!" he said when he came down. "The back room is good."

"The gutters helped, and the windows—it's good we got them painted while the weather was dry."

I wheeled Maggie's bicycle up the cinder footpath to the car on the road. Pat put the back wheel of the bicycle into the boot and secured it with rope. The two women embraced before Maggie got into the car.

"I'll be out tomorrow evening to see how the two of yous are getting on if I don't have too many runs to do off the train," Pat said awkwardly before he got into the car.

"Don't worry," my mother said. "You have done far, far too much for us already."

I was lightheaded with happiness, almost delirious as I watched the car drive away. My beloved was home and I was alone with her. The evening was clear and dry, the leaves yellow and fallen, and there was a burning red sun on the rim of the sky. We looked at the upstairs rooms, the two small bedrooms off the narrow landing, the larger bedroom where we'd sleep that night. The windowsills were low and deep enough to sit in. The ceiling boards were fixed to the rafters, only a few inches beneath the slates, and took on the shape of the roof. In wind and rain these frail rooms were thrilling at night because they brought us so close to the storm and yet kept us warm and sheltered and safe.

We walked the land together, going first through the meadows around the house. There was a spring well in the long meadow that ran to the woods. By a wooden plank we crossed into the small rough fields of the hill in front of the house. On the other side of the road was an even rougher hill that was also ours. This had been long neglected, and some of the fields were half covered with furze and briar. Close to the road stood the roofless stone walls of the old house, and beside it a wild kitchen garden rich with weeds. "This is where they should have built our house. You'd wonder what made them move into the middle of that field," my mother said. "People do strange things."

She spoke of the hospital, of two trained singers who were patients in the ward and sang for them in the evenings, of how she made friends with Mrs. Flanagan, whose son Paddy was a priest. Out of the close friendship my mother formed with Mrs. Flanagan, her dream for me took shape, and I in turn took it up and gave it a further childish shape, until it was impossible to tell to whom the dream belonged.

One day, like Paddy Flanagan, I would become a priest. After the Ordination Mass I would place my freshly anointed hands in blessing on my mother's head. We'd live together in the priest's house and she'd attend each morning Mass and take communion from my hands. When she died, I'd include her in all the Masses that I'd say until we were united in the joy of heaven, when time would cease as we were gathered into the mind of God. There was no provision for my father or any of my sisters. Was the dream selfishly mine, or was it her dream, or was it a confusion of our different dreams? When she asked me, as she often did, "Who do you love most of all?" I would answer readily and truthfully, "You, Mother," and despite her pleasure, she would correct me.

"You know that's not right, though it makes me glad."

"I love God most of all."

"And after God?"

"Mary, my mother in heaven."

"And after Mary?"

"You, Mother."

"You know that's not right either."

"I love my earthly father and mother equally."

The part of the dream that did not include my father must have been mine alone.

We walked to Ollarton's with a can for milk. We wore coats, as the night had turned cold under a clear, pale moon. We passed Brady's pool where the horses drank. Across from the pool was Brady's house and the smaller house where the old Mahon brothers lived. In the corner of the meadow below Brady's was a dark, deep quarry. At the railway bridge we turned. An avenue of great trees led up to Ollarton's, and in front of the house was a small lake ringed with reeds, still and clear as a mirror, reflecting the pale moon. When we entered the yard behind the house, we could hear them milking, which they interrupted when they saw us waiting with our can in the doorway. It was characteristic of my mother that she would have neither coughed nor spoken. By the light of a lantern milk was strained and measured into our can from a long-handled metal cup. The happiness of that walk and night under the pale moon was so intense that it brought on a light-headedness. It was as if the whole night, the dark trees, the moon in the small lake, moonlight making pale the gravel of the road we walked, my mother restored to me and giving me her free hand, which I swung heedlessly, were all filled with healing and the certainty that we'd never die. I was safe in her shadow. My chattering at times grew so wild that Mother let go of my hand and placed her fingers on my lips in reproof and amusement and love.

At home we fed the fire with the gathered sticks until flames leaped about on the ceiling and all the walls. The globe of the small lamp burned red before the picture of the Sacred Heart on the mantelpiece. The kettle began to boil and we had tea with slices of bread and jam. Before going upstairs, we knelt in the red glow of the room and the leaping firelight to say the Rosary.

"Thou, O Lord, will open my lips."

"And my tongue shall announce Thy praise."

"Tower of Ivory, House of Gold, Arc of the Covenant, Morning Star, Gate of Heaven," we prayed.

The poor slated house thrown up in the middle of the field was a frail defence against every wind and rain shower that blew, but that night it could have been one of the mansions of heaven.

In the morning we walked to school, past Brady's pool, by Brady's slated house and the thatched house where the old Mahon brothers lived, past the dark, deep quarry. Across the railway bridge Mahon's shop rose up at the foot of the hill. The little stone railway station stood a little way below the bridge. As soon as we crossed the bridge, we were joined by other children. The school stood beside the road on the top of the hill. There were two classrooms and a connecting porch in front, where the coats were hung and brooms and basins and buckets were kept. The field behind the school ran downhill, divided into two playgrounds by a wall. In the middle of the wall stood the dry lavatories, the infants' and girls' playgrounds separated from the boys' by the same wall. The whole was enclosed by thick whitethorn hedges, broken by ash and oak above the earthen banks and a deep drain.

We met Mr. McMurrough, a small, nervous, bespeckled man, who had even more ailments than my father and was forever in trouble with inspectors over unkept records and lacklustre teaching. In her letters my mother had complained about the dusty classroom and the awestruck stare of the children when she first visited the school. Now it was clean and dusted. There were jamjars filled with wild flowers in the windowsills. Almost every child had been given some small task, and they were wonderfully officious in their self-importance and anxiety to please,

which, no doubt, I shared; but there was the constraint, and difficulty as well, that she was also my mother. There were no beatings, but she had a rod with which she used to rap out a warning
if too much commotion or unruliness and competition were getting out of hand. On the rare occasion she used the rod, it
was never much more than a tap and more a disgrace than a
blow. "You've let us all down. I thought you were much better,"
she'd say.

In the boys' playground where I now belonged there were the
usual games of catch and jump and run. Teams were picked, but
sometimes the only ball we had was an inflated pig's bladder,
which, sooner or later, came to grief on the whitethorns.

All these days we had together were dry and bright, even
mildly warm until night came. Every evening we gathered dry
pieces of wood from the hedges around the house as soon as we
came from school. Mother said that the fresh air and exercise was
doing her more good than any medicine. When we came in from
the fields, we'd start a great fire in the house. Two workmen were
also there digging drains to draw the damp away from the foun-
dations. After the men had gone home for the day we'd sit in front
of the fire, glowing and pleasurably tired from the exercise, stok-
ing the flames from the heaps of dry wood. The fresh wood hissed
and spat and frothed white in the flames. I am sure I did most of
the chatting and Mother most of the listening, but I believe we
often sat happily silent. The firelight leaping on the walls as the
night came on was in itself a conversation. Later, we'd put on
coats and walk under the pale moon to Ollerton's for milk, past
Brady's pool, turning at the railway bridge to go the white road
until we came to the avenue of old trees by the lake.

One evening we came home with the can of milk to find Pat's
car outside the little iron gate. Pat and Maggie were in the house.
They had come to see how we were getting along and stayed late.
Other evenings after the lamp was lit and before we knelt to say
the Rosary, my mother helped me with the school exercises I was

having difficulty with. These days were so happy that even when we were in bed under the thin roof I was so loath to let go of the day that my mother would have to say firmly that it was time we stopped talking and trusted to sleep if we were to be bright and wide awake for school in the morning.

Suddenly, that brief space we had alone together was gone. All the others came from the barracks in a small, red turf lorry. Bridgie McGovern sat with the driver in the cab holding Dympna. Breedge and Rosaleen, Monica and Margaret were small within the crates of the lorry with beds and furniture and bedclothes and mattresses and pots and pans. When the pins were taken out and the boards dropped, they were lifted down. My mother kissed them in turn, and then took Dympna from Bridgie as they all gathered round her. She looked disappointed for a moment when Bridgie told her that our father hadn't been able to come because of certain duties, but this was soon hidden in all the cries and clamour and competition for her attention. In that frail house in the middle of the field, our whole lost world was everybody's again.

Each schoolday morning we walked with my mother up the narrow footpath of cinders to the little iron gate on the road, our few books and lunch in the school bags of dark-blue cloth our mother had made from decommissioned police trousers. We went past Brady's pool and house, the house where the old Mahon brothers lived, passed the dark, deep quarry, across the railway bridge, and up the hill past Mahon's shop. The Brady children often met us by the pool. At the foot of the hill a small crowd of children was often waiting for my mother, and we'd all climb past Mahon's shop to the school together. Master McMurrough was usually late, and our mother opened the school with her big key. Our lunches were slices of buttered bread and jam and small bottles of milk. The playgrounds were supervised by the older children, and my mother and Master McMurrough had the peace of the empty classrooms for that hour. On wet days the whole school remained indoors.

On the way home from school, Mother often shopped at Mahon's. Mrs. Mahon was a grey-haired, be-whiskered woman, a widowed sister-in-law of the two old bachelor brothers who lived on Brady's street, and she liked to talk with my mother and sometimes gave us sweets from the tall glass jars while we waited.

In my mind we acquired immediately two cows for the asbestos-roofed byre, two bullocks that belonged to Uncle Pat, a pair of goats, a flock of brown hens, a jennet and cart and harness. Reading through my mother's letters I find that everything was bought over many months. In the letters, my mother had to be very careful to defer all decisions to my father, whether they were necessary repairs or improvements to the house, purchases of any kind or the employment of workmen. When anything was done, or seemed to be done without his consent, there was trouble.

I remember one scene in Aughawillan. Only a small section of the paling had been erected where my mother planned to turn part of the field in front of the house into a small flower garden. My father came on his bicycle on a late dry evening while it was still light. Because of the war, all private cars had been taken off the roads, and the blue Ford now rested on blocks in a shed at the barracks. Usually he came at night, with the big silver carbide lamp hissing between the handlebars, his cycling cape and pullups glittering with rain. He was barely in the door when a flow of angry recrimination began, how money was being squandered left and right on the farm, how her relations were pocketing money for themselves, how everything was being done about the place without any reference to *him,* as if he wasn't of the slightest importance.

Usually he was slow and calculating in the first onset of an attack, but he must have been seething as he cycled along and could not wait to unburden himself. Now the attack raged without thought or check. The whole house was silent, frightened. My mother made no attempt to defend herself. In a lull in the tirade, the small child Monica, who was a favourite, ran towards him to be lifted in the air, and only for my mother and Bridgie, who rushed between them, he would have swept her against the table or wall in his anger.

"I think we better go outside. We can discuss it there. It's not good for the children," my mother said, and got a copybook in which she kept accounts.

He followed her out angrily. They stood by the part of the paling that had been erected, straight lengths of ash cut from the hedges and nailed to low posts. She was speaking quietly and pointing out figures in the copybook, while he continued to complain and shout.

We watched in a frightened and fascinated silence as he took the book from her hands and shook it in her face before casting it to one side. He stalked out alone into the fields. Normally, Bridgie would have closed the open door and whooshed us away, but she too must have been held by the scene. When he came back from pacing the fields, he had a new list of complaints. Then he calmed, exhausted, and was made much of by my mother and Bridgie, and soon he was eating at the table in a change of clothes, waited on by the two women and charming all around him. He was still in good humour in the morning, but by the time we returned from school that evening he was gone.

On most days—between his hackney runs—Uncle Pat came out to Aughawillan. He was always doing odd jobs about the house and on the land. On Wednesday half-days, Maggie cycled out from the town bringing sweets and bread and fruit from the shop in her carrier basket. Even my Uncle Jimmy, who had his mother, wife and three children to support, and who had less money than either of my parents, offered to loan my mother a stripper cow he did not need until the price of milking cows fell later in the year. The suspicion that they were taking from him and benefiting at his expense was all in my father's mind. In old age he grew obsessed with the idea that his second wife was stealing things from the house to give to her old mother and bachelor brother, when she was only indulging in country barter, taking them bread she had freshly baked, or plums and apples from the orchard, or pots of jam. Either way, the exchanges were trifling compared to the depths of his suspicion. They were no more than gestures or symbols, like flowers, that cement ties and affections, but of this he had no understanding.

There were also times in Aughawillan when our happiness was not threatened by his presence but sharpened and added to by the drama and excitement of his visits. I remember him most of all arriving out of wet dark nights, his black cycling cape and pull-ups and black sou'wester hat shining with rain. The hissing sound of the big silver carbide lamp fascinated us, and we used to vie with one another to get to turn the silver screw on the neck of the lamp that stilled the hissing and caused the beautiful blue flame within the glass to die. There was a definite theatricality about the way he divested himself of his wet outer clothes, letting them fall in pools of water in the middle of the floor to be gathered up and hung in the scullery by my mother and Bridgie. "How are the troops?" he would call out as he let the wet clothes fall on the cement. "Are the troops fighting fit? Are they obeying orders? Are the troops good? Are they marching in time?"

He'd towel his reddish-gold hair, his face, his neck, put on fresh socks warmed by the fire, and sit in unlaced boots to the big meal at the head of the table, waited on by my mother and Bridgie, all of us around the table, clamouring for his attention. Then he'd be gone. "How sad and lonely it was to come home from school and find you had just left," my mother wrote. Occasionally, when he took part of his holidays, he'd stay for most of a week or some days, working at various tasks about the land, and he liked "organizing the troops." He had us gather stones to fill the open drains that had been dug to draw the dampness from the house, promising a prize for the biggest heap. Now, instead of gathering dry sticks from the hedges for the fire, we rushed home from school to gather stones. Soon each of us had our replica of Queen Maeve's grave between the drains, and we were jealous and watchful that the others weren't stealing from our heap to add to their own. We got a cow which Bridgie McGovern milked in the small cowhouse beside the hedge, two young goats, a flock of brown hens with a big red rooster that woke us each morning and would flap his wings if we went too close to the pecking hens, and a brown jennet with a cart and harness. The cart was painted in the traditional blue and red, and had big iron-shod wheels. In the letters, the jennet is described as "old" when he was bought, and there was much grey and white in his brown coat. He had to be slow and quiet for a boy of eight to be able to catch and harness and manage. He was with us for eight or nine years, until he died in a snowstorm. Before he came to us he had spent time with tinkers and was addicted to smoke. Whenever an outdoor fire was lit to burn weeds or branches, he would squeal with pleasure and run to stand stock-still with his nose above the fire. He liked it best when we burned weeds, and would stand for hours hidden in the thick, white billowing smoke. He must have also spent time drawing cans of milk to the creamery, for whenever we passed a creamery can by the roadside he would stop and refuse to budge until I got down from the cart and rattled the creamery can, when he'd move on. He disliked being harnessed, and whenever he saw me come with the bridle he would squeal and gallop to the farthest corner of the meadow. The only way to catch him then was to come with a sprinkling of oats in the bottom of a can.

We loved the pair of young goats. "Springers," Bridgie called them. Because of the damage they did to shrubs and trees around the house and her plans for the flower garden, Mother tried to keep them on the hill, but they'd escape from there, and our cries of delight would ring out as they chased us round and round the house, leaping the heaps of stones and the faces of the open drains.

Most Saturdays I went to town on the train with my mother. Instead of climbing the hill past Mahon's shop to the school, we turned right at the railway bridge and up a little siding to the stone railway station. The Reillys lived in the stationhouse, and their son Paddy, who was fifteen or sixteen, often worked for us on the farm. The little narrow-gauge line ran to Ballyconnell and Belturbet and connected with the mainline Dublin–Sligo trains at Dromod. A smaller branch line went from Ballinamore to Drumshambo and the Arigna coal pits.

Because of the war, the trains had to run on the low-grade Arigna coal, and sometimes it would have been faster to walk the four miles of sleepers from Aughawillan to Ballinamore than to take the train. I think it was seen more as a social outing, when such outings were rare, than a means of transport. On the little gravelled platform there was great friendliness, talk and laughter, the excitement of meetings and greetings. Everybody was dressed in their Sunday clothes. Often my mother wore a fur with the small head and paws of a young fox clasped at her throat. Everybody came up to her on the platform and on the train, and sometimes people gave me coins.

Whenever any of the firemen who lodged at Aunt Maggie's were on the train, they shouted and waved their shovels at us from the engine. On one steep incline, we often had to climb from the train and walk to the top of the hill while the empty carriages slipped back down the track and waited for the engine to get up steam and make another run at the hill. There was never any complaint. I remember muted clapping and a shovel waved in victory from the engine when the train made it to the top of the hill, and we climbed on board again. There was a ticket conductor, Hughie McKeon, a fat man when fat men were rare, who was extremely proud of a big, ornamental gold watch he had received from America which he wore with a gold chain across his black waistcoat. People knew his weakness and never missed an opportunity to ask the time. Uncle Pat met all the trains with his hackney car but as there were seldom any fares on our train we usually rode the few hundred yards to Aunt Maggie's shop in his car.

Three stunted fir trees grew behind the high railway wall in front of the shop, and the little train to Drumshambo left from there. Close by, the white signal box stood high above the level crossing and the white railway gates. On the other side of the tracks loomed the dark, cavernous railway sheds where the engines were repaired and serviced. A hose, like a huge elephant's trunk, ran from the water tank to hang from the centre of the highest arch. Pat used his key to enter by the hall door at the side of the shop, as did the railway men, but we always entered through the shop. Maggie loved to see us come and kissed us both and unbolted the little door beneath the counter-leaf to let us into the kitchen. Pat was generally waiting for us there by then and the kitchen was always wonderfully warm. A kettle or pots simmered on the black-leaded range, and sometimes bits of the hot plates glowed red and orange.

Maggie had many young girls helping her over the years. The girl she had then was Mary. She did the bedrooms and lavatory and landing and stairs in the morning, and helped Maggie cook and clean during the day, and she served in the shop. Pat and the railwaymen ate at the big table beneath the window on the garden. Food was Pat's great pleasure, and he ate in total silence, with complete concentration and an unusual delicacy of movement. The most any question would elicit from him as he ate was an affirmative grunt or an absent, steady, look. When he finished, he'd push his plate away, and his "God bless you" was both a thanksgiving and a sigh of pure pleasure. Over tea and sweet cake he'd relax and chat, sometimes even holding forth. The food was always more delicious at Maggie's than at home. A dish I loved was wild rabbit wrapped in strips of fat bacon and roasted in the oven with carrots and shallots and small roast potatoes. Often teachers who knew my mother joined us in the big kitchen, and there was much talk and discussion.

The railwaymen wore black overalls and heavy black boots. Their smudged faces and hands and arms they washed in hot water in the scullery before sitting to the big table under the window. All of them came from railway families who lived close to the Broadstone in Dublin. They were cocky and quick-tongued and weren't liked. They looked down on the country people: for them, Ballinamore was outer Siberia. Once they had paid Maggie for their bed and board, they'd have little spending money left. Passing the time must have been hard for them in this small town in the middle of nowhere, away from their families and, in some cases, their wives. That is how I remember "Blackie," a tall, strong, aggressively cocksure fireman who had returned to Dublin to be married while working on the trains out of Ballinamore. After his honeymoon he returned to Ballinamore and the trains, and persuaded Maggie to allow his wife to come and stay with him for a week. The other railwaymen were moved into Pat's room for the week, and the young wife arrived on the train. When my mother and I came to town the next day, Maggie was already bristling with outrage—and there was still most of a week to go. I remember the young wife as luxurious and strong. She wore light dresses, heavy make-up and was loud. They spent the day in bed, in a continual rut, only coming down to the kitchen for their meals.

Faced with Maggie's outrage and passive aggression, it was not unnatural that they flaunted themselves all the more. She raged about the state of the bathroom, the bathroom that shone with cleanliness from Mary's mopping and wiping and polishing, where everything was arranged as neat and orderly as the pink wrappings from the Jaffa oranges speared on a nail beside the toilet bowl. There were complaints about towels and bedclothes and the sound of horseplay, but the real offence was never uttered. Everybody grew uncomfortable. She tried to get them to leave, but they had paid in advance and she had to suffer out the week. As soon as the wife left to return to Dublin, Blackie was given his notice and moved to a rival boarding house. Very soon he was replaced by another railwayman, and was never mentioned again, though he often waved to me from the shunting engines.

Another lodger was the line maintenance foreman. The rail bicycle with the wide metal wheels which he and his lineman pedalled at speed along the tracks fascinated me, but he disliked being asked about his work. He had a little learning and was anxious to impress Mother, and was fond of quoting wise saws that pointed up some moral: "Dirt over grease is no disgrace, but grease over dirt is a great disgrace." While the foreman didn't like to be questioned himself, he insisted on quizzing me about what I was learning in school, but this was to try to wrong-foot me in front of Maggie and my mother. He must have been lonely. His family was in Tipperary and he got home for a few days only in every month.

Whenever Uncle Jimmy cycled in from the mountains on a Saturday he joined the teachers on the sofa. He brought all the news of their mother and home place to the two sisters. He'd have all his other business in the town done by the time he came to the shop, but he still had a long cycle ahead of him back into the mountains, and he never stayed long.

Between trains, Mother would take me with her when she went through the town to buy thread and wool and things for the house that Maggie didn't stock. Everywhere people stopped her, and she'd smile and listen and give words of sympathy or congratulation or encouragement, and people looked happier when they left us. I was by her side like a shadow, carrying light parcels, glowing in the affection and warmth she created. When the shopping was done, we went to the church to pray. After the bustle and busyness of the town, the silence in the small church was intense, even the sound of someone moving between the Stations of the Cross seemed loud. After we prayed, we went together to the brass candle shrine one side of the high altar. We bought a penny candle, lit it together, fixed it on the spikes, and made a silent wish. Though she urged me to make sundry and pious wishes for Grace and Salvation and my father and sisters, I always made the same wish: that she would never go away again and be with me for ever.

When we left the church, we always felt uplifted. After tea in Maggie's, Pat drove the small distance to the station. I watched the passengers disembark from the incoming Dromod train, and felt triumphant when Pat netted a fare but disheartened after everyone had scattered and he waved to us before returning alone to the car.

The journey home must have been downhill because we never had to get out and walk. In midwinter the journey took place in darkness lit by the sparks flying from the engine. At some level crossings newspapers and other parcels were thrown from the slowly moving train to people waiting with lanterns. There was a different excitement coming home to the morning's setting out as people compared prices and purchases and spoke of their day, and sometimes there was a sideshow if some man had too much to drink during the long day in town. A lantern met us at the little station, Garradice Halt. At first, we'd have to grope and search for our footing until our eyes grew accustomed to the dark, but occasionally there was a moon and stars that lit the hedges and the yellow ghostly road.

In the house they would all have listened for the train's whistle. Sometimes Bridgie wouldn't be able to keep my sisters inside, and we'd find the twins and Margaret and Monica waiting for us in wild excitement within the little iron gate, demanding to be allowed to carry parcels down the cinder footpath to the dimly lighted house.

I had acquired a small saw by then, and was cutting trees from the hedges into lengths for firewood and using the jennet and cart to draw the firewood to the house. The wood never had time to season, and foamed white at the ends and hissed and spat as the fresh lengths burned on the hearth. After the Rosary was said, we loved sitting in front of the fire and watching the flames leap on the walls and ceiling, trying to postpone the hour when we'd be forced to climb the stairs to bed.

At this time my father began to court me. The *Irish Independent* was his newspaper and they ran a comic strip with pictures and captions, "Count Curly Wee and Gussie Goose," the comic adventures of a pig and a goose, which they published in book form as an annual, the pig an aristocrat who wore spats and a top hat. He bought me the book that Christmas and a small boy's bicycle. From the letters it appears that we spent that Christmas in the barracks. As winter gave way to early spring in Aughawillan, primroses and violets started appearing on the bank above Brady's pool on our way to school. A field for oats was ploughed and sowed and harrowed and rolled. Part of another field was turned into ridges for potatoes. The little fenced garden across the road was dug and manured and sowed with cabbage and other vegetables. As well as the workmen, Uncle Pat was much about the house. A letter from me to my father survives from that April:

> *Dear Daddy,*
>
> *Thanks very much for the pictures [Count Curly Wee and Gussie Goose]. I had great fun reading them. I hope you are well. Come to see us soon. We got two goats. Uncle Pat does not like them. Will you bring over my bicycle please and games. We are all well. I was gugering for Uncle Pat Thursday.*
>
> *Goodbye from Sean to Daddy*

My mother had the two workmen build a stronger paling around the garden she had planned. A path was made down its centre, a wooden gate constructed. High netting wire was put up all around against the goats. In the spring evenings we helped her plant a border of herbs inside the netting wire, and in the flowerbeds the workmen had prepared she sowed marigold, sweet william, lilies, nasturtium, and planted roses.

Unknown to us, there was a fresh crisis. In her letters to my father she states matter-of-factly that her "visitor" has not arrived, but by Easter she is certain she is pregnant. Their reactions could hardly have been more different. He announces from the barracks that he has started a Novena for her and has begun to fast. He also writes to Dr. Corcoran, her oncologist in the Mater Hospital. The doctor's reply is professional and sympathetic:

> 30, Fitzwilliam Square
> Dublin
> 10 April 1943

> F. McGahern Esq.
> Cootehall
> Boyle
> Co. Roscommon

> Dear Mr. McGahern
>   I have your letter of the 5th instant re Mrs. McGahern. I doubt if there is any point in her coming to Dublin at Easter, but I should like to see her about a month after Easter. I can assure you, though I have advised against what has happened, I can readily appreciate the position and I see no reason why either of you should be worried.
>   It is a fact that if the possibilities of recurrence are present, that rapid progress may be brought about by the present condition of affairs. On that score we can only wait and see, and there is nothing we can do about it

*until I see her again, when I shall consider the position
more fully. At any rate I am glad to hear that she is well
and advise her not to worry about the matter.*

Yours faithfully John Corcoran

My mother reassures my father and places her trust in God:

*I am feeling very well. Yes I know where I stand now and
so God knows best. I am sure with His help I will be
quite alright. I am not a bit worried about it at all—it is
awfully good of you to fast and I think it is too much for
you. But you know best. Still it is a lot to do. I place my
trust in God knowing all will be well.*

He presses her to see a priest, a Father Ignatius, who must
have belonged to one of the Orders. He might have belonged to
the Gran near Enniskillen, where Francie McGarry went earlier
with Uncle Jimmy to be cured of his craving for drink. There was
widespread belief in the power of the enclosed orders for all kinds
of healing. My mother bows politely but will not be rushed or
panicked:

*Yes. I will see Fr. Ignatius as early as possible but I must
write him first to see when he is available. I am in the
best of form otherwise and after all God knows best and
I am sure He will bring me safely along, and it might only
be good for me—doctors are not infallible.*

An appointment to see Dr. Corcoran was made. Uncle Jimmy
came to the house one Sunday. It was arranged that our grandmother would come to stay with Bridgie while she was away. This
time she assured me she would not be gone for long and I promised to say my prayers while she was away and to take the girls to

school and cut sticks and not cause Bridgie any trouble. Pat brought our grandmother in his car to the house, and a few hours later drove our mother to the Dublin train at Dromod.

Granny was a small, vigorous woman, with a sharp sense of humour and a strong presence. She had been a redhead but was now completely grey, and often wore a red wool cardigan over the shoulders of her long black dress. Though she was kind and never impatient, there was no way we could bend or question her decrees as we were used to doing with our mother.

Aughawillan Church is small and plain and was built in 1869. All around it is a gravel walk and the graves and headstones of the parishioners. The bell had fallen and rested on the grass beside the main door. The church was about a mile from Corramahon, and we walked to Mass every Sunday and Holy day, past Brady's pool, across the railway bridge, up the hill past Mahon's shop, and the same distance again beyond the school. In the church, men and boys went to the right, girls and women to the left, and I was in the middle of the body of men the first Sunday of our mother's absence. I made the sign of the cross and stood and knelt and sat and prayed like those around me, looking towards the altar in the spaces between the men. Despite her reassurances and promises, I must have been upset by my mother's absence, and I had one of those attacks of manic energy I was prone to. In the church this took the form of rattling my Rosary beads and pulling them vigorously through my hands. I was certainly unconscious of what I was doing and it brought no admonishment from the men around me. When the priest began his sermon he paused a number of times, but I continued to pull and rattle my beads. Then, after a long silence, he said from the pulpit, "Will that boy in the middle seats stop making that noise," and suddenly I realized that the silence and every eye in the church was fixed on me. It was as if God had spoken from on high and I was ruined for all eternity and disgraced here and now in the eyes of the world.

I don't know how I twisted and turned in my agony for the

remainder of the Mass, but as soon as it ended I pushed between the legs of the men, not waiting for Bridgie and the girls, past the men at the door, out the church gate, and ran. I ran and ran, gasping for breath, and felt that if I was able to make it across the railway bridge I was safe. I got past the lane to the football field, past the parochial hall, but before I reached the school I heard the sound of hoofs and the wheels of the traps and sidecars drawing closer. If they caught up with me, my shame and disgrace would be public and known. There was a stitch in my side. I was hardly able to run now, and the hoofs and the wheels were closer. At the school, I climbed over the gate and hid in at the back of the school. I listened to the hoofs pass, the wheels, the bicycles, the footsteps, the voices. When there was silence for a long time, I came out of my hiding place, and after making sure the road was empty, climbed back over the gate. Covered with a sense of exposure and shame, I went down the hill, past Mahon's shop, and across the railway bridge. I hurried past Brady's pool and house and the house where the old Mahon brothers lived. I had been fasting and silently ate the breakfast I was given, and quickly disappeared out the land. Nobody in the house said anything. I hung about the land for hours, but eventually was dragged back to the house by hunger. I couldn't face going in, but stood in the flower garden pretending to be interested in the newly planted herbs and flowerbeds. I couldn't have been more visible.

Suddenly, one of the upstairs windows opened, and Granny stuck her head out. "I hear, Sean, you knocked the priest off his stroke at Mass this morning." She laughed, and said the words as if I had accidentally struck a blow for freedom. My sense of shame and disgrace lifted. I had been restored to the world. I had been condemned from on high and had been given human absolution.

In another week Mother came home. She was well and happy and went straight back to school. With her each morning we went up the cinder footpath to the little iron gate, past Brady's house and pool and the house where the old Mahon brothers lived, past the deep, dark quarry and across the railway bridge and up the hill by Mahon's shop to the school, and returned the same way in the evening. I am sure it is from those days that I take the belief that the best of life is life lived quietly, where nothing happens but our calm journey through the day, where change is imperceptible and the precious life is everything.

All this time, my father was still courting me, and I was charmed and delighted by his favour. When he came to stay, I went with him everywhere through the field. The rich green of the young oats now glistened in the rolled field. The potato shoots broke the sides of the ridges and were moulded. A bank of mud turf belonged to Corramahon, less than a mile away near Garradice. My father was there when the workmen put out the mud on the spread. We ploughed through the plot of mud in our bare feet, leading the jennet and borrowed donkeys while the workmen drew up buckets of water with ropes from the boghole and splashed it on to the mud until it all was trampled into a black paste. Then it was shaped with flat spades into rows and cross-rows and left like loaves of bread to cast the rain and to dry in the wind and sun.

The flowers appeared in the garden in front of the house and my mother tended them in the evenings. When my father came and joked that nobody can eat flowers, she looked at him and smiled. A new cow was bought, which Bridgie milked. When she finished milking, she sometimes allowed me to sit on the stool to strug the dregs from the loose elder. We also had a black kitten now. On the small bicycle I cycled into Ballinamore with my mother on pleasant Saturdays instead of taking the train.

My father promised to take me with him to the Ulster Final. Every year he attended the Ulster Final like a ritual. On the Sunday morning of the Final he arrived early in a borrowed car. He decided that we'd both go to Second Mass in Ballinamore and leave for Clones from there, getting something to eat along the way. This alarmed me. Canon Reilly was the parish priest in Balli-namore, a large, powerful, headstrong man. He had been the manager of the school in Lisacarn I attended with my mother as an infant.

Canon Reilly always came to the school carrying a small brown suitcase. It was said to contain the viaticum and the holy oils used in anointing the sick. One lunch hour he arrived in a rage. The whole school was immediately afraid. A boy of the Cannings, a poor family of many children on the Willowfield Road, had broken into the poor box in the church and later had a feast of chocolates and sweets in the town. Having first extracted a confession from the boy, the priest offered him the choice of being taken to the guards or accepting his punishment there and then. The pale, whimpering boy chose to take his punishment from the priest. With a key, Canon Reilly opened the small brown suitcase and took from it a length of electric flex. In the clearing, between the two sets of benches in the middle of the schoolroom, the beat-ing took place. The whole school watched in stricken fascination, the priest holding the boy with one arm and wielding the length of flex with the other, the beating moving in a slow circle as the boy sought to drop to the floor and to move away from the wire cut-ting into his bare legs. When it was over, crying and bleeding, the boy returned to bury his head in his arms on his bench, while the priest returned the length of flex to the suitcase and gave a short lecture to the whole school on the example they had just witnessed.

I had watched in awe, but by now I also knew of Canon Reilly's fearsome reputation in the town where he was his own law. I was told he had lifted the heavy railway gates off their hinges when he found them closed against him on his way to a sick call, and drove across the tracks in front of the train, frighten-ing everybody and almost causing a terrible accident.

In certain dioceses—our diocese of Kilmore was one, Armagh was another—the teachers had to conduct catechism classes after

Second Mass on Sundays. This was enforced with varying degrees of rigidity, depending on the priest. In Aughawillan there were never any classes. Every child for miles around knew not to go to Second Mass in Ballinamore on Sunday. After Mass, Canon Reilly stood in the church gates, and it was his delight to deliver any child back into the catechism class by the ear. He brooked no argument, accepted no excuses, and it did not matter whether you came from the parish or not. He had also closed all gaps around the church, and it was almost impossible to get by him at the gate.

I explained this to my father and why it would be better for us to leave a little early and attend Mass at some other church on the way to Clones.

"But you're not from his parish," my father argued.

"It doesn't matter. He brings everybody back to the catechism class whether they're from the parish or not."

"You'll get by him," my father laughed, as if he was already interested in the confrontation.

"They say it is hard to get by him."

"We'll give it a shot anyhow. We'll manage," my father said. We attended Mass in the little church with the yew trees at the end of Chapel Lane, and when we came out, the huge bulk of Canon Reilly stood alarmingly between the gates. "Run on ahead while there's still a crowd," my father said.

I attempted to slip through, hidden in a crowd of men, and when I was almost clear, a hand took me by the ear. He held me, waiting to see if there were any other boys trying to slip through late. There were none.

We were joined by my father. By this time, all the Mass-goers had gone except those gossiping outside the church gates.

"We are on our way to the Ulster Final and stopped to attend Mass," my father explained politely enough.

"I couldn't care less if you were on your way to Timbuktu. Every child who comes to Mass here has to attend catechism class. There are no exceptions."

"We'll be late."

"That's no concern of mine."

"Let go his ear." My father was now angry, and the priest looked at him in amazement. Canon Reilly wasn't used to opposition.

"He's going back into the catechism class and nowhere else," the priest said, and began to move me by the ear towards the church.

"If you don't let go his ear, I'm taking your ear in a citizen's arrest. You are preventing us from going about our lawful business."

The Canon looked at my father in further amazement, but when he showed no sign of complying with the demand, my father took hold of the priest's ear. I'm not sure what other words ensued, if any, as this strange procession proceeded through the porch and up the centre aisle, until we stood beneath the sanctuary lamp in front of the high altar, Canon Reilly in the centre holding my ear, my father, who wasn't as large as the Canon, holding the priest's ear. The church was completely empty except for the two catechism classes. A nun was conducting a class for girls in one of the side chapels. In the opposite side chapel Master Gannon stood in front of a class of boys.

Beneath the red sanctuary lamp negotiations took place between these two wilful men, my father and the Canon, and it was agreed that if I joined Master Gannon's class and was able to answer whatever question was put to me we could then both leave. On the other hand, if I failed to answer the question, the matter would have to be considered further. I joined the class in trepidation, as everything now depended on my religious knowledge, which was, at best, uncertain.

"Ask him one question and if he can answer it let him go. And there will never be an exception in this church ever again. Next Sunday I'll declare it from the altar."

I was the centre of attention. Master Gannon was highly amused, but he couldn't allow it to show openly.

"Who made the world?" he asked, and I could hardly believe my ears or my luck. I hadn't expected anything so easy.

"God made the world."

"Go! Both of yous go before I lose control of myself," the Canon roared.

I have a vague memory that the hawthorn was in blossom all along the way to Clones and of waiting about the streets of the town after the match as my father talked with Cavan people he had grown up with, but these memories could as easily belong to other years and Finals. I remember that I was inordinately proud of my father for taking Canon Reilly by the ear and had no sense of sacrilege or outrage. I tried to bring up the incident a number of times, with my mother, with Pat, with Maggie, but every attempt was ignored. Nobody would talk. What they said among themselves I do not know. They all would have known of the strange procession of the ears down the centre aisle of the church, and they must have felt that some dangerous boundary had been crossed.

———————

The weather grew warm and we were allowed to throw our boots away and run barefoot. The soft touch of grass was cool and delicious to our feet as we ran about like young cattle in the first discovery of a fresh field. Grass that had only flourished in the shelter of the hedgerows now covered entire fields. All the hedgerows were a mass of green thick leaf, the banks sprinkled with wild flowers. The potato stalks pushed through the mould to spread out and lock above the ridges, showing tiny blue and white blossoms. I brought water in iron barrels covered with wet sacking with the jennet and cart to the wooden barrel on the headland. When it was filled, the bluestone was set to steep in a bag hung from the broken handle of a spade, and once it had melted and soda was added, the blue turned a rich turquoise. I stood by the barrel with the resting jennet and watched the workmen back up and down the matted furrows with their knapsack sprayers. When the spraying was done and the blue wash was drying on the potato leaves, I helped them rinse the barrels and the machines and take the barrels home. The field of oats was now so tall that I could neither see nor be seen once I entered its green walls. The once playful goats kept to the hill with their kids and could not be enticed back to the house, and they lowered their horns threateningly if we came too close. Uncle Pat's two white bullocks were grazing on the hill. I accompanied him over the fields when he came to look at the bullocks, and I looked at them when he wasn't able to come. He was now very busy. Because of the war that was still raging in Europe, all fuel was scarce and expensive. He had bought an old lorry, stripped it down, and with the mechanic Billy Keegan converted it to a travelling sawmill. The big circular saw was set in a steel platform above the chassis and driven by the heavy engine. The advantage it had over conventional sawmills was that it could move easily from site to site where trees were for sale and convert their timber into firewood along the edges of the wood.

Billy Keegan ran the saw with three huge workmen, who were all members of the Ballinamore tug-of-war team. There were no chainsaws then, and the trees had to be felled with crosscuts and somehow levered on to the steel platform. The scheme may have been my father's brainchild. There were few trees in Leitrim but there were many plantations and small woods in Roscommon, especially around walled estates like Rockingham and Wood-brook and Oakport, and this ingenious mill worked for most of its short life there. My father probably helped with the purchase of the trees and the supervision of the workmen, and as he was fascinated with anything mechanical he would have enjoyed this hugely, especially so since no money of his own was at risk.

Pat continued his hackney business—it was his main source of income—but he didn't like it and he talked of selling his plate if the sawmill was a success. Trees then became more expensive; the sawmill had breakdowns; the men were largely unsupervised. Billy Keegan was clever and notoriously untrustworthy and found ways to sell off some of the firewood in spite of my father's suspicious watchfulness. Once the war ended, the venture was doomed anyhow, but it did not last that long. If the incident of the ears in Ballinamore Church did not make it into the communal memory, one detail from the life of the sawmill did.

Bill Keegan was lecherous as well as clever, and though small and unprepossessing in appearance, he was attractive to women. When he was running the sawmill, he had lodgings with a widow near Knockvicar, a couple of miles from the barracks, and started an affair. My father brought word of the scandal to Pat. He may have demanded that Pat, as Billy's employer, take some action, as it would have been out of character for Pat if left to himself to bother about the affair. Late one Saturday night Pat called on Billy's wife. "We are going up to visit Billy after First Mass tomorrow," he said without explanation. The pair left in Pat's car immediately after First Mass the next morning, and when they reached the house near Knockvicar, Billy and the widow were still in bed. The knocking wasn't timorous. Upstairs, the corners of blinds or curtains moved. The widow came down and opened the door in her nightdress. Pat cleared his throat: "This is Billy's wife," he said. I heard different versions of this story over so many years that it could be said to have lived across a generation, but the fact that Pat had lost all his savings in the travelling sawmill never found a place in the story. After the war he did make serious money meeting returning Americans at Shannon in the hackney car, driving them around to visit relatives or find their roots, before taking them back to Shannon, but he hated this trade more than any other—the boasting, the loud talk, the excessive consumption of alcohol and a skinflint regard for money that belied the open hand of America that was so extolled. Sometimes, too, the poor relatives they visited plied them with so much whiskey in misguided hospitality and pride that they were sick in the car.

His next venture succeeded and he sold the hackney plate and was free. He put down petrol and diesel pumps and sold and serviced the cars and tractors and farm machinery that started to come into the country once the war ended. When my father wanted to join him and invest money at the start of the business, he turned him down with surprising forthrightness. "With you in charge, Frank, I'd have a great run business, but I'd have no customers!" Once the sawmill failed, he was about Aughawillan again. His two white bullocks were on the hill, and he gave my mother every help he could.

She passed these days in deep self-effacement. "He has brought me through forty years with hardly a day's sickness and why should I complain that He should choose to test me now?" And it was this faith and love that was like hidden strength through the happiness of our days in Aughawillan. She no longer read any more. She had no books or time. Such hours that were her own were spent in the flower garden, which was now fenced and temporarily safe.

Sometimes I helped her with the roses or the weeding of the flowerbeds, but more often it was my sisters who were with her there. I went with the workmen or Pat out on the land, or cut sticks from the hedges, drawing them to the house with the jennet. For a boy of eight I had unusual freedom, though I thought it completely normal. With a hazel rod cut from the hedge, I was able to go to Garradice to fish for perch or venture up the canal bank when there was no take along the lake shore. I went along the railway line to Keegan's regularly on my own, leaping the white stones between the sleepers, hoping to meet the line maintenance men on their great bicycle. The Keegans' Aunt Bridie had come home from America to marry Uncle Jimmy. Jim and Christy

Keegan were a few classes ahead of me at school. Their sister Bridie must have been seventeen or eighteen, and had kept house since their mother's death. Jim and Christy had a white ferret with beady red eyes and a fawn greyhound, and they promised to take me hunting with them in the winter. That summer Jim Keegan and I drew all the turf from the bog with the jennet and cart. I was childishly in love with Bridie Keegan, and when I found her alone we would chat away for hours; she would bake scones and give me hot milk or tea.

My father came every few weeks on his bicycle from Roscommon and stayed sometimes for just a day, other times for several days, and then he'd be gone. Whether it was the summer and the green open fields and newness of the farm or because he was still courting me, his strictness instilled less dread. I went about with him at various tasks. He must have heard me talk of the Keegans and their fawn greyhound, because late one wet summer's night he came in out of the rain, his black cycling cape and pull-ups shiny with rain, the big silver carbide lamp hissing, and a small, exhausted, black whippet called Toby trailing behind him on a long lead. I was delighted with the whippet and he went with me everywhere in the evenings.

My father's new restraint may have been connected to our mother's pregnancy. She wasn't feeling well, but she tried to keep it from us, and the rest lay beyond our world. That there was trouble with Bridgie we didn't know either. Bridgie was complaining that she had already nursed and brought up one infant on her own and didn't relish having to do the same for the child that was soon due. My father thought it was just a ploy on her part to get more money. In a letter, my mother wasn't so certain. At the end of the school holidays we all went to the barracks in Cootehall for a week. I had a great time, my father taking me fishing in the tarred boat up through Oakport and the Gut and on towards Knockvicar. If he was out on patrol and one or other of the guards was taking the boat out and they had room, I went with them.

My mother was having a bad time and couldn't wait for the week to be over. She was in pain and had to visit the wives of the guards and be visited. My father arranged a formal evening for her at Guard Walshe's. Mrs. Walshe went to a great deal of trouble to entertain her without having either the money or the social skills, when it would have been a far happier evening, my mother said, if they could have sat in some corner and talked over a cup of tea or a glass of water. Towards the end of the evening, Guard Walshe came in off patrol. He was starving and gobbled up all that was left of the meal. She told this humorously, but my father was angry at what he took to be her ingratitude. For him the outward shows could least belie themselves. As usual, when it didn't greatly matter to her, she deferred and backtracked, praising the trouble the Walshes had gone to and blaming the bad evening solely on the fact that she was feeling out of sorts. Years later, a daughter of the Mrs. Finan who had taught me in Cootehall told me that in the very early hours of one morning in that summer her mother had come on my mother walking barefooted in her nightdress in a field close to the barracks. She told Mrs. Finan that she hadn't been able to sleep and that the cold dew of the grass on her feet eased her pain. Marie Finan was herself a child in Lenihan's Bawn then. She later became a nun in the Ursuline Convent in Sligo. At the time she told me this, she had become a revolutionary nun who still belonged to the Church, though estranged from much of its social teaching, and was running a shelter for the homeless in Sligo. I was so plunged back into time and memory by the images of the nightdress and her bare feet in Gilligan's field or Lenihan's orchard that I neglected to ask Marie what she thought her own mother was doing walking about on her own in the fields in those grey hours.

Soon after we had all returned to Aughawillan from the barracks, Bridgie McGovern said goodbye to us in tears, and left in Pat's car. That same evening Pat brought the new maid, Katie McManus, to the house. Bridgie had continued to complain. My mother feared that she'd leave her when the baby came, and decided to let her go if that was what she wanted. In a letter to my father she describes the drama in her matter-of-fact, practical way:

Well, Bridgie departed yesterday in tears. She was in a bad way and said if the new maid didn't suit she would come back at any time, that I should know in a week and that she could return then. Of course I believe she didn't intend leaving at all, that it was as you state—that she was leaving for more wages etc. Pat said she cried all the way down but Bridgie's grief will be quickly forgotten and it wouldn't be very deep-seated. Be that as it may, Pat arrived back bringing Katie McManus with him. She is small of build, fat and not such a dash to her as Bridgie—seems quiet and cool but can get through the work nevertheless. She gets on well with the children. She would be a direct contrast to Bridgie. She was 2 1/2 years with Mrs. King and 1 year with Mrs. Smith in Ballinagh. So that's that now and as much as I know for the present.

She had to be careful as well as firm. Having allowed her to make this decision, my father started to row back in favour of Bridgie. In another letter, my mother writes that just before Bridgie left she bought my father—above all things—a connection for his bicycle pump. "I don't know about Bridgie," my mother writes diplomatically but firmly. "This girl seems alright and I could not bring back Bridgie just yet. She chose to go and I was tired listening to her say so since she came to Aughawillan, and so be it now." In a further letter she adds that "Katie gets on well with the children and unlike Bridgie never stirs out at night and that is another blessing."

The meadows were cut and saved. My mother and Katie were cooking the whole day for the five workmen when the haycocks were drawn in with horses and built into ricks. The field of green oats ripened. Scarecrows were set up against the birds. In blue September weather workmen with scythes mowed the oatfield in a single day and bound the sheaves. The tresses of hard grain swished and rustled as the sheaves were lifted and gathered into stooks. "The sound of money," a workman laughed. Later, the stooked sheaves were brought in with the jennet and stacked close to the hayrick.

In October, a crowd of men, some carrying pitchforks, came behind a Ferguson tractor pulling the big red threshing mill through the opened gap on the road and past the house. All morning we had listened to the whine and fall of the thresher at Brady's. The mill almost heeled over close to the stack and had to be righted by the men. A wide, thick belt connected the mill to the pulley wheel of the tractor, and there was a different sound when it was threshing and when it was running free. A man on the stack pitchforked the sheaves to the man on the ground, who in turn pitched it to a man high on the thresher. The tying was cut and the sheaf fed evenly into the whirling mill. There were stories of hands and fingers lost. I winced as I watched the calm concentration of the man feeding the sheaves to the mill. At the side of the mill the bright grain spilled into sacks. Where the straw from the broken sheaves was pulped out, another man was pitching to men building and tramping the straw into a rick. The sheaves were full of fieldmice, and as they escaped from the stack they were gobbled up by Toby. The tiny creatures seemed to run towards the black whippet and vanish in a flash of teeth. He swallowed so many mice I was afraid he'd burst and die.

When all the sheaves were threshed, the mill was wound down, the wide belt removed and the mill cleaned. Once it was hitched again to the tractor, all the men trooped into the house for their meal. Then they were on their way, the tractor and the cumbersome big red mill lurching out to the road in the direction of the next threshing. A few men stayed behind to store the bags of grain and head and rope the straw rick. Then they too followed the thresher.

Mother had to go to Dublin for some days to see Dr. Corcoran and make arrangements for the coming birth. I was hoping for a boy after so many girls. "Why would you want a boy rather than what God chooses to send us?" "Because I'd have someone to play football with and to help me with the jennet." Earlier, my father wanted his friend from Cootehall, Mary Ellen Kilboy, to come to visit us in Aughawillan, and my mother wrote him that there was nothing but children and workmen in her life and she had no way of entertaining anybody, but that if Mary E. insisted on coming she would do her best. Now, to please him, she writes from the guest house where she was staying while seeing her doctors that she had written Mary Ellen "and told her she must visit us either before this coming event or after, but probably afterwards would be better owing to circumstances, and so I did not let down either you or Mary E."

He wanted her to go to the Boyle nursing home where Dympna was born because it would be less expensive than Dublin. This she refused to do. Maggie accompanied her to Dublin but she had to be careful to allay his suspicions that she was taking advice from her and others and not from him:

Thursday

I was not feeling so well last night, and so I intend going to Dublin one of these days, probably tomorrow if symptoms increase further.

I discussed going to Holles Street with nobody but Mr. Corcoran. Maggie didn't know of it until I asked her if she would come with me as far as Holles St., that I had to call there. When in Cootehall for the week's holiday I felt very much out of sorts, and I decided I wouldn't stay there for birth, just because of that.

ALL WILL BE WELL

Sub. turned in on Monday and so that much is settled.

Jim Keegan and Sean drew 3 load of turf on Saturday and they are finishing them by drawing a load after school this week.

That is all my news. I know you are praying for me and so God will do what is best.

While waiting to go into Holles Street, she stayed at the small Cumberland Hotel in Westland Row and recalled that it was almost exactly nine years ago that she was in Dublin at Percy Place expecting her first child. She was afraid the birth would be delayed and that she would have to wait on into the middle of the month at the Cumberland, and she is relieved when a son, her seventh child, is born "a healthy lump" on November 4th, 1943. There was difficulty over the boy's name. My father wanted the child to be christened Jude, after the patron saint of hopeless cases, because of her cancer, and here she stood firm against him again, objecting that such an unusual name would single him out too much among other children. He was christened Frances Jude Anthony and grew up as Frank, though in his young years my father insisted on calling him Jude.

The potato stalks that had been such a sea of green leaf and delicate blossom under the July breezes were now withered and white on the ridges. Pat got Eddie McIniff to dig the potatoes, and I picked them for Eddie after school. Of all the work, I disliked picking the potatoes most, the evenings cold, sometimes rain, hands blue from the wet clay, dragging the bucket along the ridge and over to the pit, the dead potato stalks matting the sticky clay about boots so that they too felt as heavy and cumbersome as buckets. With Eddie McIniff this was almost a pleasure. Nearly everybody brightened when Eddie was around. He was small and curly-haired, a good footballer in spite of his size, who took all the close-in frees for the Ballinamore team, played the drums in the town band, and remained a child for the whole of his short life.

When he went to England after the war, his homecoming every Christmas outshone Midnight Mass. The town band with an army of friends met the train at the station. After the handshakes, the slaps, the embraces, the jokes, the laughter, he was carried shoulder high down the platform. Even Pat in his hackney car would sound his horn. Once outside the station, Eddie would climb from the shoulders and take over the drums. The band would lead the crowd through the town to whatever bar had been decided upon. Shopkeepers and their customers would crowd to the doors to watch.

Pat, who disliked drinkers and drink, would shake with silent laughter at the mention of his name. "Oh Eddie. Poor Eddie. Eddie wouldn't harm a fly. Eddie's a child." Each Christmas Eddie bought drinks for everybody until the savings he had brought from England disappeared. Then his friends in turn bought drinks for Eddie until the party reached its inevitable close. A secret collection was made, a ticket bought, notes put in an envelope for the journey, and a last big party held before the band played Eddie to the departing train.

For the boy I was then, Eddie was perfect company, ready to talk of football or anything under the sun, without giving the impression that he was talking to a child. If the potatoes weren't picked with night coming on, he was happy to leave them on the ridges, even if they were going to be exposed to a night of frost, and to pick them himself before he started digging the next morning: "The country will be full of auld spuds and eejits long after we are dead and gone."

One evening, after I had picked all the eating potatoes and was gathering the small potatoes that were put in a separate pit to be fed to the hens, Eddie stopped digging as it was getting dark and helped me finish the picking. The talk got round to football, and Eddie began to show me how to take free kicks, using the potatoes as footballs, the whitethorn hedge bordering the field as the goal and goalposts. Eddie showed me how to slice the ball with the side of the boot, sending a number of potatoes sailing effortlessly over the whitethorns, and then it was my turn. I missed the first few kicks, but soon, with Eddie's help, was managing to send the occasional potato clear of the hedge.

In Aughawillan we hadn't seen my father in weeks. In a letter to him from the Cumberland at this time, my mother wrote, fairly sharply for her: "I hope your rheumatism is improved and that you were able to go and see the children." Whether it was the result of this reminder or not, Eddie and I had the very bad luck that he decided to cycle down from Cootehall that evening. Eddie was applauding a potato I had sent high over the whitethorns, when to our dismay we found my father standing silently beside us.

"The child is bad enough but I don't even know how to begin to describe you," he began.

We stood listening until Eddie whispered, "We better gather up those while there's still light." We picked the small potatoes silently and covered the pits with rushes. "I'll see you tomorrow," Eddie said.

"You'll see nobody tomorrow."

Eddie didn't answer but went and took his spade from the ridge. Instead of coming down with us to the house for his tea, where the lamplight already shone from the kitchen window, he left us at the little iron gate. My father made no attempt to dissuade him, and I felt deeply shamed.

"Will Eddie get paid?" I asked Pat anxiously when Paddy Reilly from the railway station arrived to finish the digging.

"Oh Eddie. Oh the sergeant. Yous were a fine pair," Pat laughed, but reassured me: "Eddie needs money from time to time and will come to me."

In the spring, Aughawillan played Ballinamore in the field down from the church. Like all the other boys in the school, I was supporting Aughawillan, but wasn't too downcast when Balli-namore won because Eddie was one of their stars. He had scored a goal from play and converted all the close frees. Many people had gathered around him after the match, and I went towards him uncertainly. As soon as he saw me, it was as if nobody else on the whole field existed. He lifted me in the air.

"Shawneen boy!"

"You played great, Eddie." I was in tears.

"We'll always have spuds and eejits," he laughed, without a care. I felt proud and absolved and happy.

Pat met my mother and baby brother off the Dublin train at Dromod and drove them to Aughawillan. Again, there was no question of my father meeting them because he was busy in the barracks. I was overjoyed to have her home, but dismayed by the first sight of my brother: it would be a long time before he would be any use at football or at catching the jennet in the mornings.

The next evening we rushed home from school to be with our mother and the new baby, and soon our precious daily life was restored. She was walking with us again past Brady's pool and Brady's house and the house where the old Mahon brothers lived, past the deep, dark quarry and across the railway bridge and up the hill past Mahon's shop to the school. There were now five of us walking with her, the twins Breedge and Rosaleen, Margaret, Monica, myself. The baby and Dympna were with Katie.

I was training to be an altar boy. Three of us had been selected, and the training was conducted by the priest in the sacristy of the church after school. The Latin responses we learned by heart without understanding. I advanced much more quickly than the other boys, as my mother helped me practise Latin in the evenings. She hadn't studied Latin but knew the responses intimately and their general meaning from years of devotion. I had always liked reciting words to myself, when I was driving the jennet or gathering sticks about the fields, and now had as much pleasure from the Latin words as words I understood. I learned when to genuflect, when to kneel, to stand, to sit, to bow, to pour wine and water, to ring the bell, to walk with the priest along the altar rail, holding the plate beneath each communicant to catch any grains that fell from the sacred Host. I was advancing into the world. The priest who had terrified me from the altar a few short months before for rattling my beads was now talking pleasantly to me about the weather. A white surplice and black soutane was made for me. My mother and sisters were in the church to watch me serve my first Mass as if it was a step on the way to ordination.

My father came more often. Eddie McIniff and the free kicks with the potatoes were not mentioned. I remember most of the visits as warily pleasant. There was one bad row over the oats, in which, luckily, I wasn't involved. Mice had been holing the bags of grain and they were taken in and spilled on the floor of the other downstairs room. The room was intended as a sitting room or parlour, but, like most such rooms in the Ireland of the time, it was never used. This hadn't even been put through the pretence: it was never furnished. My sisters loved to play in the loose oats, and as long as they didn't bring clay and dirt into the room my mother didn't mind. She thought they could do no harm, but as soon as my father saw the marks their play had made in the smooth wall of grain, he went wild and could hardly be contained when he discovered traces of urine in the oats. He lined the girls up and they began to accuse one another. They were all crying as he ordered them to bed and said they wouldn't be given anything to eat till morning. Long after their cries and sobbing had ceased, he continued to scold my mother, and then the usual exhausted, uncomfortable silence descended on the whole house. The next day he and I gathered the loose oats into bags and took them to the mill at Templeport with the jennet and cart. We saw the great water wheel turning in the stream by the side of the mill, and then felt the dryness and dust and heat when my father carried in the bags. The grain was spread out on a drying floor, and when fully dried was winnowed of its chaff. Deprived of their shining husk, the little grains looked dull and naked; then they were ground into oatmeal. People like us who had brought grain did much of the lifting and carrying because the miller had no assistant. The miller's payment could be either in cash or a percentage of the grain, and my father paid in grain. He was in extraordinary good humour on the way home, and in the house lifted the oatmeal and let it trickle like coins through his fingers to show my mother and Katie its goodness. For the remainder of the evening he played with my sisters and charmed them and told them stories as if the evening before had never occurred. My mother baked biscuits with the oatmeal, sprinkled the rolled dough with sugar, and cut it into circular shapes with the lid of a canister. The biscuits were rock hard and plain, made palatable by the glistening sugar, but my father praised them as if they were manna from heaven. For the rest of that winter we took them to school with our bottles of milk for lunch.

That winter was hard but dry. We woke into white mornings. Ice had to be broken in buckets, in barrels, on ponds, even on the spring well. The goats came off the hill. Mother was afraid they'd strip the bark of the good trees around the house and break into the flower garden, so Pat put an extra fence to keep them out of the flower garden, which made it look even more like a beleaguered fortress in the middle of the bare field, itself in the middle of a winter wilderness. A slide was made all the way downhill from the school until we could race past Mahon's shop and up to the railway bridge. The ice on Garradice was so thick that a horse and cart was driven across the ice with fodder to give to cattle on one of the islands. On Sundays, I went hunting with the Keegans, taking Toby the black whippet. Toby turned out to have been better at swallowing mice than running down hares and rabbits, though the Keegans said he was useful at turning them back into the path of their big fawn. Any Sunday they caught two or more hares they gave me one, and I was as delighted taking them home as my father was taking the sacks of oatmeal from the mill. It was ideal hunting weather, but the ground became too hard, and soon the nails of both the greyhound and whippet were torn and bleeding and we had to stop. The rabbits that were netted with the ferret the Keegans sold to the Delahoydes. There was always a sudden muffled thundering within the warren after the muzzled ferret was slipped into the burrow before the terrified creatures crashed into the nets.

This was perfect weather for cutting and gathering sticks. The jennet and cart were able to go anywhere over the hard ground. After our lessons were done and the Rosary said and the lamp turned low, we'd all sit in front of a great fire of sticks, following the light as it frolicked from wall to ceiling to wall, glittering on the white cups and plates of the dresser, on the glass of the religious pictures on the walls. Sometimes we'd cry out in excitement when a collapsing piece of wood sent light flaring and leaping and dancing in every direction. On the high mantelpiece, above the fire, the blood-red light from the small copper lamp before the picture of the Sacred Heart burned serenely, unaffected by the riot of light. "One more minute. One more minute," the girls would plead at bedtime. I was allowed to stay up a little later and was sometimes there to help my mother or Katie add sods of turf to the burning wood before the ashes were raked over the coals.

My father continued coming regularly. This hard, dramatic weather appeared to change his mood. He complained less of his ailments and pains and was, mostly, in good humour, finding work to do about the land. Amazingly, they were still risking sexual intercourse in the light of all that had gone before—fasting, Novenas, Dr. Corcoran's warnings. In a letter written that February, my mother reassures my father that he has no cause to worry further since "her visitor" had just arrived.

On certain Saturdays when something heavy or cumbersome had to be collected, I drove the jennet and cart to town. My mother might have liked to have come with me, but as a teacher she couldn't be seen on the cart. She took the train and we met at Maggie's and spent the day as if we had both come together, meeting the teachers who came into Maggie's to see her, shopping together in the town, and I'd leave early. Sometimes I galloped the old jennet in order to be at home before the train.

She and I drew even closer. Now that I was serving on the altar, her dream for me was that step nearer. "One day I will say Mass for her." All through Lent she came with me to the Devotions at which I served. In my black soutane and white surplice, I carried a lighted candle. By the priest's side we went from Station to Station while she prayed among the few people huddled beneath the organ loft. I remember the wind and rain, the drip of rain from the eaves, but there must have been dry and windless evenings as well.

Walking back in the dark with my mother from one of these Lenten evenings, I had a frightening premonition that the world of Aughawillan was not as completely restored and safe as I had wanted to believe. She had come home after that terrible absence; she would never leave us again; I was taking all that completely for granted. Our steps had been uncertain on leaving the church, but as our eyes grew accustomed to the dark we were soon able to make out easily the potholes and the grass margins as we went past the football field, the parish hall, the school, and down the hill past Mahon's shop and across the railway bridge. "Do you think when you grow up that you could change your mind about becoming a priest?"

We had been chattering happily and carelessly along the whole length of the dark road and the question occurred naturally. "No. I'll not change."

"What makes you so certain?"

I disliked the direction the conversation was taking, and shivered at the very thought of death and the possibility of eternal damnation that awaited us all. The prayers at the Stations of the

Cross in the church had been no more than movements and words. "It's too hard to get to heaven if you are not a priest," I said.

"I'm not a priest or a man and I have to hope for heaven."

"That's different. You're a good person."

"Sometimes I think I'm far from good, and Daddy as well has to hope to go to heaven, and all the others."

I became unusually silent. "If you're a priest it's a great deal easier to get to heaven," I said finally.

This was a formulation I had even then, though it was to grow clearer in the years ahead when it became intricately linked with its opposite, a dream of love and sex and worldly happiness. To enter the priesthood was to die in life, and by giving back our life into the hands and service of God we were circumventing death and the judgment while still in life.

"If God was to take me early would you still go on to be a priest and say Mass for me?"

"What do you mean?"

"We are in God's hands. We have no choice if He calls us."

"People do not die until they are old," I said. I saw too clearly what she was saying. Its unfairness enraged me. God had all the angels and saints and His own blessed Mother in the company of the Faithful in heaven, and I had but the one beloved. She was all that I had.

"God can call people at any age," she said, but faced with my intense alarm she desisted. "I pray that I'll grow old, but that is in the hands of God."

"You'll come to my ordination in a big car. When the bandages are taken from my hands, you'll be the first to receive the new priest's blessing. We'll live together in an old presbytery close to the church, and when you die I'll say so many Masses for you that you'll hardly have to spend any time in purgatory." I was talking wildly to try to keep all harm away. She would stay with us for ever. She would never go away again.

"Then we'll be forever with God in heaven," she said.

"For the whole of eternity," I said, partly by rote and partly in awe. Our heaven was here in Aughawillan. With her our world was without end.

Master McMurrough was many days absent because of illness that spring. On these days the heavy folding partition between the rooms was pushed back and my mother took charge of the whole school. She could do very little with our classes other than to keep us quiet with various exercises and copying work, and she seemed to have remarkably little trouble with discipline. Nearly all the pupils were anxious to please her. Any of the older girls or boys she found feuding or at horseplay she took down to her own room, where she put them sitting in the small infant desks until they were ready to promise to behave normally. In her letters to my father she complained in passing of the extra work these absences entailed, but we never heard a word of complaint.

My father and I were still getting on wonderfully well. At times he made the two of us appear like a small opposition party of men in a house and government of women. This was all done playfully, but there was an edge to his play. In March he was there for all the spring ploughing, when a new field of oats was ploughed and the ridges for potatoes turned. I helped him dig the small vegetable garden across the road. We drew manure with the jennet and he shovelled and shaped the loose clay into beds. We drew the rest of the manure to the potato field, where he spread it before harting the ploughed ridges. He could work quickly in short bursts, but he wasn't like the other workmen who seemed able to continue evenly through the long grind of the day. After a while he would need some change or excitement, and if it didn't come he would fall into a state of lethargy or grow angry or start to complain. This didn't affect me, and I used to hurry from school to join him in the work. He would have the seed potatoes cut and dusted with lime and be waiting for me. I would drop the splits into the holes he made in the ridges with his *sciveen*. The *sciveen* he was proud of because he had made it himself from a straight sally cut from the hedges—peeling the bark away, whittling the end to a sharp point, and inserting a peg for his foot. While we worked, the whippet rested on the empty sacks underneath the heeled-up cart. Each of the goats now had a pair of kids and they were never far from the house. In the evenings the girls played with them, but I no longer joined in this play, feeling perhaps that it wasn't manly enough or that I was too busy or too important. I would hear their excited shrieks as the goats and kids chased them round the house while gathering sticks or sawing wood. I remember one evening when our father was explaining something important to us, completely absorbed in what he was saying. One of the mother goats, accustomed to the play round and round the house, recognized him as strange and lowered her horns a number of times, plainly thinking of charging him from behind. We weren't able to say a word: if the goat had charged and floored him, he would have taken it personally and we would not have been able to keep straight faces; an investigation would have followed. To our relief, something else distracted the goat's attention, and we were able to breathe again.

Before he left, it was arranged that I should visit him and spend a long weekend in the barracks. I was so excited by the prospect that I could hardly wait. I would take my small bicycle with me on the train to Drumshambo. He would meet me there and we would cycle back to Cootehall together. Reading through my mother's letters, I was surprised to discover how anxious she was about the visit. My father was cavalier about any schooldays I might miss, while my mother was adamant that I could take one day off but not another single day.

My mother saw me off from the station, the bicycle travelling in the guard's van, a small suitcase strapped to the carrier. I was taking a freshly baked cake and a pair of newly knitted heavy socks as presents. Pat met the train in Ballinamore. When no one off the train wanted a hackney car, he insisted on putting my bicycle into the boot and drove me the short distance to Maggie's shop. I spent a delicious hour drinking tea with biscuits and telling about the goats and the cows and the whippet and the white bullocks. The Drumshambo train left from the end of the platform beside the three stunted fir trees across from the shop, and I watched the engine being shunted into place and hitched to the wagons. All the wagons were empty coal wagons. There was just the one carriage and a guard's van.

In Drumshambo I looked eagerly for my father. He was nowhere in sight. Anxiously I enquired if a sergeant in uniform had been at the station, thinking he might have come early and gone into the town. No man in uniform had been at the station. I asked the way to Cootehall. The road went in the same direction as the train was going and after a mile or so there was a left turn for Cootehall. I'd have to be careful as it wasn't signposted. After that they thought it was more or less plain sailing. I'd cross the Shannon at the new stone bridge, go straight on through the Tinker's Cross at Derrynorgan, and after about a mile I'd come on the turn for Cootehall. "I'll have met up with my father before then," I said. On the road out from Drumshambo I met miners on bicycles coming home from their work in the pits, wearing hats with the miner's lamp, their faces and hands black, their clothes black. What was strange and frightening were the eyes shining out of the black faces under the hats.

I found the turn for Cootehall by asking at a house. The road was stony, potholed and narrow. The only even path was on the high shoulder and it was easy to slide off its slope. There was little traffic, a few carts, people walking, one or two on bicycles, a few cattle out on the long acre. I rested on the bridge when I got to the Shannon and looked upriver at the piles of huge rocks along the banks that had been blasted when the river was deepened and widened for the Shannon Hydroelectric Scheme. I had heard of the French engineers who had worked on the Scheme, many of them good musicians. Some had married local girls who went to live with them in France when the work was finished. After the bridge, a long stretch of straight road ran to the Tinker's Cross; it was troubling not to see any sight of my father, even in the far distance. At the Cross there was a small encampment of caravans and some wattle tents huddled beneath the hedge, but there were no fires. At Drumboylan I missed the turn for Cootehall. I was exhausted and afraid I was lost when I recognized the bridge and post office at Knockvicar from the excursions in the tarred boat. I had missed the turn and travelled in a wide circle. Though I was tired and sore from the shaking of the road, I felt triumphant at having made the journey on my own. I wouldn't have wanted to meet my father now. After another half-hour I passed the parochial hall and Gerald Flynn's and the school and saw the familiar church and shops and houses scattered about the walled triangular field.

Guard Cannon, the barrack orderly, welcomed me and started to laugh. "Lord bless us, Seaneen, but you must have missed the Sergeant. You came round the world for nearways. Your father thought he'd meet up with you before you got to the turn. He's not that long left. You must have done fierce tracks on that small bicycle."

He took me into the living quarters, where old deaf Biddy was cooking and cleaning. She worked half-days, coming to the barracks in the late morning and leaving in the early evening. She had stayed late because I was coming. I was starving. Soon she had a meal on the table that was a portion of heaven: a fried egg, a slice of bacon, a piece of black pudding, fried bread and scalding tea. She could lip-read, but I had difficulty answering her deafness and Guard Cannon rephrased my words. Whenever she understood something she clapped her hands together and shouted the words joyously out. All three of us were in the big living room when my father returned.

"The prisoner is here," Guard Cannon called out.

"You were too quick. You beat me to it. I was hoping to get to the Cross before you," my father said agreeably as we kissed.

"I knew where I was when I got to Knockvicar," I said uncertainly, and took the cake and knitted socks from the suitcase. I saw that he had made little effort to meet me. Though children are seldom fair, they have a passion for fairness. In their need of certainty in an uncertain world, they demand that all promises be kept.

"Round the world for nearways," Guard Cannon repeated as he prepared to troop back down to the dayroom.

Biddy showed my father the porridge she had prepared for our breakfast and the bread she had baked and placed two eggs to one side. All we had to do in the morning was light the fire, heat the porridge and boil the eggs and make tea. My father grew impatient with all these instructions and ushered her to the door, but she insisted on returning to kiss me before she left.

My father could not have done more to make me welcome. My one disappointment was that the boat hadn't yet been tarred and we weren't able to go on the river. Biddy came back the next day. I think she was delighted to have a child to care for. The meals she cooked were delicious and there was no sparing on food as there had been when we all lived here.

On Sunday, I was proud of how handsome my father was after he shone the silver buttons of his uniform, his badge and the three silver stripes of his rank, and we walked together all the way up the church to kneel in the front seat.

The evening before I was to return to Aughawillan he took me with him into Oakport to shoot rabbits with the twenty-two rifle. He had run very low on ammunition and gave me the three shells he had left to carry. We went by the broken stone avenue along the lake shore on which carriages had once travelled to Oakport House. The great iron gates were now fallen and lay on the broken stone, but out on the lake the gulls were screaming and clamouring and wheeling about overhead, much as they must have cried out and circled and wheeled above their island of rocks at the time of the carriages. Over Nutley's boathouse a red sun was sinking towards the dark woods of Oakport. We stole silently along a high wall until we came to a place where the wall was broken. With his hand my father indicated that we were going to wait here, and I gave him one of the three shells. On the far side of the wall there was a grove of tall trees and wide, short-grassed fields. With a rifle my father could wait patiently for hours, and it never seemed long because of the excitement of the hunt. As the light weakened, the rabbits began to come out to graze. Through the break in the wall I saw that he was trying to line up two rabbits for the one shot. When the shot rang out, he called, "Run! Get him!" When I brought the wounded rabbit back, he killed it with a single stroke of his hand.

I carried the rabbit as we walked back. The red sun had sunk into the tallest trees of Oakport and streaked the lake in glowing shades of red and orange. Close to the great stone piers and the fallen gates, my father came to what I believe he had planned all along. "Would you think of coming to live with me in the barracks?"

I did not know what to say. "What would the others do?"

"They'd stay in Aughawillan. Everything there would be just as it is now."

"I have to go to school in Aughawillan."

"You could go to school just as well here in Cootehall. That would be no bother."

"There's the sticks to be gathered and there's the jennet and Toby."

"The jennet and Toby could be brought here. We are not cutting any turf in Aughawillan this year. That old mud turf is a waste of time and money. We are cutting the turf here and taking it to Aughawillan with a lorry. You could help me save the turf and draw it out to the road with the jennet."

"What would Mammy do?" I could no longer obscure from myself what was being proposed.

"She has more than enough to contend with. She'd have one less. And it must be hard for you living in a house of women."

"How?"

"Could you say *shit* or *piss* in front of women?"

"No, Daddy."

"You'd have to say something silly like *wee-wee* or *job*."

"Something like that, Daddy."

"We could have great times together. We could go in the boat once it's tarred. You wouldn't know yourself in a while here. You'd be able to practise with the other boys in the football field. In a house full of women you could turn into a molly. You'd be a half a woman before you'd know."

"I have to be back for school."

"You don't have to go back to school unless you want to."

Fear was now apparent in all the half-perceived feelings that harried and jostled and closed on one another.

"Mammy said I could take one day off but not two."

"That wouldn't matter. It's what I say here that counts. A few old schooldays wouldn't make any difference one way or another. I thought I'd be able to get back with you tomorrow but can't. You could wait till later in the week and we could be back together. We could give them the news together."

"She'd be worried. I'd need to tell her first."

As we crossed the bridge into the village, we could hear the rising frenzy of the hounds all the way back across the lake at Oakport House as they were about to be fed.

"I know all this is very sudden and you need to think about it." He became less pressing; and then when I stayed silent he said, "I don't want you to tell anybody what we have been talking about. Women can be very quick to read things wrong. When you think about it you can come straight back to me and we'll take it from there."

"I'll not say anything," I promised as we went in the short avenue.

The next day he cycled with me all the way to the stone bridge across the Shannon.

"My jurisdiction ends here. As I'm on duty, it wouldn't look good if I was seen in Drumshambo."

"The rest of the way will be no bother. There's hours yet to the train," I said.

"You'll think about coming to live here but don't tell anybody."

"I'll not say a word."

"People can take things up wrong. Tell them I couldn't get away but I'll be down for certain later in the week."

As we kissed, I saw a look of hatred in his eyes, but shut it out of mind. I didn't want to recognize it, but later I came to know it well: he hadn't got his way.

I would normally have blown and boasted about this visit on my own with my father, but I was such a model of restraint that my sisters grew suspicious. They were sure I had received a beating. I told of old deaf Biddy and the boat still waiting under the sycamore to be tarred. I had a rabbit to show for the evening in Oakport. I told of the long cycle out of Drumshambo and the black faces of the miners coming down from the Arigna pits and how I was beginning to think I was lost until I saw Knockvicar. My mother looked at me anxiously but didn't press. My father had no need to warn me to secrecy: it was as if I had glimpsed instinctively that what had occurred between us was too dark and shameful for speech.

My mother began to miss days in school. Now Master McMurrough had to supervise the whole school, placing two of the senior girls in charge of the infants, while trying to teach his own classes. As well as being unpunctual and taking much sick leave, he was not a natural teacher. There was a boy called Michael Campbell he had a set on. Once when McMurrough was punishing him for some failure, Campbell ran from the school. McMurrough pursued him with the cane, through the porch, out into the yard and across the ditch. The teacher seized him there, and they both rolled together down into the briars of the deep dry drain, where Campbell broke free again. The whole school was delighted by this diversion and a little frightened. An angry, dishevelled McMurrough returned alone to the classroom. Campbell came back with both his parents the next day. There were loud words. Law, or worse, was threatened if such an incident was to occur again, and the boy would be taken out of the school. Campbell was more or less left alone after that.

Though I had little interest in school and schoolwork at this time—all my passion was for the fields and gathering wood and the jennet and Toby and the white bullocks—I got into very little trouble with McMurrough, probably because of Mother, and I may have done enough schoolwork to get by. On days when she was sick, instead of tackling the jennet I would go to her and sit on the low windowsill beside her bed, and I'd stay there for the whole evening. We were nearly always alone. We'd hear the cries of the girls playing round the house with the goats, and sometimes one of them would come in angry tears to the room for comfort after a fall or a fight. Katie McManus brought the baby up to the room when she had to go outside to milk the cows or draw water or do some other task.

My brother was a strong, winning baby who seldom cried. Dympna was two years old now and much more attached to Katie than to my mother. When my mother and I were alone we talked of school and church and the fields, but seldom an evening went by that we didn't talk of our life together, when I would be a priest and we'd live in the priest's house beside the church. She never tired of this dream, and looking back I think I must have sensed instinctively that there was something wrong and that I was talking out the dream to try to hold her in my life, in the way we sing or pray. There were times when the conversation took more unwelcome directions.

"You'll have to study hard if you want to become a priest. You'll not be able to be all the time around the fields. You'll have to learn Greek and Latin. Very high marks are needed to get into Maynooth."

"That's a long time off yet," I said.

"There's only one good time to make a start. That time is now."

"I *do* study now," I said, but I knew it wasn't true. I did the bare minimum.

"I know you do, love."

Whenever my mother was more than a day or two in bed, Dr. Dolan was sent for, and he came in his car, carrying his satchel down the cinder path. After one of his calls I had to cycle into the town for a prescription. I remember that it made her instantly better, and in two days' time she was walking with us to school again: every primrose, violet, white strawberry blossom glowed anew on the banks, and we were able again to immerse ourselves completely in our own long days.

The brown hens stopped laying. It was discovered Toby was the thief, swallowing eggs as he had swallowed mice escaping from the stack. I might have been able to save him if it was only the eggs, but when Breedge tried to take eggs from him he bit her hand. She said that he had attacked her face too. I promised to tie him up and take him everywhere on a lead. It was no use. He had to go. I was distraught when the two workmen took him away in the evening, and went in and hid among the cows to cry my grief out on their warm necks. I was still there when a wet and shivering Toby came leaping into the cowhouse and placed his paws on my shoulders and began to lick my face. I cried now for joy. The workmen had put him into a sack weighted with stones, tied the mouth of the sack, and threw him into the deep part of the lake out from the avenue of trees that ran to Ollerton's. As it was sinking, he ate his way out of the sack, swam ashore, and was home before the workmen reached their homes. All this escape earned him and me was a few days' reprieve. They took him away another evening, and I stood for a long time dry-eyed between the cows, praying for a second miracle, but this time he did not come back.

There were now much longer spaces between my father's visits, and sometimes he left us after only a few hours. His courting of me was over. He no longer wanted me with him when he went about the fields, and he appeared to lose all interest in the land, even in the crops we had planted together. Uncle Pat shovelled the potato ridges. The youngest of the workmen, Paddy Reilly from the railway station, went to Cootehall to live in the barracks and help my father with the garden and the cutting of turf.

The distant war in Europe was drawing to a close. Rationing was easing. On my way home from school, on a day my mother was absent, I was given a loaf of white bread in Mahon's shop. "Only a half-dozen came on the train and I kept this one for your mother," Mrs. Mahon said. I hadn't seen a white loaf in years and took it home in high excitement to show it to Katie, and then took it upstairs to my mother. That evening we were all given a slice, and we ate it in wonder. I still gathered and cut sticks about the hedges and went to town with the jennet and cart. My mother no longer went to town on the train. I bought whatever provisions the house needed. When I had difficulty in the shops, I showed them the list she had given me. Always I was made much of, and feasted in Maggie's before leading the jennet out through the railway gates for home. Once outside the town, I sat into the cart.

Whenever my mother was back at school and feeling better,

on good evenings she'd spend hours in the flower garden. We vied with one another to help her, and were probably more of a hindrance than a help, but she liked our company and gave us separate tasks when we quarrelled. The little I know of cultivated flowers derives from that garden. The rose bushes were now sturdier, with many blooms; the nasturtiums, lilies, pansies, wallflowers looked happier and more secure in their beds. The fences had been further reinforced, and the garden became even more like a small fortress in the middle of the wilderness. Next spring, she said, we would plant whitethorn slips all around, and in time we could have an arch of whitethorns above the gate, as they had in her old house in Drumderg.

Around this time, the first note of despair enters my mother's letters: "I was at school today after a few days in bed. I am improved but still suffering and it seems I must suffer on—maybe if the weather improved the sunshine might help. God is great."

She suspects that the cancer might have returned, but everybody around her conspires to drive her from this knowledge. Her stomach pain and recurrent bouts of constipation and diarrhoea, she is told, are an unrelated sickness that she can recover from if she will only make the effort. She asks my father to write to Dr. Corcoran in Dublin, which he is understandably reluctant to do, since he has already written to him secretly.

He came on his bicycle one last time. He hardly noticed us and was gone in a few hours. All the time was spent in grave conversation with my mother. When he left, she was able to walk him all the way out to the little iron gate at the road. We were not allowed to accompany them. They spent a long time in conversation, and were never to see one another again.

From this time on my father's only contact with my mother was by letter. He began to write to Maggie as well. As Pat couldn't read or write, my father rang the guards in Ballinamore regularly asking them to get Pat to telephone. There would never have been any great urgency for Pat to call my father, but my father would have enjoyed the drama and attention. Maggie and Pat were constantly at the house. One of the white bullocks Pat kept on the hill was thriving, but the other was failing, and I was given a new task of feeding him crushed oats in the morning before I went to school and again in the evening.

In another of my mother's letters there is the same note: "I am still grunny and stayed in bed to see Dr. Dolan. I am not anything worse but just wish if there could be something done before they stay too long. Maggie was out today and said that she had a letter from you. The children are all well. Best love now. Your loving wife, Sue." Her complaints are all brief. She enquires about his health and all the hard work he is doing in the barracks and garden and on the bog. She tells him that the oatfield has been rolled and that Pat has moulded all the potatoes. They got ammonia from James McGovern and it had been mixed with compound and put on the potatoes Tuesday evening. She had been in bed at the time and hadn't been able to see it put on but she supposed it had been done all right. The letter to Maggie that she mentioned included a proposal that my mother move to the barracks in order to rest and recuperate. That it was made to Maggie inclines me to believe that it was meant for public consumption rather than anything he wanted or deemed practical, and it was Maggie and not my mother who answered: "Just to say Sue is very much improved thank God and I asked her if she would wish to go to Cootehall for a rest and she said that when she was getting better at home in Corramahon that she would stay on for the present till she would get built up."

In the light of the medical knowledge from Dr. Corcoran already in his possession, my father then sent an extraordinary letter. When he went to Drumshambo to the convent of the Poor Clares, he was almost halfway to Corramahon, yet he would not visit her. She was to live for more than another month:

Cootehall
23–5–1944

Dearest Mammy,

I arrived home safely Saturday morning after an interview with Mr. Murphy, your auld sparring partner [a guest of Maggie's, and probably an earlier admirer of my mother]. He was quite drunk, much the same but older. Saturday all day I was in a poor way until I heard that you had a good night yesterday evening. I heard that you were "well improved." I went to Drumshambo [the convent of the Poor Clares] and enrolled you in Perp. adoration and by the way I have resumed my fast for you. I also sent Margaret a letter on the train telling her of a cure for her neuritis. I hope she got it. Hazel nuts carried on the person but I don't know where I may get them, for a few months longer, so that is that. In my letter to Mgt. I suggested that you should come over here for a while when you are able but of course you must be very very careful about moving out. Even when all trace of it is gone you must only move out to the road first day, a little further next and so on. It is so easy to get relapsed. Cut out meats, rice and rhubarb, use oat porridge sparingly, reduce potatoes. Take greens and milk foods and watch constipation and indigestion above all. You seem to have lost confidence in God and to be worrying unnecessarily. The nuns who spoke to me yesterday say you'd be better giving up the teaching and I think if you act reasonably you have nothing to fear. The only thing I fear is your going against me in your quiet way as regards the children and you can get over it. The responsibility is too much for you and I am suffering also. So may God direct you. I wrote to Corcoran but I know there was no need. Don't be stubborn. Look at Mgt.'s history of stubbornness and your own of recent date and see that your family is that way inclined and realize that it can only bring you more trouble and all will be well. I am wicked and contrary but am as good as most and can be very easily led if taken the right way.

I don't know whether to send this to Carramahon or not but I am chancing it in any case.

Best love dearest and stop worrying,
Daddy

The "hazel nuts carried on the person," and whatever other advice he offered Maggie, received a shirty response: "I had two letters from you on Monday. There was a lot of stuff in them—but I just passed them. I don't mind when Sue is getting better," Maggie wrote.

On one teeming day, Dr. Dolan came with his satchel to the house and spent a long time with my mother. As soon as he left she rose and dressed for the rain. She was intent on cycling to the priest's house in order to get his signature on a form that would allow her to employ a substitute teacher. Katie tried to dissuade her because of the downpour, but she had made up her mind. She wanted me to dress up and come with her on the small bicycle. "Those short stays in bed are doing no good and they are not fair to Master McMurrough. The doctor wants me to take a long sick leave to see if I can get cured once and for all," she said.

I remember the journey vividly. There wasn't a breath of wind, but the rain poured steadily down. Streams were cutting tracks in the road and there was flooding in parts of the fields. We went past Brady's pool, past Brady's house and street, and the street where the old Mahon brothers lived, by the deep, dark quarry, and across the railway bridge. There we dismounted and wheeled the bicycles past Mahon's shop and up the steep hill to the school. We cycled past the hall and lane to the football field and dismounted again below the church. By the time we reached the priest's house we were soaking. She left me to hold the two bicycles at the gate. The housekeeper answered the door and allowed her inside. My mother was a long time in the house. It was Father McGrail who showed her out. He waved to me from the door.

"I'm sorry to be so long. Father McGrail wanted to talk about the school. He didn't see I was drownded."

"He should by right have come to you instead of you having to get out of bed to come to him in all this wet," I said angrily.

To question the priest in anything at the time was close to sacrilege.

"That's not the world," she smiled. "The priest didn't have to get anything signed."

"I could have taken the papers to him."

"It wouldn't look right. There are some things that not even you can do, but he said you have become very good on the altar."

"Father McGrail is nice," I said, warmed by the praise.

"If we're lucky we could have a sub in by Monday and I wouldn't have to worry about school. I'd have those weeks and then the long holidays to get on my feet again." But she was never to feel the rain again or see the roadside hedges bent low with rain or the open or closed day.

Pat came to the house in the car later that evening and set out at once to do the rounds of the substitute teachers she thought were free. He had luck at the very first house. The next day, a Saturday, a girl came on a bicycle and spent some time with my mother in the bedroom. She took my mother's syllabus and notes away and was given tea by Katie downstairs. We were all quiet and curious as we watched her drink tea with thin buttered slices of bread and jam. We would be seeing her in school on Monday.

The world of the dying is different. When well they may have sometimes wondered in momentary fear or idle apprehension what this Time would bring, the shape it would take, whether by age or accident, stroke or cancer . . . the list is long. Then, that blinding fear could be dismissed as idle introspection, an impairment to the constant alertness needed to answer all the demands of the day. Inevitably, the dreaded and discarded time arrives and has its own shape: suddenly, the waitress pouring coffee at tables, the builder laying blocks, a girl opening a window, the men collecting refuse, belong to a world that went mostly unregarded when it was ours but now becomes a place of unobtainable happiness, in even the meanest of forms. The truth of what the ghost of Achilles spoke to Odysseus from the underworld takes on a new poignancy: "Speak not soothingly to me of death, Oh glorious Odysseus. I would choose so that I might live on earth to be the servant of a penniless man than to be lord over all the dead."

Those who are dying are marked not only by themselves but by the world they are losing. They have become the other people who die and threaten the illusion of endless continuity. Life goes on, but not for the dying, and this must be hidden or obscured or denied. The only way it can be articulated openly is as a joke, when the clash between the inevitable and the unimaginable can be resolved in laughter. No one knowingly makes plans around someone who will not be there, and that this knowledge is unconscious ensures a ruthless efficiency. All the pious platitudes are like a covering of dust or chaff.

My mother's faith must have been a strength, but even this was used against her when my father accused her of losing her faith in God. No matter how strong that faith was, it could hardly alleviate the human pain of losing everyone who depended on her whom she loved and held dear. She had no one to communicate this to after her forty-two years in a world where many loved her.

Each day when I came from school, I went upstairs to her room, seldom immediately. The girls generally raced upstairs as soon as they were in the door, but as quickly they tired of the room and were away outside to play. What I wanted most was to be alone with her. I either sat on the edge of the bed or on the low windowsill. I told her the school news, and then our talk would wander. When I had to tear myself from the room to go and gather sticks or feed the ailing white bullock on the hill, I'd return as soon as these tasks were done. The Rosary was now said in her bedroom. Katie would bring my brother upstairs and we'd all kneel around the bed.

One evening when I was sitting on the low windowsill, she said, "Will you promise me something?"

"It's to say Mass for you?"

"No, no, though I hope you will one day. It's something else. Will you promise?"

"What is it?"

"Will you promise first?"

"I can't promise without knowing."

"I don't want you to be too upset if I have to go away. And I want you to do all that you can to help the others and to keep them together."

"Go where?"

"If God calls me and I have to go."

I thought first it was to Dublin, as in those long months when we were in the barracks without knowing where she was, but this was unimaginably worse. This way she would never come home.

"No, no."

"You know I'd be safe with God and I'd be waiting for you all in heaven."

"No!" I ran from the sill to the bed. "God has lots in heaven. I have nobody."

We talked until she promised me that she would not die. Soon we'd go together on the train to town. She'd come to my first Mass and she'd be the first person I'd bless with the new priest's hands when she came to the rails. With the substitute in the school and the long summer holidays stretching ahead, she'd be well again by September. We'd walk again past Brady's pool, past Brady's house and street, and the street where the old Mahon brothers lived, past the deep, dark quarry, across the railway bridge and up the steep hill past Mahon's shop to the school.

Katie had to call me several times before I left the room that evening. I left it uneasily and didn't think I'd be able to face Katie and the others, and as I dragged myself away I noticed that she too was trying to hide her face.

Pat came almost every day to the house and always climbed the stairs to her room. He'd cough loudly as he crossed the narrow wooden corridor to the room, and never went further than the bedroom door. "How is the patient?" he always asked, clearing his throat. She nearly always said she was improved or a little better, and this heartened him. He'd mention the coming summer and the good weather and how all these things take time. They were very fond of one another. Only once did she answer, "Not so good. Sometimes I think I'll never get out of this. I don't know what will happen." He was shaken and didn't speak for a long time, clearing his throat several times. "There's no use in that way of thinking, Sue. If you were to go on like that you would be surely calling it a day soon."

"I don't want that but sometimes it's not in our hands."

"You'll be all right, Sue. Far worse than you who thought they were finished are walking around today without a care."

Maggie came on her bicycle one evening in great excitement. She had heard of a young woman who won the gold medal in her finals in the London Hospital and was home. She wanted me to go with her to see if we could get her to come and nurse Mother. They lived only a few miles away on the far side of Garradice. As we cycled along the narrow roads around Garradice, it seemed as if everything would be made whole again if we could persuade this girl to come.

An old woman in black came to the door. I was left holding

the bicycles again, but this time there was no rain and the light was of the lengthening evenings. Maggie explained the purpose of the visit, pointing me out.

"She came home for a rest. She's worn out by the bombings and all that's going on in England."

"Couldn't I have a word with her anyhow?" Maggie pleaded.

A confident young woman came to the door and her mother disappeared into the house. She was plainly reluctant at first. Maggie pleaded with her, pointing me out, explaining how young my mother was, a teacher, with children: there was a maid, she'd get all her meals, she'd have no housework. I could hardly bear the tension, and then my heart sang when I heard them agree hours and wages. We cycled home full of happiness.

The nurse came the next day. She was shocked by the state of the bedroom, perhaps by the house as well, and spent the whole morning cleaning and rearranging the room. Dr. Dolan came, and he and the nurse spent some time talking on the cinder path a little way up from the house after the visit. It was decided that the baby would no longer sleep at night with our mother but with Katie. Rosaleen now slept with our mother, and a small bed for me was moved into the room. At six in the morning Mother woke Rosaleen, who then woke me to go down and light the fire. When I had the fire going and the kettle boiling, I took the hot water upstairs where we helped Mother mix a white powder. Rosaleen thinks it was probably morphine. I then went downstairs to put more turf on the fire so that it would be lit for Katie when the house rose. A new strictness was imposed by the nurse. I could no longer go to the room as soon as we came from school or stay very long when we were allowed to climb the stairs to her room. My mother seemed to spend a great deal of time sleeping during the day.

The good weather came in June. The goats were back on the hill. The little fortress of a flower garden in front of the house remained intact, but no one tended it any more and the smaller flowers were barely visible in the grass. Sometimes I went up the railway tracks to the Keegans. In this good weather Jim and Christy and the father were nearly always in the fields or on the bog, and I was sure of finding Bridie alone in the house. She made much of me and gave me tea with slices of fresh buttered bread with jam or honey.

"Your mother is still in bed?"

"Still in bed. She has a nurse now."

"I know. She's a long time laid up. She didn't look all that well when I was over to see her last week."

"She got wet that bad evening we went to the priest's."

"You got wet on that evening too and you are not laid up."

"No, but I wasn't sick. She'll be better soon. We were very lucky to get the nurse."

"What would you do if she didn't get better?"

That was unimaginable. This was not the pleasant, happy visit I had come for. "She'll get better. After the holidays she'll be back in school with us."

"Say, if she wasn't able to get back?"

"She'll be back. There's oceans of time yet for her to get better. There's the whole holidays."

"Say if she died?"

"She can't die. She's too young to die. Only old people die."

"Our mother wasn't old when she died. I had to give up school before I was fourteen when she died. God calls people away at every age."

"She can't die!" I went silent as I heard footsteps and voices approaching the house. Jim and Christy and the father were coming in from the fields. They all welcomed me. Ordinarily, I would have wanted Bridie all to myself, but at this moment I was never more glad to see them.

As I went back down the sleepers and white stones of the railway track, Bridie's questions would not go away, "What if she doesn't get better? What if . . ." was too terrible, but the doubts and fears kept coming. Why would Bridie want to torture me?

What terrible thing was she trying to say? I sat down on one of the sleepers in the middle of the track and put my head in my arms. I wouldn't have cared if the train was coming.

Dr. Dolan arrived every day. Another nurse was hired to be with her during the night, and Rosaleen and I went back to our old rooms. The fire was never raked but kept going by the nurse during the night. If there was any fighting and shouting, we were warned to be quiet. Pat and Maggie came every day from the town. Uncle Jimmy came. Aunt Katie. Father McGrail. Master McMurrough; and on Saturdays and Sundays other teachers came, some of them cycling distances. My father never appeared.

We were less protected now. The three Brady children waited for us by the pool each school morning, and we went home with them after school. The Whelans wanted to fight us as soon as we left the Bradys. I fought one of them and was beaten. I didn't tell anybody. I felt too humiliated, but word must have gone round, and after that Hugh Patrick Brady, who was older, came with us all the way past the pool to the iron gate opening on to the foot-path of cinders. Sometimes when he was gone the Whelans would return to the gate and shout down to the house, challenging us to come out and fight. Now that our mother was no longer at school we were seen as vulnerable and weak.

On the last Sunday in June I was invited over to Aunt Katie's. Breedge and Rosaleen, Margaret and Monica were going to Brady's for the day. I think it was a way of clearing the small house, lightening Katie McManus's work and possibly ensuring quiet as well. As soon as I came from serving Mass, I cycled towards the town and out the Willowfield Road. The narrow road ended at McGarry's gate. Their thatched house overlooked a small lake with an island and several swans. Many wildfowl gathered on the lake and stood out like clusters of dark fruit on the unruffled water.

The canal also ran along their fields and was full of eels and bright yellow roach and small perch. I had a wonderful day with my first cousins, exploring the shores of the lake where Emmet had a setline for pike attached to a bottle floating outside the drowning leaves. We ran, we jumped, we played marbles on the earthen floor of the living room and caught many small perch in the canal, and I came home very late, dog tired and happy to find myself the centre of a storm of anxiety. "Where were you all this time? What kept you? Your mother nearly left us while you were away. She was asking for you and we couldn't find you anywhere."

She had nearly left us and I wasn't there. She had not gone. That was relief, but, mortified, I climbed the stairs. She was not gone. She was there. We kissed, and I sat close to her on the edge of the bed. "I didn't mean to be so late."

"It doesn't matter, love. How were the McGarrys?"

The nurse was in the room. We did not speak of what had nearly happened while I was away or of our dream of life together. Constraint was now all around us. Her voice was low and she looked very tired, but I would have sat there for ever. After a long time the nurse came towards me and touched me very gently, indicating that I should leave. My mother was sleeping deeply.

My father must have heard from Maggie or Pat that the end was close. Margaret and Monica went by Brady's pool, by Brady's house and street, and the street where the old Mahon brothers lived, by the deep, dark quarry, across the railway bridge and up the steep hill past Mahon's shop to the school; but the rest of us were kept from school. A lorry was coming to take us to the barracks. It must have been decided the night before, because the brown hens weren't let out in the morning and were packed into crates for the journey. Pat and Maggie were in the house and the two workmen who hadn't been with us for weeks were there. The morning was a perfect late June morning. Everywhere birds were singing. Pat heard the lorry coming and went out to the road to direct it through the open gap and down the cart path to the house. The lorry had just enough space to turn and park on the cinders between the house and the flower garden. There was only the driver.

The driver handed Pat a note which he gave to Maggie to read. Maggie told him what was in the note in a voice so low and rapid that no one could hear. The men began to take the furniture out of the house and to lift it on to the back of the lorry, moving what was downstairs first: the table, chairs, the yellow dresser, pots, buckets, basins, the flour bin, the milk churn, tea chests filled with cups and plates and saucers wrapped in towels and dishcloths, the lamps emptied of their oil, the religious pictures from the walls. Then they began to clear the upstairs rooms: the wardrobe, the chest of drawers, the mattresses, the bed clothes, the white enamel pots. This was slow and difficult because of the narrow, rickety stairs. My mother's bicycle was lifted on to the lorry with my small bicycle. The iron beds were left till last. The joints had rusted in the dampness and the sections would not pull apart. Bicycle oil and brute strength were tried. Neither worked. A hammer was found. They started to beat the sections apart. The sound of the metal on iron rang out and the thin walls of the house shook in the beating. A man swore at the noise the beating made. When the sections were finally separated, they fell with a light clang. It must have taken no more than an hour or two hours to clear the small house, but it seemed like a whole day.

I stood beside the overgrown flower garden watching the lorry fill, trying to put off the time when I'd have to climb the stairs and cross the landing and enter the room to see her for the last time. Earlier I had said goodbye to the cows and the white bullocks and the goats on the hill, and when I went towards the old jennet he galloped away thinking I had come to harness him for work. Breedge and Rosaleen and little Dympna had been to the room, as had Katie with my baby brother. Breedge and Rosaleen were excited by all the moving and commotion and tried to draw me into their gaiety. I looked at them in incomprehension and silent hatred: how could they not know what was happening? The window of the sickroom opened and the nurse motioned to me to come to the room. It could not be put off any longer. Inside, the house looked much larger emptied of all the furniture. In a terrible numbness, I climbed the stairs, crossed the landing by the open doors of the small empty bedrooms, entered the room and went towards the bed. Maggie and the nurse were in the room.

"The lorry will be going soon, Mammy."

"Not for a little time yet, love."

Her voice was so low I was hardly able to hear.

"I came to say goodbye, Mammy."

Her eyes were fixed on my face; she seemed to be very tired. I bent to kiss her. She did not move. I was bewildered. Both Maggie and the nurse turned away. I tried to hurry. If I did not get away quickly I'd never be able to walk out of the room. I wanted to put arms round the leg of the bed so that they wouldn't be able to drag me away and they'd be forced to leave me with her in the room for ever. I went out the door, crossed the landing, went down the stairs and out into the blinding day.

My uncle put his hand on my head but, blessedly, did not speak. "Will the lorry be going soon?" I started to pester the driver. "Any minute now. We are almost there." The crates of alarmed clucking hens were the last to be put in among the furniture in the back of the lorry.

I could not tear my eyes from the upstairs window. I wanted to rush to the room. But how would I ever be able to leave a second time? The engine started. Katie, with the baby in her arms, sat into the cab with the driver. Breedge, Rosaleen, Dympna were lifted into the lorry. I climbed up beside them. The end board was raised and the pins dropped into place. The high crate was closed. Dympna sat between Breedge and Rosaleen on a mattress, and they were warned not to let her stray. The two workmen and Pat and Maggie were gathered outside the door. Maggie was shaking. Pat looked lost, but as the lorry bumped along the cart path to the gap on the road, I saw him turn towards the workmen. On the main road the lorry gathered speed, but with each pothole we hit, the furniture shook and jumped and would have fallen if it hadn't been roped to the crates. The hens clucked their alarm for the whole of the journey, only falling quiet on rare moments. We went through the railway gates, past Maggie's open shop, down High Street, past the barracks where my father lived when he came as a young sergeant to the town, across the canal, and we blessed ourselves at the blue-and-white statue of the Virgin outside the convent where our mother first taught. We went through Fenagh, Keshcarrigan, Leitrim village, crossed the shallow, angry Shannon at Battlebridge, and into the narrow roads leading to Cootehall. The girls were still excited by all the moving and newness, and after a while I joined them in putting my hand out through the crate to comb the rushing air with my fingers.

We were in Cootehall: the church, Henry's field, Lenihan's Bawn, the barracks. We went past Charlie Reegan's bar, the post office, Packie McCabe's, turned in the short avenue of sycamores to the barracks. Beyond it stood the black and red navigation signs at the entrance to Oakport, the slow river and glittering lake and the dark woods of Oakport in the far distance.

On the white gravel my father waited with all the guards, Guard Walshe, Guard Cannon, Guard Murray, and two of their wives, Mrs. Walshe and Mrs. Cannon. The two women were wearing light summer dresses, and Mrs. Cannon's long bare legs were in white tennis shoes. All my father's silver buttons and stripes and badges were shining as if it were a court day, the high collar unclasped. He lifted each of us off the lorry and kissed us before setting us down on the gravel. The two women were crying, and it worsened when Katie got out of the cab carrying our baby brother.

"The poor children. The poor children. The poor children." This pitying was almost as hard as entering and leaving the upstairs room.

The ropes that held the furniture together were loosened. The three guards removed their tunics to help carry the furniture and boxes into the barracks. My father alone remained in full uniform. Mrs. Walshe left for her own house below the quay. Mrs. Cannon stayed. There were already a few hens at the barracks picking about in the big rhubarb beds in front of the lavatory. The brown hens were closed into their henhouse in the crates until they grew used to their new place.

The whole mood of the day lightened as soon as they started to carry in the furniture. There were even quiet jokes and laughter as pieces were edged through doors and around corners and up the wide barrack stairs. My father alone remained gravely silent. Mrs. Cannon stood smoking and talking to Katie in the big barrack kitchen, and I became fascinated by the pale, bleached hairs on her bare legs above the tennis shoes, and stealthily, guiltily, let a coin roll towards her across the cement to try to see further up the short dress when I bent to lift the coin.

The barracks had been empty for so long that the big rooms gave back echoes. The girls started to call out and to listen for the echo and to laugh when it came back, and then called out again even louder, until my father roared at them to be quiet; then they began to cry. The furniture was soon all taken in. The lorry drove away. I moved outside into the day.

The barrack boat had been tarred and was floating in the inlet down from the dayroom, tied up to the clump of sallies. All the arable part of the big barrack garden had been tilled, and the rich green mass of potato stalks, with their tiny white and purple blossoms, moved like water under the various breezes. That night I slept with my father in the big iron bed with the broken brass bells, the single window looking out on the river and Oakport. I was too numb and heartsick to care where I slept.

Strangely, we were not sent to school the next day, or the next, and it was on that third day that the news of her death came. We were in the big barrack living room when we heard the telephone ringing down in the dayroom. The dayroom door opened and Guard Cannon's steps came up the long hallway. He knocked timidly. "There's a personal call for you, sergeant." My father went down to the dayroom, shutting the door behind him. Guard Cannon stayed with us in the living room. His face was grave. "Is it from Corramahon?" Katie asked, and when he nodded she burst into tears and, as if a dam had broken, I joined her, weeping uncontrollably. She was gone. She would never answer to her name again. She was gone for ever.

At the sight of our sudden weeping, Breedge and Rosaleen started to laugh, but went quiet when the dayroom door opened and my father's footsteps came slowly up the hallway. He stood silently in the doorway for what seemed an age. "The children's mother died at a quarter to three. May the Lord have mercy on her soul."

"I'm sorry, sergeant, very sorry," Guard Cannon gripped his hand.

I had no control over my grief and was joined by Breedge and Rosaleen. My father asked Guard Cannon to see if Packie McCabe could drive him to Aughawillan. "Later you can phone compassionate leave for me into the Super's office." Guard Cannon left all the doors to the dayroom open when he went for Packie McCabe.

Slowly my father took his beads from the small purse. He put a newspaper down on the cement and knelt with both elbows on the table facing the big sideboard mirror. "We will offer this Holy Rosary for the repose of the soul of the children's mother."

We found chairs and knelt, all the time crying.

"Thou, O Lord, wilt open my lips."

When no response came but our crying, he gave the response impatiently, staring fixedly into the big mirror. "And my tongue shall announce Thy praise.

"We offer up this Holy Rosary to Almighty God that He may grant the children's mother eternal rest in heaven."

We struggled through the Our Fathers and Hail Marys of the Five Sorrowful Mysteries. The girls were confused by all the emotion and strangeness and had reverted to laughing again, looking at one another mischievously through latticed fingers, until my father paused and said, "Can no respect be shown to the dead or do I have to enforce respect?"

They were frightened and began crying again.

"Crying isn't respect. The respect your poor mother needs now is prayer."

We rose from our knees. He asked for shaving water and a white shirt. Katie poured the hot water into the basin on its iron stand in front of the wooden-framed mirror in the scullery window and draped a white shirt on the back of a chair in front of the fire. He took the white shirt with him when he went upstairs to change. Guard Cannon came back to say that Packie McCabe would be outside any minute now. He must also have gone to their house in the Bawn to tell his wife of the death, as very soon afterwards a weeping Mrs. Cannon, who barely knew my mother, arrived and embraced us all. My father had changed into the brown suit and the white shirt and a black tie. He stood in silence with his grey gabardine coat on his arm until Guard Cannon came up from the dayroom to say that Packie McCabe was outside. We all followed my father out to the waiting car. We watched the small blue Vauxhall as it went out the short avenue, turned at the bridge, was hidden briefly by the post office, and then disappeared down Lavin's Hill.

"It makes you think," Guard Cannon said.

The news had gone around and the village women started to come. They gathered round Katie and Mrs. Cannon in the big living room.

"The poor children. The poor children. The poor children."

I had to be alone. Why had he alone gone to see her, he who never went to see her all those weeks when she was still living? I crossed by the rhubarb beds to the darkness of the lavatory, but even there it was too open. I thought of the little room beneath the stairs where old clothes and ravelled sweaters were kept, and it was warm and dark as night when I bolted the small door. There were bags among the old clothes in which woollens were kept, and I put my face in the wool and camphor, and for the first time started to weep purely.

I remembered her in the world, walking those lanes to school. To Lisacarn, to Beaghmore, to Aughawillan; on the train, in Maggie's, going from shop to shop by her side in the town, watching with her the great fires of sticks in Aughawillan evenings, the flames leaping around the walls and ceilings, going with her for milk to Ollarton's when the moon showed us the way . . . She was gone where I could not follow. I would never lay eyes again on her face. The time I had spent in the flower garden by the lorry instead of going to her in the room came back to torture me. If I could have had but one minute of it back, to go up the stairs and be with her again. What must she have thought when she heard the lorry leave?

I heard them calling my name. I must have been hours among the bags of wool and discarded clothes. They were looking for me down by the river. I had to appear and face them in what was left of this day.

"Your mother will be far happier. She'll be in heaven looking down on you. She'll be able to do far more for you there," a woman said as she forced me to drink tea and eat.

"Are any of them going to the funeral?"

"He said they weren't to go."

"It's probably better that they remember her the way she was in life."

Night came so slowly that it seemed it would never come. The women started to leave.

"Will we be going to Aughawillan tomorrow?" I asked Katie after they had all gone. It was a last hope.

"No. We'll not be going, love," Katie said.

She decided that there was no need to say the Rosary before going to bed as it had already been said. "Tomorrow is a Holy Day. We all have to go to Mass as if it was a Sunday. We should go to First Mass and go to Holy Communion for your mother."

The day was the feast of St. Peter and St. Paul. I didn't know how I'd be able to face into people at Mass and tried not to go, but Katie was adamant. "I'll have to tell your father when he comes back if you don't go. It wouldn't look right for you not to go on this day above all days."

"His mother is dead, his mother is dead, his mother is dead." I had to steel myself to run the gauntlet of men standing along the chapel wall. Inside the church I was able to hide among people until the priest read the announcements before the sermon. "Your prayers are requested for the soul of Susan McGahern, wife of Sergeant McGahern, who passed from this life yesterday. For those of the parish wishing to attend, her body will be removed to Aughawillan Church, arriving at six this evening. The burial will take place immediately after eleven o'clock Mass tomorrow. May her soul and the souls of all the faithful through the mercy of God rest in eternal life for ever, Amen."

I would have run from the church but was seated in the middle of a bench, hemmed in between men. They were praying for my mother. Always we had prayed for others, but that was never close or real or near. They were now praying for *her*.

She would be taken to the church at six this evening. She would remain all night in the church beneath the sanctuary lamp. Tomorrow, after eleven o'clock Mass, she would be buried. There was no longer any hope it could be wrong or changed or denied.

I ran from the church as I had run when the priest admonished me from the pulpit. I hadn't as far to run: down Henry's street, by Jimmy Shivnan's forge, past Gilligan's shop, and across the stone wall into Gilligan's field where the horse that drew the travelling shop was grazing, across the stone wall and through the arch and into the barracks. My heart was thumping but I was safe inside the barracks long before the bicycles and traps and sidecars and people walking started to move in a stream towards the bridge.

All day people trickled to the still house in my mind. Down the cinder path they'd come, shake hands at the door. "I am very sorry for your trouble," climb the stairs to look on her face a last time, the living face I had a whole hour to look on and threw away. They'd kneel at the foot of the bed, watched by the woman who had taken over the night vigil, and afterwards they'd have tea or wine or whiskey. As she lay cold in the light of the candles, she'd never move or smile again, whether they were there or not.

All day I watched the clock. At six they'd take her to the church. Once the hands of the clock passed five, I was close to panic as I pictured the house: the brown coffin came in the glass of the hearse; the hearse stopped by the little iron gate; the empty coffin was taken out, and carried down the cinder path to the house; as the coffin was taken in, the people would leave the house and gather outside on the street of cinders or in the flower garden. How must the house have looked to the people with the furniture already taken away? Only those close to her would remain in the house. The door would be shut, the night blinds drawn. Outside in the open day a single voice would call out the Rosary. All the voices together would murmur back the responses. On chairs beside the bed the coffin would rest while my father and Maggie and Katie and Pat and Jimmy gathered to look on her a last time.

They'd lift her from the bed and place her in the wood. They'd put the lid in place and turn the screws. Never would her face be seen again. They'd carry her down, past the empty rooms, shakily down the stairs. Outside in the day, the single voice calling out the prayers was being answered by the sea of voices. Once through the door, she'd be raised on shoulders, my father's, Uncle Jimmy's, Pat's, Francie McGarry's. They'd carry her up the path of cinders to the hearse at the gate. The hearse would move slowly at first, gathering speed as it went by Brady's pool and Brady's house and the street where the old Mahon brothers lived, past the deep, dark quarry, across the railway bridge, and up the hill past Mahon's closed shop to the school, the hearse halting at the school gate, past the hall and the football field and up the small hill to the church, all the banks of the way covered with the small flowers she loved. The bell would be tolling now if it was in the bell tower instead of resting on the grass.

All night they'd leave her before the high altar under the red sanctuary lamp, candles in tall black candlesticks about the coffin. They'd leave her there all night in the brown coffin, the church empty, the doors locked, the coffin beneath the lamp in that weird stillness, but at least she was not in the earth yet; somehow it all might be turned back yet.

There was a clear blue sky in the morning without a wisp of cloud, a promise of yet another true day. We saw a small group gather at the bridge and leave in three cars.

All morning I watched the clock, seeing the minutes that were left beat away. Close to eleven I was frantic. I made sure no one was watching, and took the blue clock from the sideboard and stole out with it to the avenue by the elder tree along the footpath to the arch. She'd never see again the flat fragrant blossom turn into clusters of tiny black grapes. Under the evergreens it was dark on the avenue. There was no one in sight, but I hurried until I reached the great oak halfway up the hill to the Bawn, and entered the deep thick laurels. I held the cold glass of the clock to my face as the minutes beat away. The church was now full. The altar boys in black and white were coming out on the altar ahead of the priests. I had only a wren for company, flitting from branch to bare branch under the thick covering of leaves. The four candles were lit around the coffin under the sanctuary lamp. *Introibo ad altere dei. Ad Deum qui laetificat juventutem meam.* I could stop nothing now. I followed the Mass from movement to movement, holding the clock in my hands, weeping.

At the end of the Mass the priests go to chairs at the side of the altar. The altar boys sit on the altar steps. My father and Uncle Jimmy stand at a small table outside the rail. Silently the mourners come to place offerings of money on the table in front of my father and uncle. As soon as the line ends, the two men count the money into small blue bags and write the sum that has been gathered on a slip of paper. They bring the slip of paper and the blue bags to the priest. The sum that is read out is unusually large. My mother was a teacher and she was young. Father McGrail faces the people and talks of the life she lived in the world, her devotion, her modesty, her gentleness, her care for everything placed in her trust. I cried out as I listened and thought the hands of the clock were about to stop.

The priests come through the altar gate to bless the coffin. An altar boy holds the vessel of holy water; another carries the smoking thurible, and yet another the small boat that holds the incense. The boy carrying the cross moves a little way down the aisle and stops.

She has waited for the Lord as sentinels wait for the dawn, and now she goes to the Lord; but the Lord has many servants, and I had but the one beloved. The clock beats in my hands in the shelter of the laurels. The candles smoke as they are quenched and put aside. My father and uncles struggle as they raise the coffin to their shoulders, the cross moving ahead, and the crowd follow behind the coffin that rides a last time on living shoulders; it moves from the porch out into the sunlight, its brass glittering, swaying a little as the bearers change step on the gravel. Slowly it moves round the sacristy, as far as the footpath to Dolan's gate, where there's a gash of fresh clay among the crosses and flowers. They have lined the grave with moss so that the coffin will go softly down on the ropes. The crowd circles the grave, the priest's clay falls on the boards. Heads are bowed as the quick shovelfuls thud on the hollow boards. The brown wood is covered. The grave is filled. Green sods are replaced on the clay. The crowd moves slowly away to the graves of their own dead or out the gate into the open day.

I was almost blind when I came out of the laurels though the whole long avenue was all in shade. When I reached the archway I saw two men with fishing rods coming in the short avenue of sycamores to the barracks. They must have been given the loan of the boat. I ran to meet them before they got to the barrack gate. I wanted to go with them on the river in the boat.

"You are going out in the boat?"

"We are thinking of giving it an old try anyhow."

"Could I come with you?" I must have looked a strange sight, my face tearstained, the clock in my hands.

"You know the day that it is," they reminded me very carefully.

"The funeral is over now. I don't think it'd be any harm to go."

"I'd give it a miss today. It wouldn't look good if you were missing when they get home."

"I don't think they'd mind."

"I'd give it a miss today anyhow. They'll be other days. What are you doing with the clock?"

I was taken aback. "I brought it out to look at the time," I answered lamely.

I followed them down through the long grass to the river in the hope that they'd relent. I listened to the rustle of the boat against the big drowning leaves as they pushed it out into the current, using the oar as a pole. When they started to row, the oars squealed fiercely, and they stopped to pour water on the dry rowing pins. They waved to me as they rowed towards Oakport and I waved in return before turning back to the house.

The brown hens were pecking and scratching around the rhubarb beds as if they no longer had any memory of Aughawillan. I hid the clock under my arm as I went into the house, and was able to leave it back on the sideboard without anybody noticing. I was ashamed of my quick desire to go on the river. She had hardly been buried when I was willing to abandon her for my own selfish pursuit of life and pleasure. I was unable to watch even one hour with her. One day I would make everything up to her by saying Mass for her, and then, with a pang of anguish, I remembered that our dream was now changed: she would not be there.

Suddenly, they were home from the funeral, three carloads, all relatives of my father—Smiths and Bradys and Leddys. My father looked tired but stood impressively robed in his position and prominence. Katie made tea for everyone. "The poor children, the poor children, the poor children," women repeated, and it was no easier to endure. They made much of my seven-month-old brother who was sleeping in his cot by the window.

I looked at them with curiosity. They had seen her laid out on the bed, they followed the coffin; they had watched the grave fill while I followed it on the beating clock. When I could stand their talk no longer, I slipped out of the house without being noticed and headed towards the river.

A terrible new life was beginning, a life without her, this evening and tomorrow and the next day and the next. If I could have that hour or hours out on the cinders by the lorry back, I could portion out the time so that I could lay eyes on her face from time to time and she would not be gone for ever.

Maria, the barracks' old grey cat, was out on the stones waiting for the return of the boat. I picked out the boat, the oars flashing in the late sun as it left the Gut, and headed out into Oakport. I tried to catch Maria to lift her ragged fur to my face, but she did not want to be caught. She escaped into the sallies but returned to the stones as soon as I moved back from the water. I decided to stay and meet the boat, but before it reached the navigation signs at the end of Oakport, I heard them calling my name from the house. They wanted me for the Rosary.

The Sunday following the funeral I had a hard time slowing my step to keep behind the march of my father's blue uniform up to the front seat of the church. With eyes closed and hands joined he returned from the altar rail after receiving the sacraments as if he was already in communion with the dead in heaven. After Mass I had to stand by his side for what seemed hours as a crowd gathered about him at the church gate to offer their condolences. "The poor children, the poor children, the poor children" became too much for me again, and I began to weep, but my anger wasn't noticed. In the weeks following the funeral, my father was like a man possessed.

The Month's Mind Mass is traditionally a low-key remembrance of the dead for close members of the family, but he wanted a High Mass. Maggie was dismayed. She had paid the priest herself for a Low Mass in Corleehan. She wrote that there would also have to be a Mass in the town where my mother lived and taught for years as well as in Aughawillan. Priests who had been fond of my mother had written to her that they had said Mass privately for her, and if money was to be spent it was better that it be spread around and that they be offered something.

Ten priests would be required for a High Mass. They would all have to be paid and given lunch in the hotel in town afterwards. Not to leave any room, she went to Father McGrail herself, who had already been approached by my father concerning the High Mass. She reported that the priest had advised strongly against it, as it was neither customary nor necessary. She then took the liberty of booking a Low Mass because Father McGrail was going on holiday and was anxious to fix on a day. The day couldn't be changed and she hoped it was suitable. The spectacle of a High Mass with ten priests had been avoided.

He had a free field when it came to choosing the headstone, and took me with him when he went to Smith's. He spent ages in the yard, going from monument to monument, and eventually picked a large limestone cross in a Celtic design with a thin Italian Jesus in white marble nailed to the centre, the most expensive headstone on display.

Sitting at the table in front of the big mirror, he spent a number of nights drawing up the plan for the grave until he was satisfied. He had a natural talent for mathematics and measurement as well as for expressing himself in writing. Though he had purchased a family plot and had been given a favoured position close to the church, when they were complete his plans could not be contained within the plot. Trouble came quickly. I was dispatched with the letter to Mr. Callaghan, the Aughawillan contractor and stonemason. I have only a vague memory of this errand. Over the years I was sent on many of his errands. I probably travelled by bicycle to Drumshambo, and then by train to Ballinamore, and stayed the night at Maggie's:

> *Garda Siochana*
> *Cootehall*
> *Boyle*
> *Co. Roscommon*
> *24/11/1945*

Dear Mr. Callaghan
> *I am sending Sean down with this letter to you as I cannot get away myself. I am terribly annoyed having heard that you erected part of the cross foundation on some person's plot named McBrien. I cannot understand why you should do this, you will appreciate this must be rectified. Please send up a letter with Sean telling me about the whole matter, you will appreciate how awkward it is for me. I don't even know the family and to think we have annoyed them.*

> *Yours faithfully*
> *Francis McGahern*

Mr. Callaghan must have written his reply while I waited:

Garradice P. O.
Co. Leitrim
24.11.45

Dear Mr. McGahern
I'm sorry to learn that there's trouble about the cross
foundation. I'm enclosing a copy of plan you gave me
which shows that the base for the cross is 2' x 10" and
1' x 10": and that it had to be on the centre of the plot.
Now I put it up according to the plan and I don't think
any blame lies on me.

Yours faithfully
Patrick Callaghan

I don't know how it was resolved. There would certainly have been shouts and roars when I returned with Callaghan's letter, and soon there was further trouble. The plan had strayed into Dolan's private path as well. The Dolans were a relatively wealthy family, who had an attractive house in trees beside the church. Many of them had been to America and some of them had settled there. When the church was being built they gave the field to the church, and in return were granted the right to this private path through the churchyard. A footpath ran from the house, through the trees—I remember lilacs along the way—to a small gate in the church wall. From the gate, the path threaded its way between the graves to the wide, gravelled footpath that ran all around the church. The Dolans didn't come through the church gates like the rest of the congregation. Such are the symbols of privilege, and the Dolans were probably jealous of their right. I remember an old uncle of theirs vividly, Charlie Dolan, who had spent years in America and was fond of fishing. Most days in summer he passed our house in Corramahon on his way to and from Garradice. Whenever he caught a big fish he hung it from the handlebars of the bicycle even though the tail trailed in the dust and the body of the fish slapped awkwardly against his knee as he cycled along. The lesser fish were packed in a bag strapped to the carrier, the fishing rod pointing ahead like a long spear tied to the cross-bar. It was a childish world. People knew his weakness in the same way they knew Hughie McKeon's pride in his gold watch when they went on the train to town, and Charlie was stopped at every turn of the road. The huge fish was admired in wonderment: it must have taken a near miracle to get such a monster up on the shore, and Charlie never failed to rise to the bait. This need for recognition and glory must have its roots in human loneliness.

I am not sure how the trespass into their private path was resolved, but I know that the Dolans threatened law. Probably Maggie or Pat went to Father McGrail and the Dolans, in the light of the whole story, allowed the wall to stand, as it didn't in any significant way affect their access to the church or their old right. The trespass into the McBrien plot was much more serious and had to be removed at my father's expense, the plan redrawn. Probably the trespass into the private path was corrected at this time as well. Today the thin white Italian Jesus looks green and forlorn on the Celtic cross, and the rain has eaten away the lettering on the limestone.

Margaret and Monica went as usual to Aughawillan School on the day the rest of us were taken from Corramahon on the lorry. I didn't discover why the two girls had been kept behind until many years later. Maggie had agreed to keep her godchild Margaret, but my father had insisted that the girls couldn't be separated. He was dispersing and arranging the family while my mother was still alive. On the day that she died they were at school. She died shortly before school was out, and someone was dispatched to intercept the two girls before they reached the house. They were met at Brady's pool and were taken to Brady's house. They did not understand what had happened and were charmed by the fuss. They remained with the Bradys over the days of the funeral and did not see the hearse go slowly past Brady's pool and Brady's house and street where the old Mahon brothers lived. Immediately after the funeral my father demanded that Maggie take the two youngest children—my baby brother and Dympna—instead of Margaret and Monica. When Maggie refused this new arrangement after agreeing to his earlier demand, he took the two older girls from her, and the whole seven of us were together again.

A High Mass with ten priests, the large limestone cross . . . his next grand plan was marriage. This was extraordinary for the time. People wore a black mourning diamond on their suits for a year after the death of a close relation. They didn't go to dances or parties, they kept to their own houses, and any exhibition of high spirits was seen as lacking in feeling and respect for the dead. If a wedding or engagement was already arranged, it had to be deferred for a year. When a death was known to be imminent within a family, weddings were often hastened. If his rush to marriage in this context was extraordinary, that he should propose to Maggie, given the level of antipathy between them, was more amazing still. She disregarded it at first, or didn't want to believe it, but he pressed her a second time. When she came to reply, her response is restrained and carefully thought out. She certainly sought advice. The letter begins with practicalities. It was written soon after he took Monica and Margaret away; he demands clothes that have been left behind:

High Street
Ballinamore

Dear Frank,

I have just come across Monica's coat, as I think that is the one you are looking for. There are 2 school bags and 2 stockings, one for Monica and one for Margaret. I wish I could have a pair for each of them as they would

*be useful as I well know poor Sue R.I.P. how she was
always so busy knitting and sewing for them in her spare
time. God help us what a world that we should bother
about it and to think that she is gone and all still goes on
without her help but such is life.*

She deals with snaps and negatives he has asked for, probably for
a memoriam card, and then describes a visit she made to Drumderg. She probably went for advice on how to handle the proposal.
The children are those of my Uncle Jimmy and Bridie Keegan:

*I was out home one evening and they are all very well
and happy thank God. It does me good to look at them,
there are 3 very good little children there, and they are
very cute, but poor Mother she is happy despite all but
heartbroken, only keeping her good side out.*

Last of all, she comes to his proposal:

*You mentioned about marrying in your second last letter.
It is only since I thought of it. I am sure you wouldn't
think of the like for at least 12 months. Then if you think
well of it I wouldn't mind if you mention it then, but not
till then. I will pray that God will send you a suitable
person if it is for the best. Still if you held such love for
poor Sue R.I.P. I can't see how you should be so
anxious to marry again but of course you know best
yourself, but I hope you get a good one if you do, and I
hope Sue's children won't be forgot, that is all I would
worry about, but God sees after all these things they say
and I think he must.*

*Kind regards,
Margaret*

I was surprised that the proposal was entertained. My sisters think otherwise. Maggie had been devastated by her sister's death. She had difficulty sleeping and couldn't pray at the grave because so many painful memories and questions kept crowding in on her. She had to enter the church to be able to pray. Stemming from religious doctrine, the spirit of self-sacrifice was everywhere in the air, only coming to earth on rocks of common sense, and it was not uncommon for a deceased wife's sister to marry the widower, to safeguard the children and to exclude a potentially hostile step-mother. It was also a position at a time when positions of any kind, especially for women, were scarce. Maggie had a shop, probably some money, and she was lively and attractive, and all these considerations would have drawn my father. Once they were married, she would be in his power. Those were my sisters' arguments. Maggie discussed the proposal with them years after-wards, and concluded, characteristically, "I might have been hard up but I wasn't *that* hard up." I don't believe she ever took the proposal seriously. Her whole family hated confrontation. What she appears to have done is to use custom in the same way as she used it to avoid the spectacle of a High Mass, this time to sideline the proposal and deliver the rebuke. If the proposal was ever renewed after the year's lapse, it was rejected. Even while he was waiting for Maggie's response, he was courting Mollie Waters, a beautiful sister of Mrs. Cannon who was visiting them in the Bawn. Each day the two sisters were with Katie in the barracks, and my father was always around at his most charming. In the late evenings he dressed carefully, warning us to be on our best behaviour in front of Mollie, and went in his uniform to the Bawn. We thought vaguely, if we thought at all, that it would be strange and flattering to have such a beautiful stepmother, but then the thought of her in place of my mother would come with all its heartbreak.

At the end of the week, without any warning, a big shining car drove fast in the avenue and went through the archway up to the Bawn. A few hours later it left. A young, well-groomed man was driving. He did not look to left or right as the car passed the barracks at speed. The beautiful black-haired Mollie was by his side. Guard Cannon and Mrs. Cannon arrived. There was a long, hushed conversation down in the dayroom. As Mrs. Cannon had become friendly with Katie and spent a great deal of her time around the barracks, news of what happened quickly filtered down even to us. Mollie Waters had been doing a line for some time with a young solicitor in Donegal who came from a powerful political family. His father was a district justice, Mrs. Cannon told Katie proudly. Recently, for some reason that wasn't clear, Mollie broke it off. Hearing of her interest in someone in Roscommon, he drove down at once and took her home. They were planning to announce their engagement. Whether or not my father was used as a pawn in the affair, he took it badly and was in foul humour for weeks.

Within a few weeks of the funeral, the house and farm were sold, the cows, the goats, the one thriving white bullock. Either my father had exaggerated the financial risk of the purchases when writing to Dr. Corcoran, or he was lucky in the sale, or both. The ailing white bullock and the jennet were kept. There was enough grass for the jennet on the boundaries of the barrack garden, and he was needed for drawing turf. My father found grazing for the bullock with the Kellys of Longmeadow on the Plains. I was dispatched to bring the bullock and jennet and cart to Cootehall.

By then, I was overcoming the instinct to hide when I saw people, and I did want badly to look on her grave and to pray for her there, but I was unsure how I'd be able to manage when faced with Aughawillan again.

I left Cootehall in the middle of the hot summer, cycling on the small bicycle to Drumshambo. I travelled with a few other passengers in the train's single carriage to Ballinamore. The rest of the train was as usual made up of wagons of coal from the Arigna pits. Pat wasn't at the station, and I wheeled the bicycle down to Maggie's. As soon as I walked into the shop and we greeted one another, we both burst into tears. She lifted the counter leaf and shepherded me inside and sent the new girl out to serve in the shop. She wiped and dried my face, and before long we were talking. I wasn't able to stop talking. She made tea and cooked a big fry with halves of tomato, which was a great luxury then.

In the evening Pat cycled with me out to the grave on Maggie's bicycle. He said he was tired of sitting in the car. We prayed in the church and then went round by the sacristy door to the grave. The big limestone cross hadn't been erected yet, and the fresh clay lay in an angle between the path that ran along the church wall and the footpath that led to Dolan's gate.

I tried to imagine her lying in the coffin under the clay, but could not. I knelt with Pat to pray. Wilted flowers were scattered on the clay near where Maggie had planted a small bush of rosemary in a corner of the grave. As we rose to leave, I remarked on the largeness of the plot, remembering how small her hands and feet were. "That man will want plenty of space for himself when it comes round to his turn," Pat said.

Maggie still had the line foreman from Tipperary and the two Dublin firemen as lodgers, but the house was subdued. Pat did not join the three men as he usually did when they played cards for small stakes after supper.

I slept in the spare bed in Pat's room and woke to the shunting of the morning trains. The early part of the day I spent happily with Maggie. Then I cycled out alone to the grave. All that came to me as I stood at the grave was the dull light from the fresh clay. When I put my fingers down into the clay, as if into water, and brought them to my mouth, all they tasted of was clay. I then knelt and willed myself to pray in the empty church.

After he met all the trains and had returned from an evening run, Pat drove me out to the Aughawillan farm. We opened the gap on the road and went down the field to the house. The fences of the flower garden had been broken down, and all the flowers had been trampled on and eaten, except for a few roses. The cinder path running to the little iron gate on the road was still free of grass and weeds. Pat unlocked the door. The big fireplace was full of ashes and we climbed the stairs and went through all the empty rooms. We spent a long time standing in the room where she died, where I had not gone to her other than for a brief moment in all the time I had on the day the lorry took us away. I looked at the low, deep windowsill, where I used to sit chatting away to her for hours, as if it was a hostile place, but found that nothing was as sharp or vivid or as painful as it had been in my mind, and that both the house and fields were dully reassuring in their solidity, empty now forever of her presence and her precious life.

"If you were to give this house a good shaking, it would come down around our ears," Pat said as we came down the stairs. "He was lucky to get rid of it so quick. There are no better men than two eejits of farmers when they start bidding against each other."

We took the bridle and went in search of the jennet and bullock. We found them on the hill. The jennet had done no work since we left and was sleek and fat from the summer grass. He squealed when he saw us and galloped off.

"He's no dope," Pat shook with laughter. "He had Bundoran here on his own for a long time. Now he's off to Cootehall."

The jennet eluded us several times, but eventually was cornered and caught. The bullock went quietly ahead of us down to the house. There we harnessed and tackled the jennet. Pat followed behind in the car until we turned for the town. Then he left us. The bullock ambled ahead of the jennet and cart. An hour or so later Pat met us at the railway gates. The bullock and jennet were driven down to the waste ground at the back of Maggie's sheds and garden. The jennet was untackled. They were both watered and fed and left for the night.

In the morning we were on our way before the shops opened.

Pat went with us through the town and then said goodbye after we passed the convent. Cootehall was eighteen miles away. The little village of Keshcarrigan was halfway, and my father had arranged that I be given a meal in the Garda barracks and the bullock and jennet be watered and rested. The bullock was lively at first, and I had to cycle ahead to guide him past the various crossroads and turns while the jennet jogged along at his own slow pace behind. Soon the bullock started to flag. I put the bicycle on the cart and sat up in front with the reins. We reached Fenagh in not much more than an hour, but the next six miles to Keshcarrigan took several hours, our pace slowing with every hour. The jennet was untackled, and he and the bullock were watered and left to recover in the barrack garden. I was given a big meal by the sergeant's wife in the living room of the barracks. Keshcarrigan is close to where I now live and very little ever happens there. For many years it was a penal station for guards who had got into trouble elsewhere. So little happened on the poor farms, and the place was so remote in the shadow of the mountain, that the Garda authorities felt that drunkards couldn't get in the way of much harm or trouble there. One such guard, who had been shooting game and drinking *poteen* for several days on the mountain without leave, on his return climbed to an upstairs window of the barracks to discharge both barrels of his shotgun up the wide empty street.

"What are you doing that for?" someone who happened to be around on that dead Sunday evening enquired sensibly.

"To let them know the law is back in town," came the trenchant answer from the upstairs window.

A boy with a jennet and a white bullock on his way to Cootehall must have been novelty enough, as I remember all the guards coming into the living room of the barracks and asking me questions while I ate. My father telephoned while I was in Keshcarrigan, and I was brought down to the dayroom. He was in great good humour. I don't think I ever had spoken on the telephone before, but I was able to tell him that the white bullock was slowing and everything was going well.

When I was ready to leave, we had difficulty in getting the white bullock to his feet, but eventually got going, hoping to reach Cootehall by evening. I remember people saving hay in fields all along the road, the white dust of the road and the intense, airless heat, of asking for a drink of water at a roadside house, and being given a slice of apple tart and cold sweetened tea instead of water by an old woman. By this time, the white bullock was coming to the end of his tether. Twice he lay down in the middle of the road, and twice, with great difficulty, I forced him to rise again. There was no traffic. We reached Leitrim village by the narrow back road, and when he lay down in the middle of the village between the canal bridge and the turn for Cootehall, even I knew he was finished for the day. A small crowd gathered. I was questioned. Who was I? Where had I come from? Where was I going? Who owned the white bullock? I heard an old man say, "That bullock has more sense than the men that sent the *gorsoon* out on such an errand," and his words were a comfort, as I was beginning to feel I had failed. Someone crossed to the Garda station beside the bridge. One of the guards rang my father, and it was decided to leave the bullock with the guards in Leitrim because it was already evening and Cootehall was still four miles away. I was to go ahead on my own with the jennet and cart. We reached Cootehall as the dew of the summer's night was beginning to fall.

The white bullock remained in a field close to the Leitrim barracks for two or three days. I collected him there early one morning, and we completed the remainder of the journey without difficulty, though his hoofs were still sore. He went to graze with the Kellys on the Plains, and immediately began to thrive on the short sweet grass. There was some difference between the Kellys and my father, and the bullock was then moved to an outlying farm of the Morahans along the river, way in past Moran's well. I fed him hay and oats in an abandoned house that winter during snow. In a room of the house I saw a beautiful white owl dragging a steel trap by a partly severed foot across the floor when I went to feed the bullock, blood on the snow that had drifted in through the windows and covered the floor. The trap had been set for the same rats the owl was hunting. A man released the owl, but it could hardly have survived that harsh winter. When the bullock was sold in the spring Pat gave me a pound.

The jennet and I drew all the turf to the barracks that summer. Drawing the turf from the bank out to the road was the worst part of the work. Only small loads could be carried. The gaps across the drains were made from sally branches and sods of heather, which softened in rain. Once a wheel sank, the jennet went down. I'd have to untackle him then and get him out of the cart. What I was most afraid of as he struggled free was that he'd break a leg and be lost. I'd have to unload the cart and go for help because I wasn't strong enough to drag the empty cart free on my own. Men would come from their own banks, and after they had dragged the cart free and mended the gap, they'd warn me not to stand on the lower side of the cart in case it turned over in one of the deep ruts. Once out on the road, the crates could be filled to the top. I didn't mind the work. I was able to be on my own. It numbed all thought. While I was working I could generally stay in my father's good graces. As I came in the short avenue to the barracks with the load of turf, I often saw my sisters at various tasks in the garden under his watchful eye, and knew I had the better deal.

The jennet, the white bullock, the brown hens and Katie McManus were all that was left to us of the world of Aughawillan. Katie was as hard-working and pleasant as ever and had grown very fond of our baby brother. Mrs. Cannon was much with us in the barracks that summer. After the debacle with her beautiful sister, when my father felt very hard done by, she would have been well advised to be careful, but she was a natural meddler. She had become friendly with Katie. She would sit for hours smoking and gossiping and drinking tea in the living room of the barracks, while Katie went on with her housework, pausing good humouredly from time to time to comment or listen more carefully. Without consulting Katie, Mrs. Cannon went to my father and proposed that he marry Katie. She got on so well with Katie that she felt confident of winning her around if he agreed, as Katie was already fond of us. Every way the plan was a disaster.

My father was incensed. He was snobbish. Katie was a maid. She was small and plain, though with her energy and uncomplicated sensuality she was attractive to certain men. Katie would have been too loyal to my mother to have ever looked at my father sexually, and they disliked one another instinctively. In that last year, knowing how ill and harassed my mother was, Katie hardly left the house other than to go to Mass and the occasional dance or concert. In Cootehall her social life blossomed. She went out most nights, leaving the baby with my sisters. My father disapproved, but there was very little he could do about it as she would have worked a very long day. He always sought to keep the world around him closed; he discouraged us from mixing with the villagers, and he would have hated to see Katie going out among other people and taking with her a knowledge of him and his house that he couldn't control. He was also puritanical enough to write to Maggie of Katie's "fondness for boys." Maggie replied sharply, "Sure, that is only natural," and went on to praise Katie for all she had done for our mother.

By this time, Katie had a steady boyfriend, Peter McLoughlin, who lived with an older brother on a small farm on the edge of the bog. He was handsome and quiet and penniless. To have to compete with such a man for Katie's hand would have been anathema to my father. No matter how Mrs. Cannon's proposal was viewed, it was not only hopeless but ridiculous. Before she had finished her case he roared at her in rage, ordered her out of the house, and warned her never to set foot in the living quarters of the barracks again. Theatrically, he wrote "Private Quarters" in large letters on official paper and tacked it on the door to our living room. After this, whenever any of the guards came up with messages, they always knocked timidly and waited for his "Come in" before entering.

One Sunday Katie asked me if she and Peter could come with me on the river in the tarred boat. I was delighted. They were company I liked. There were already objections that I was too young to be on the river so much on my own, and their presence in the boat guaranteed the Sunday. Though I had no idea of this at the time, my presence was equally useful to them as a chaperone. Peter rowed. I sat on the stern seat, Katie on the seat between us. I let out the spoons and gave a line to Katie to hold. She was happy and excited but a little frightened of a fish coming on the line. Peter teased her, laughing, and let go of the oars to squeeze her bare arm.

"When you feel the fish you can hand the line to me or Peter but it is probably too bright," I said. They laughed at my serious-ness, but I didn't understand or mind. I was glad they were happy. The day was bright. All the wide water of Oakport glistened. Peter was strong and the boat raced quickly across the lake. When we reached the black and red navigation pans at the Gut and moved into the shade of the Oakport Woods, I asked Peter to slow and to draw closer to the edge of the reeds and drowning leaves. The boat was moving too fast and was too far out in the current for us to have any hope of a strike. At the platform above the Gut, made of great tree trunks, we drew in the lines. Here, the low tim-ber boats that plied the Shannon were loaded. We spent a while examining the platform and the metal rails on which the trolleys took the timber from the sawmill deep in the woods. By the time we reached Tohran's Island we had caught no fish.

"Our only chance is perch. There's always perch round here and at the Golden Bush." I had brought a jamjar of worms and two fishing poles.

"Didn't you say there were great strawberries some place round here?" Katie asked.

"In the woods between here and the Black Lake."

The wood strawberries were not as sweet as the wild strawberries that grew on the banks but were much larger, a dark deep red.

"If you want to try for the perch, me and Peter could pick some of the strawberries," Katie said.

I showed them where the wood strawberries could be found, and left them off on the shore. They both disappeared into the woods and I rowed across to Tohran's Island. There wasn't another boat on the river that Sunday. I caught several perch but they were all small. There were flagstones out from the island and I could see the fish on the bottom in the clear light. The small perch ran with the worm over the flagstones. They were difficult to hook but fun. Not until I saw that the sun was well down did I begin to think about Katie and Peter. I didn't know how much time had passed and was worried. I called out to the woods across the river, but no answer came back. I rolled up the fishing line and rowed across and tied up the boat. Several times I called out, but nothing came back from the woods but an echo. After the river light, it was dark in the woods. I went towards the strawberry beds. There was plenty of fruit still left but no tracks or trace of any recent presence on the big strawberry leaves. I was worried. I knew I could row home alone but I couldn't go without them. I had heard there were many dangerous places in the woods near the Black Lake. I went back towards the boat, calling out all the time, when, to my intense relief, Peter and Katie emerged without any warning out of bushes. They were both dishevelled, with bits of twigs and leaves caught in their hair and clothes.

"Did you get much strawberries?"

"We had no luck. We sort of got lost."

Katie's face was red, though no sun ever got through to this part of the wood. "We better head for home. They'll all be wanting their tea," she said.

On the way home we let out the spoons, but Peter rowed so fast that the spoons rose and skimmed over the surface behind the boat. As we went through Oakport, Katie asked me not to tell that they had gone alone into the woods. "Especially since we never got a strawberry it wouldn't look too good," Peter said. I promised not to tell, but couldn't for the life of me see why they had such a need for secrecy. Maria, the barracks' grey cat, was waiting out on the stones for our return. We hadn't much to show for our day, but Maria had the small perch.

As well as keeping the house and bringing up the baby, Katie had, to some extent, fallen into my mother's role of trying to protect us from our father's rages. This was done passively and carefully, whooshing us out of his way, scolding us herself to divert his attention, comforting us, allowing her disapproval to show; but Katie had a poor position compared to our mother. Going out most nights into the village fuelled his resentment further, and the presence of Peter McLoughlin was probably the final straw.

In the delicate social shadings of the place, the McLoughlins were unusual. Their farm was small, on the edge of the bog. Two of their neighbours on similar farms, Langan and Casey, worked regularly for my father at turfcutting and the planting of the potatoes, but both of these men were fond of drink. The two McLoughlin brothers were hard-working and too proud to work for anybody as day labourers, though they did work on the roads for the council. My father would have looked down on them, but their independence placed them outside his control. These were the two worst possible combinations. If they were people he could look up to, he would have been full of an unsteady charm; if they deferred to him and were useful, he could be capriciously avuncular and solicitous: at the very worst, they would be guaranteed unlimited free advice. All these things played a part, but for Katie there was as well an antipathy that went back to her time with our mother: he identified her with our mother and our mother's relatives, and from his point of view she knew too much.

In one of his rages he threatened her physically, and she warned him that there would be consequences if he struck her and that she wouldn't stay on if things continued as they were. Nobody was going to dictate to him what he could do or couldn't do in his own house, he told her in his fury, and she could go whenever she wanted. She didn't want to leave, but eventually she had no choice. Pat came to take her home in the hackney car.

It turned out that my father had been preparing for her departure by placing ads in which he combined his need of a domestic with his romantic quest: *Young widower, Garda Sergeant, with young family, seeks* . . . Over the months that followed we saw a number of these women. Whether he was unlucky in his choices or inefficient, in the way he was with his windmill and lighting plant and engines, each of these women proved to be spectacularly unsuitable.

I remember only one of them. She was around the same age as he was, strong and handsome in a masculine way, the daughter of a teacher, with either brothers or sisters in the profession. She came from Castleisland in Co. Kerry, was devoted to Shakespeare, all of whose works she seemed to know by heart and to quote throughout the day. I don't remember any of the quotations; a few years later it would have been different and I'd have been fascinated. She was a forceful, theatrical extrovert and maybe a little mad. She went to Henry's. She went to the priest's well for water. She called to Gilligan's. She posted letters in the post office. She talked to everybody. I think she was the occasion of enormous curiosity and excitement and suppressed merriment, especially among the guards in the barracks, and my father didn't know how to handle her.

In the gentle manners of the village, she would have been at a great disadvantage. Everybody would listen with sympathy and much friendliness; nobody would say anything outright; most of the responses would be no more than echoes of her own speech. What she would have taken for agreement with her position and views would have been no more than the room to allow her to turn in her own hall of mirrors.

After a few weeks she was determined to marry my father, and told everybody. The betrayed person in any affair is generally the last to discover what is happening, and my father was now in this position, he who was manic about controlling everything. I don't know if she tried more circumspect approaches and was frustrated. One morning while he was sitting at the table taking his breakfast in front of the big mirror before going down to the day-room for the morning inspection, she told him that the whole village was talking: he was a healthy, able-bodied man; she was a strong, vigorous woman. They were both free and living alone together in this big house. Many people were talking and saying that it was time—and past time—their situation was regularized. With her education and connections she hadn't come all the way from Castleisland to be somebody's scullion!

He would have been incensed enough, but particularly incensed that all this was delivered in front of us sitting with big ears around the table beneath the window looking out on Coote's Archway. From time to time he raised his face from his plate to glare at her in undisguised hatred, but it had no effect on the flow of words. Not until he rose to go down to the dayroom did he speak. "So you think," he said savagely between gritted teeth, "so you think you're the man for the job?" Then he was gone, banging the door on which "Private Quarters" was still printed, and banging the dayroom door as well for good measure. By the time we came from school that evening, she had left on the bus.

When Katie left us, we were desolate. The last vestiges of our link with our mother's protection were now gone. What we didn't know was that Katie, hearing of the succession of disastrous housekeepers from Maggie, was willing to return. This and much else can be discerned in the letter Maggie wrote my father at the time:

High Street
Ballinamore

My dear Frank
How are you getting on since. I hope your foot is improving and that the pain is going, but of course you could expect pain as I will never forget poor Sue R.I.P. all she suffered with hers, so I suppose we have to go through a bit of suffering in this world, otherwise it would be too easy for us, and of course I always say there is no real happiness this side of the grave, but what about this if we get it in the next world as well. How are all the children. I hope the poor wee things they are all well, but indeed I can imagine they have their school trouble, as they wouldn't like the slaps, as they were never used to them with their poor mammy . . .
How is the new housekeeper doing? I hope well & that she is good to the children. You mentioned something about Katie that she was fond of boys, she might be but sure that is only natural, and everyone has their good & bad points but Kate was so good to Sue R.I.P. that I will never forget—long may I live. At the same time don't think for a minute that I'm telling you to take her back, as I wouldn't dream of doing so. I am only giving my opinion on the matter, and I know that you are quite capable of acting on this matter yourself, and don't think afterwards that I said or did anything, as it all is in your own hands, and you know what is best to do yourself as you have experience of

both of them. I have nothing else to say so I will finish.
Remember me to all the children.

Kind Regards
Margaret

In another letter she has to assure him that she would not dream of discussing his affairs with Katie. At this stage between the two of them, he had plenty to hide, and I am certain that they did discuss him. Again, Maggie defends Katie:

High Street
Ballinamore
27/9/44

Dear Frank
Had your letter yesterday and was glad to hear that
you were all fairly well but I was sorry to hear that your
housekeeper is not a success, but it may be that she does
not know the run of the place. Of course you can be sure
that you won't get any of them with all qualifications if
you get near to it you may be thankful and smile at the
rest. Anything further about them I can't or won't say as
I know you have a better idea yourself than what I have,
I will pray that God will do what is best for you and I
hope the good one will turn up for you. As for Katie I
have nothing to say or comment on her but what I
always said that she was an awfully good girl to
Sue R.I.P. and I hope she will have her reward for it
anywhere she goes, but I wouldn't dream of discussing
you with her and why should I, only I heard Katie say
she got on very well in Cootehall, and was quite happy in
it, and very fond of Jude. I was also glad to hear that you
had made a start to get dresses & coats for the children,

*as they will want them now as the weather is getting
cold.*

*How is your ankle. I hope it is getting better but it
just takes time and of course you will have to be careful. I
will conclude hoping you are all well. Give my love to all
the wee children and I hope to see them sometime.*

*Kind Regards
Margaret*

A succession of maids followed, none staying for long, and
for most of the time my sisters cleaned and cooked and sewed and
looked after their baby brother and me and our father.

When I went back to school in September, I was so blinded by
change and grief that a young woman teacher substituting for
Mrs. Finan, who was having another baby, sent for my father to
ask if I was retarded. "He may very well be," was the enigmatic
reply. Privately, he upbraided me. My sisters played with one
another; they talked, they fought as if no great change had happened. Even when they talked about their mother, it was clear
they hadn't fully taken in all that had happened. I had nobody I
could talk to, but even if I had, I am not sure I would have been
able to talk, or would have wanted to.

"You miss your mother very much," my father surprised me
once. He appeared drawn to the fit of weeping the enquiry pro-
voked. "I miss her very much too, miss her every single day," he
said. "If she had got better, even though she wasn't able to walk,
I'd have carried her up and down the stairs and taken her outside
to sit in the sun on good days."

He probably believed his own words. I knew that he was
lying, as he had lied when he said he'd meet me off the Drumshambo train, though I would have given the whole world for the
mercy of the picture he painted.

No matter what we did, his resentment of us seemed to increase, and we heard as often as the refrains of the Rosary:

O God, O God, O God, what did I do to deserve such a pack? I'll put you all in a bag like Toby and bring you down to the flagstones and sail ye all out under the arches of Cootehall Bridge. I'll pack you all off to the orphanage where the nuns and brothers won't be long in bringing you to your senses. They'll soon put manners on you. Of course this old fool gets no thanks when another man would lock the doors and drive you out on the side of the road to eat grass.

So completely had the normal world been subverted that some years later I told a priest who knew the family well, "We owe our father a great debt since he made so many sacrifices in order to bring us up." I spoke in all sincerity. My father had repeated this so many times that I had come to believe it. The priest was amazed. "On the contrary, you owe him nothing, and you should tell him that. You didn't ask him to bring you into the world. He brought you into the world of his own free will, and in so doing incurred responsibility for you all before God and the world." Not surprisingly, I refrained from informing my father of this reversal of his view, but I began to look at him and us from that day forward in a new, changed light.

All our groceries we bought in Henry's. We took a small note-book which my father had carefully covered with blue police-man's cloth from an old tunic or trousers. Whatever we bought was written into our account in Henry's big ledger and then into the notebook. At the end of each month it was totted up and the account settled, at which time he would line us up as if in class and read out from the blue notebook all that we had eaten during the month. If the account was slightly higher than the usual—it never varied much—he would question us about expensive items, such as butter. The reading aloud of everything we had eaten during the month was mortifying. We were made to feel a burden and to feel ashamed. Sometimes he'd order cuts to be made. "If you larrup up butter like that there has to be some stop. Once four pounds is crossed you can all go and eat dry bread."

We hardly ever ate meat other than the pig we killed each year and the occasional chicken or hare or rabbit, until he discovered cows' heads. They were so cheap that the butcher wouldn't saw them up. They had to be taken away whole. I took them home on the carrier of the bicycle from Carrick because he wouldn't be seen buying them. We had no pot large enough, and I had to quarter the head with a hacksaw and an old cleaver. My father used to exude pleasure when he saw the head boiling on the range: "That's what will put muscle and sinew into the troops." He enjoyed, or pretended to enjoy, the soup from the bones and the pieces of meat we gave him, but we hardly touched it ourselves. We hated the sight of the thick black lips with their rubber-like feelers—the grey brains, the living eyes.

At the time, I was keeping a fawn greyhound, Nellie, for Tom Gleeson, an agricultural instructor who had rooms in the tower of the Bawn. The Finans had moved to a better school on the far side of Boyle. The Cannons had transferred to their more spacious rooms in the Bawn, leaving the tower free for the Gleesons and their young family. I used to go with Tom Gleeson when he hunted hares with Nellie over the open fields of the Plains on Sundays, and when Tom fell seriously ill, I was given Nellie to feed and mind until he recovered. The fawn bitch and I were attached to one another. Every evening she used to meet me at the bridge on my way home from school. Secretly we fed the cows' heads to Nellie. She loved the brains, the eyes, the black lips, and buried the larger bones. "There wasn't a pick left," we'd tell our father to his great pleasure while trying not to appear to lie.

Another of his obsessions was with boots. Every summer,

once May arrived, we went joyously barefoot. The agony of the boots began in October. He complained endlessly about what our boots were costing and demanded that they be made to last as long as possible. As soon as they were bought, he nailed strips of worn bicycle tyres to the soles to protect the leather. This made walking difficult, but we did not care. We were warned that once a tear or crack showed they had to be taken to him immediately for repair. The trouble was that when we did take him a small tear or crack, he'd threaten and scold, endlessly scold, and we learned to prefer wet feet. At night we'd hide the leaking boots.

Then a night came when he'd go in search of the hidden boots. We were all hauled out of bed to find them lined up in a row on the living-room floor. By this time, many of the boots would have been worn beyond repair. In a fury of complaint, he would put on his brown apron and sit to fix whatever pair was picked from the row. The rest of us were beaten and sent back to bed, but the owner of the boots he decided to repair had to stay up to hand him tacks and nails and hold the waxed thread and listen to the litany and receive the occasional blow when he was handed the wrong tack or something was let drop. This went on until the grey light entered the big living room and we were falling asleep on our feet. Other nights the repairs were abandoned in frustration after a few minutes.

Compared to the boots, and the groceries we ate, there was no trouble over clothes he bought us, and he usually made a display of taking us to the various drapers in the town. I imagine this was because we were at church and the communion rail every Sunday, and what he bought us would be on show. We changed into old clothes as soon as we came from Mass. We hadn't to be told. All the girls became skilled seamstresses and knitters and darners.

Young as we were, we were soon forming our own defences and adapting to the harsher laws of the world. We were very close together in years, and drew closer. Natural rivalries were suppressed. They couldn't be afforded. All our energies were concentrated on surviving under our father. If any of us went to him with a complaint against another, or even tried to curry favour, they were ostracized. When there was a bad beating and the storm had died, we'd gather round whoever was beaten to comfort and affirm its unfairness, and it lessened our misery and gave strength to our anger. We learned to read his moods and to send out warnings in an instant so that we could vanish or take some defence, such as the simulated appearance of abject misery. This was instinctive and perfected over time, and while it did not protect us from his worst excesses, it did much to soften and make them tolerable. Above all, it prevented him from charming us when he was in his good moods, since we knew it would only leave us more vulnerable to the next attack, which was never far away. This gathering into a single band formed gradually over a number of years.

In the years immediately after our mother's death we were in disarray. We had no defence against the sudden rages, the beatings, the punishments, the constant scolding. Many of us started to walk in our sleep. I woke and fell in the shallows beside the tarred boat one night, another time on the stairs, but Rosaleen was by far the worst: she was sleepwalking everywhere within the house, and going into the dayroom at night to startle the barrack orderly in his bed, where it could not be concealed. She was beaten and warned, but that only made it worse. She feels that it was as much a delayed reaction to our mother's death as it was to the brutality of the house. My father eventually had to send for Dr. Vesey. She was diagnosed to be suffering a trauma, and was sent to Roscommon Hospital where she was ordered complete rest. She was two months in hospital. Whether he had been warned or given a fright, he never beat her physically again, but he continued to scold her at every turn. She was probably the most intelligent and sensitive of the girls, and this went very hard on her, but she didn't sleepwalk again. We were learning never to trust any of his moods and to deal with them as they came. Eventually, he stood more isolated than we were within his own barracks and family.

As the bonds between us strengthened, they were given expression in impromptu concerts when we felt the coast was clear. We were mastering our master.

"O God, O God, O God," Monica would play on her imaginary piano. "What did I do to deserve such a cross? I'll put yous into a bag like Toby. I'll sail yous out under the arches of Coote-hall Bridge. I'll have peace at last."

"God, O God," Rosaleen took up on the drums. "I'll send yous to the orphanage. The priests and nuns will soon bring you to your senses. God, O God, O God, have pity on me and grant me patience."

"God, O God, O God," I played on the trumpet. "I must—I must have committed some great crime in a former life—(indeed you must have)—to have been saddled with such a pack. God succour me and save me. (He won't.) O God, O God, O God. What did I do to deserve such a cross?"

Once and once only did we find him standing in the room while we improvised and played. We would have scattered like chaff, but found ourselves nailed to the floor.

"What's going on?" he roared when he recovered from his amazement.

"We're only fooling and play-acting," I said.

"We were only codding, Daddy," Monica added.

"Is there no work to be done in this house? Did I not say before I left that the carrots had to be weeded and thinned? I'll soon teach you all a lesson. O God, O God, what did I do to deserve such a crowd? What did I do to walk into such a life?"

I don't think he was able to admit what he saw and heard. For some time after this we never played without first posting a sentry, but after a while, without warning, we would suddenly break into impromptu play, especially when we knew he was away. Breedge, who adored him but knew the consequences of going over to his side, never joined in. My brother and Dympna were too young.

In the time he was hiring the succession of unsatisfactory maids, Katie McManus remained willing to return. She was very fond of my brother and was still attached to the memory of our mother, and she was interested in Peter McLoughlin. Stubbornly, my father refused to have her back. Eventually, the house grew so chaotic that he was forced to turn to Maggie, and she made the necessary face-saving arrangements to allow Katie to return.

We were overjoyed, but quickly discovered that it was to make no great difference to our lives. The big living room was made more orderly and clean. There was always a fire in the small range. Meals were more regular. We had clean changes of clothes, but we remained even more firmly under our father's rule. This must have been part of the arrangement for her return. She had complete charge of Dympna and Frankie, but, regarding us, it must have been made clear that she was not in any way to attempt to interfere with his authority. Secretly, she comforted us in many small ways after we were beaten, but no longer made any attempt to protect us from his rages. When he was beating and scolding us, she bent over her own tasks, or turned away, or went outside. On most nights she changed into her good clothes and went out into the village. This must have been part of the arrangement as well, as my father did not object to this or complain. We knew that she often went to Gilligan's where there was music and dancing and that Peter McLoughlin was always with her there. He never came near the barracks now. In good weather I often asked her if the two of them would come with me again on the river in the tarred boat, but she only smiled as she turned the invitation aside, and after a while I learned not to press. Sometime later Peter McLoughlin went to England and Katie left us soon after. By then, she must have been with us this second time for the best part of two years. We were all fond of her, but the main effect of her stay was to turn Dympna and Frankie into a younger, different family to the rest of us, and this became more pronounced with the years.

Katie was succeeded by two Kelleher sisters provided by Maggie. They were young and pleasant but did not stay long. My father then went back to hiring his own maids, and for long periods of time we managed on our own without any maid. Maggie eventually told us that Katie had married a nice man who worked for the council on the roads and that they were living not far away from her home place.

During all this time, my father was "organizing the troops" for work in the barrack garden and on the bog and in the conacre he took. He managed to get a contract from the Reverend Mother in the Mercy Convent in Boyle to supply the convent laundry with turf, and he retained the contract for a number of years. I am sure he used his good looks and the role of widower with seven small children to obtain the contract, as there were many who needed it more than he did. From March till September of those years we were hardly ever off the bog except on Sundays or on schooldays. This was hard, backbreaking work, but a child can do almost as much as a man, scattering the sods, footing, windrowing, clamping. Because I was the most useful, I was often kept from school, which at that time I didn't mind at all. He bought a new car, of which, in the way of children, we were intensely proud. In old age he was fond of remembering the money he had made out of the "auld Rev," as he jocularly called the Reverend Mother.

I never resented the work. Though not muscularly strong, I had almost limitless stamina, and I have always liked the mindless absence that hard physical work gives. This work was much harder for the girls. I did resent his attempts to make me force the girls to work whenever he was absent from the bog, when they just wanted to roll around or play house or make daisy chains or jump from the banks. When no work was being done and he was soon expected, I used to threaten to report them if they didn't work, but I don't think I ever did. I grew to love Gloria Bog, its acres of pale sedge, an inland sea broken by stunted birch trees, the trees like green flowers, the dark gashes of the turf banks, the soft light on the heather. Whether we came barefoot across the stone stiles and through the fields by Langan's or in the bog road with the jennet and cart, once we saw the sea of heather and pale sedge stretching from the evergreens in the graveyard high on Kileelan to the low mountains, we were in a different world. At the end of those summers, I drew most of the saved turf out to the road with the jennet and cart to be stacked there for the lorries that took them to the convent laundry. Being able to work hard physically gave me a bargaining counter: as long as it stayed partially hidden I could go on the river in the boat on my own whenever I wanted. If I couldn't be trusted to go on the river on my own, I couldn't be trusted on the bog.

I was soon setting nightlines for eels and rowing as far as Knockvicar. Sometimes one of the girls would come with me to hold the lines. If we had a few coins, we'd rest at Knockvicar and buy biscuits and lemonade, the yellow, fizzy lemonade we loved, and we'd prolong this royal feast for as long as possible before turning the boat for home. My father liked that I was catching fish; he preferred fish to meat; they cost nothing, and he believed they were good for his health. Whenever the river didn't take me from work or prayer, I could go in the boat unregarded: it grew to be a passion and an incredible freedom. I came to love that river, the red and black navigation signs, the reeds, rushes, drowning lilies, the changing lights, the wildfowl, the circles the feeding fish made on the water, the two islands of Oakport, the fields like lawns sloping down to the water from Oakport House, the spring well on the edge of the woods that held water as clear and cold as ice, the wild mushrooms that could be gathered there by the bucketful and were roasted with butter and salt, even the howling of the hounds as they were being fed at Oakport House in the evenings; but far more than any of these things was the blessed fact that I could be completely alone on the river.

In our first summer in the barracks, the Roscommon team that had won the All-Ireland in 1943 was advancing towards the Double. I became an avid follower. I read everything I could get my hands on about the players. In our games in Charlie's field we took high balls out of the air like Jimmy Murray, did solo runs like Frankie Kinlough, and took angled points like John Joe Nerney, who was the postman in Boyle. My father had the only radio in the village, and every Sunday that Roscommon played, the barracks was crammed with men, the air thick with cigarette smoke. Small bets were made, and once Michael O hEither's voice crackled from the Cossor, the tension was unbearable: *Bail O Dhia oraibh go leir a chairde Gael o Phairc an Chrocaigh*. The intense silences were interrupted by cheers and shouts and groans and clapping and the stamping of feet. At half-times, I went down to the river to get away from the excitement. At the start of the second half I was always torn between my need to know how the match was going when the second half resumed and the desire to escape the painful excitement. First, I listened outside the window. As soon as I found that Roscommon was winning, I would rush back into the living room, where there was hardly space between the chairs and the long benches brought up from the dayroom, and where the men were leaning against walls and smoking.

My father loved the excitement and the big crowd and that it all circled around him and his radio. There was always a long, happy, heated discussion afterwards. Once the men dispersed, there was that sense of absence that can be found in public gardens and by the sea at the end of bank holidays.

The brown hens that had come with us on the lorry from Aughawillan remained with us in the barracks until they were old. They were added to by fluffy, golden, day-old chicks that arrived on the bus in cardboard boxes with circular holes. The chirping from these boxes was a familiar sound in buses of the time. They were reared in a wooden box covered with netting wire beneath our table under the window until they were strong enough to survive outside. The hens were fed on small potatoes that were boiled in a big pot and mashed in a wooden tub with a pounder. The tub was kept in the scullery. To this day my memory of the scullery is of the wooden mirror in the window, the view on to Lenihan's field rising to the outlying stone houses of the Bawn, the iron washstand and the sour smell of mashed potatoes from the tub beneath the long trestle table.

A wooden house was built between the barracks and the river for a pig that we acquired. He too was fed mostly on potatoes and, in the autumn, windfall apples from the orchards around because they cost nothing and were said to sweeten the bacon. Each year a local farmer came and killed the pig, shaved and quartered the sides and set them to cure in rough salt in tea chests. They were kept in a small room off the living room, and news-papers were put down against seepage from the chests. After some days the sides were wrapped in gauze against the flies and hung from hooks on the ceiling. As on the big match days, my father was in great good humour on the day the pig was killed. In the evening I was sent around neighbouring houses with the parts that wouldn't cure—ribs, cutlets from the bones, liver—and the neighbours in their turn gave back this bounty when they killed their own pig. I remember most the piercing screams, the blood being gathered in a white enamel basin for black pudding, and the sweet taste of the fresh cutlets that were called *grisceens*.

My father had hopes of making money from potatoes as well as turf, and planted much more than the other guards. He didn't succeed. Potatoes were too plentiful. The only potatoes I remem-ber him selling were a few bags of seed potatoes in the spring. One year he took to giving away bags as presents. They were not appreciated because of their association with the famine, but peo-ple were polite and accepted the presents even if they were to dump the potatoes later. Some hid their amusement as they trot-ted out the clichés, "You can't beat yer spud. We'd be lost without them. They're your only man." If it had been pointed out to him that a bag of potatoes wasn't exactly a suitable present, my father would have been furious. From his point of view he was doing a Christian act, when he could have, with less trouble to himself, dumped them in the ash pit or allowed them to rot.

Our schooling continued to be broken. After a year, Breedge and Rosaleen and I were taken from Cootehall and sent to Mrs. Watson about two miles away in Laphoil. We walked the two miles to and from the school with the Murray children. Mrs. Watson had once a reputation as a good teacher but now did very little work. Her husband, an army officer, was dead. She had three young daughters and spent most of the day knitting. Before inspections, she flew into a panic. After one inspection, when my answers attracted the Inspector's interest, she showered me with presents and I became a favourite, but I didn't enjoy this for long because soon afterwards my father moved me again to Master Kelly in Knockvicar.

I cycled the three miles to the school. Master Kelly had a reputation for winning scholarships and wasn't popular with the other teachers because he poached their brighter students. He was tall, good-looking in a dark way, nationalistic, a Fianna Fàil member of the County Council, intellectually conceited and brutal. He spent many hours in the barracks talking Irish with Guard Cannon, sitting in the dayroom or outside on the yellow chairs on good evenings. "He has the Irish all right but he'll never have the *blas*. It's all book Irish," Guard Cannon used to laugh good-naturedly. My father and he never got on because they were both competitive. Why he sent me to him I have never fully understood. Perhaps Kelly heard I was bright; if so, he was quickly disillusioned. My Irish was passable, but no more than that, and he soon saw that I had no hope of a county scholarship.

It did not help that in most of the other subjects I was a threat to the boy he was preparing for the scholarship, a gentle, pleasant boy, Tommy Moran, who later became a priest and whose uncle, Paddy Moran, had fought in the GPO in 1916 and was hanged in

1920. There is an affectionate portrait of Paddy Moran in Ernie O'Malley's classic autobiography *On Another Man's Wound*. To pass the time when they were in prison together, O'Malley and Moran would walk in their minds down one bank of the Boyle River as far as Carrick-on-Shannon in the morning, and in the evening return by the opposite bank, noting everything they saw along the way, even the changed colour of the Curlew Mountains after rain. Kelly saw Paddy Moran as a heroic figure and did everything he could to advance his nephews and nieces, while he hounded the children from the Rockingham estate. The walls of Rockingham came within a mile of the school, and he saw the Rockingham estate, with its high walls and gatehouses and the great white house that Nash designed above Lough Key, of which it was said "there was a window for every day of the year," as a surviving symbol of British rule and dominance. The children were guilty by association.

Sir John Maffey, the British Ambassador, came every year for the annual pheasant shoot in Rockingham. This was a high point in the life of the barracks. Armed detectives came from Dublin to protect the Ambassador. When I brought them tea down to the dayroom, I was startled to see their revolvers lying around among the ledgers on the big trestle table while they played cards. My father and all the guards, except the barrack orderly, attended the shoot and the grand ball that was held in Rockingham House, when all the Anglo-Irish gentry gathered for miles around.

At the end of the shoot, a gamekeeper came each year to the barracks with a brace of pheasants for my father and a single pheasant for each of the guards, a card *With the compliments of Sir Cecil and Lady Stafford King-Harmon* attached to the legs.

Most of the children from the estate were kept from school for the great Rockingham shoot. The boys acted as beaters and the girls helped their mothers with the cleaning and catering, and this threw Kelly into a rage. "The peasants are still beating the pheasants out of the bushes for Milords." When the Rockingham children returned to school at the end of the shoot, Kelly would set them tests for which they were unprepared. Then he would line them up against the wall and administer an unmerciful beating, a blow for every error or unanswered question, fulminating all the time against the whole sordid, brutal history of British rule in Ireland. "Is this what Padraig Pearce and Paddy Moran died for?" One of the ironies was that he expected us to climb on the grass margins and to salute him when he passed in his car as if he was a member of a new aristocracy.

Knockvicar was the first school I attended that had Protestants as pupils. They came from the rich farms scattered outside the walls of the estate. In the mornings while we received religious instruction they took their books out into the porch where they studied or chatted or idled among the mops and buckets and the hung coats. Other than that, they were no different to other pupils, learning Irish and playing football with us in Bruen's field, and Kelly treated them respectfully. I looked on them with a mixture of fascination and awe and pity, as I had been taught that no matter how well they conducted their lives they were bound for certain hell in the next world. I spent a miserable year in Knockvicar, but it wasn't as miserable as it was for the children from the Rockingham estate.

And then I had my first great good luck with schools. I was thirteen years old and had already attended seven schools. A Mrs. Lynch opened a secretarial school for girls in Carrick-on-Shannon; then she saw there was a need for secondary schooling and opened the Rosary High School for boys and girls. The Marist Convent for girls that my mother had attended was long established, but there was no secondary school for boys in this county town. A married woman in charge of a mixed school of adolescent boys and girls set off all kinds of ecclesiastical alarms. Mrs. Lynch must have been a remarkable woman. The Church tried to get her to close. She refused. They then brought in the Presentation Brothers to close her down. They didn't succeed. Both schools prospered. The result was that this small country town and its poor hinterland had three very good schools at a time when secondary education was open only to the rich or the academically bright.

Brother Damien was the first principal of Presentation College. In the evenings and during weekends of the early summer of 1948 he cycled around the countryside looking for suitable students for the new school, and he persuaded my father to allow me to sit for the house scholarships. I sat the exam, won a half-scholarship, and that September started cycling the eight miles from the barracks to Carrick-on-Shannon. A number of boys came from the town, but most, like myself, cycled in from the countryside.

The monastery in Carrick-on-Shannon had been a British military barracks. The Brothers lived in a wing of the building. The school was in the other part, on three floors. What had been the drilling square became lawns and trees and a sanded yard on which we played soccer with a tennis ball. A handball alley and a large vegetable garden were at the back. A high wall ran all around the grounds. In a big downstairs room we stacked our bicycles, and on wet days during the lunch hour ate sandwiches with our bottles of milk. A boy or two or more was always fixing punctures on an upturned bicycle in corners of the room.

A beautiful deaf girl from one of the religious institutions cooked and cleaned and answered the door for the seven Brothers. When we wanted to see any of the Brothers outside school hours, we went to the monastery door and gave the name of the Brother to the girl. She then struck a brass gong in the hallway. Each Brother answered to a certain number of strikes. She retreated as soon as the Brother we wanted came down the stairs. In classes, most of the English texts we were given I soon learned by heart—*Macbeth, Henry IV, Wordsworth's Prelude, Tintern Abbey,* Tennyson's *In Memoriam, The Ode to Virgil*—"Thou that singest wheat and woodland/tilth and vineyard, hive and horse and herd." I used to chant them aloud when I was cycling alone in and out to school on those empty roads. Sometimes I chanted the Ordinary of the Mass, since I now knew the words by heart and they were beginning to take on meaning through Caesar and Virgil and Cicero and Horace.

Brother Placid replaced Brother Damien as principal. Placid was a handsome Kerryman, a good footballer who played for the town team, and was fond of drink, which never appeared to do him any harm: he would sparkle in the morning after a heavy late-night session in Joe Lowe's. He was an exceptional teacher, whose eyes glinted with humour or encouragement or disapproval behind thick spectacles, which he had a habit of polishing with a white handkerchief throughout the day. In my third year my exam results were particularly good. Placid had checked my attendance and noticed that I was missing for several weeks each spring and autumn. His eyes danced with merriment behind the glasses when I told him that those were the times of the bog and the potato field. The previous Christmas my father had given him a present of a bag of potatoes, when a bottle of Redbreast whiskey would have been much more appreciated. He said I could win a university scholarship in two years' time if I worked, but not if I continued to miss chunks of the year.

We had the conacre that year in Coxhill, and Brother Placid cycled out to the field on a bitterly cold evening in late October. My father was digging potatoes and I was picking. Placid chatted agreeably with us for some time, and then asked to speak to my father. They went out towards the road and spent a long time talking. Naturally, I tried to listen, but they were too far off. My father came slowly back when they separated. I continued picking and dragging the buckets to the pit. He did not speak for a long time.

"I'm surprised, but that Brother seems to think he may be

able to make something of you if you are prepared to work. You better go back to that school in the morning. I'll manage somehow on my own," he said heavily.

I could hardly believe my luck. Only a year before I had to use all my wiles and determination to prevent him from putting me into a job as an accounts clerk and general factotum in a hardware store in a small town close to Dublin. Now I had the heady feeling that my life was gathering like cupped rainfall in my own hands.

Also teaching with Brother Placid in that small school was the blond, curly-haired Brother Francis, who blushed like a girl at the slightest sexual reference and who made mathematics exciting. There was the ramrod-straight ex-army officer, Mr. Mannion, addicted to golf and whiskey, who loaned me all his own volumes of Dickens and would talk to me about them inside and outside school hours. I look back on those years as the beginning of an adventure that has never stopped. Each day as I cycled towards Carrick was an anticipation of delights. The fear and drudgery of school disappeared. Without realizing it, through the pleasures of the mind, I was beginning to know and to love the world. The Brothers took me in, sat me down, and gave me tools. I look back on my time there with nothing but gratitude, as years of luck and privilege—and of grace, actual grace.

Around the same time I began life in Carrick I had more luck. I was given the run of a library. My father had become friendly with Andy Moroney, who lived with his father, Old Willie, in their big stone house surrounded by handsome stone outhouses and a great orchard. They were Protestants. Andy had joined the local company of the FCA at the outbreak of the war with the rank of lieutenant, was promoted captain and put in charge of the company, and he and my father became friendly. They would have had to interact over drilling exercises and rifle practice and marches through the village. My father was greatly impressed by Protestants. He considered them superior in every way to the general run of his fellow Catholics, less devious, morally more correct, more honest, better mannered, and much more abstemious. Before joining the FCA, Andy Moroney had led an isolated, eccentric life; he had a vast store of general knowledge and was devoted to astronomy. When he went on Joe Linnane's radio programme, *Question Time,* he caused great local merriment by describing himself as a "gentleman farmer." Everybody knew the word "farmer" and had some idea as to what constituted a "gentleman," but the conjunction of the two was thought to be hilarious. Like my father, he was a crack shot and had won the Western Shield a number of times. Though they were completely different in upbringing and temperament, they had a genuine relationship. His father, Old Willie, is brought to life wonderfully in David Thompson's *Woodbrook*—the old beekeeper, with his great beard and fondness for St. Ambrose and Plato: "The Athenian bee, the good and the wise . . . because his words glowed with the sweetness of honey." Willie had not gone upstairs since his wife's death, nor had he washed, and he slept in royal untidiness in what had once been the dining room, directly across the stone hallway from the library, that dear hallway, with its barometer and antlered coat rack and the huge silent clock. The front door, with a brass plate shaped into the stone for the white doorbell, was never opened. All access to the house was through the back door, up long stone steps from the farmyard and through the littered kitchen to the hallway and stairs and front rooms.

David Thompson described the Moroneys as landless, which is inexact, for they owned a hundred and seventy acres of the sweetest land on the lower plains of Boyle, itself some of the best limestone land in all of Ireland. The farm was beautifully enclosed by roads which ran from the high demesne walls of Rockingham to the broken walls of Oakport. The Moroneys should have been wealthy. They had to have money to build the big stone house in the first place, to build and slate the stone houses that enclosed the farmyard, to acquire the hundreds of books that lined the walls of the library. David Thompson's observation, though, is right in spirit: Willie and Andy had all the appearance of being landless.

A great deal of Andy's time was taken up with astronomy, which must have been a frustrating pursuit in north Roscommon, with its low skies and heavy rainfall. Clear nights were spent in the open with his telescope. He kept very neat charts and notes which reflected his precise military speech and contrasted with his genteel, careless dress. He slept during the day. Old Willie lived for his bees. In his wife's time he gave lectures to bee societies all over the country, but now he no longer left the house and its immediate surroundings. His many hives were kept at the foot of the great orchard. They were beautiful, gentle, impractical men. They lived for the most part on tea and bread and honey and now and again made a big stew. They had an unusual method of housekeeping. There was much cutlery, glass, cups, plates from the days when the house had entertained. They would continue using them until they were all dirty, and then, every month or so, father and son would do a big washing-up and start all over again. They gathered apples, stored them on wooden shelves in the stone outhouses, sold them by the bucketful, and seemed glad of the half-crowns they received.

I was sent to buy apples, fell into conversation with Willie about books, and was given the run of the library. There was Scott, Dickens, popular romances, Meredith, Shakespeare, books by Zane Grey and Jeffrey Farnol, and many books about the Rocky Mountains. Some person in that nineteenth-century house must have been fascinated by the Rocky Mountains. I picked the books with nothing but pleasure in mind and read them the way a boy now might watch countless TV dramas. Every week or fort-night, for years, I'd return with five or six books in my oilcloth shopping bag and take five or six away. Nobody gave me direc-tion or advice. There was a tall, slender ladder for getting to the books on the high shelves. In the cluttered kitchen Willie would sometimes ask me about the books. "Master Sean, what are you reading? Master Sean, what do you think?" He no longer read, and he questioned me more out of the need for company than any real curiosity.

I remember one morning vividly, one of those still, true mornings in summer before the heat comes, the door open on the yard. We were drinking tea with bread and jam—raspberry jam and not honey—and talking about a book I had returned. As we talked, jam fell into his beard. His long, flat, greasy beard completely covered his shirt front and was stained with all colours of food and drink. The jam set off an immediate loud buzzing within the beard. Early that morning he must have gone through his hives. He rose and walked to the door, extracting the bees with his long, delicate fingers, and tossed them into the air of the yard without interrupting the flow of talk.

I continued coming to the house after the old beekeeper's death, but there was no longer any talk of books. Andy began to spend less time on astronomy and more on the land, and sometimes I was sent to help him. He had little small talk and we worked mostly in silence. He was remarkably trusting, or foolhardy. The farm had a small tractor. Once, when he didn't want to go to town, he sent me on the tractor for wood or cement or hardware to Sloan's in Boyle. I told him I had never driven anything mechanical before. "There's nothing to it," he said in the clipped accent of command, and showed me how to start the tractor, how to work the clutch and gears and brakes. After a few lessons and a practice run about the field, I set off for Boyle in second gear. Along the way I started experimenting with the gears, and by the time I reached Boyle was bowling dangerously and confidently along in third gear. In the excitement of the town, I forgot where the throttle was. It is a testament to the scarcity of traffic at the time that I met nothing before I managed to find the throttle and clutch and change down. There was a parking place in front of Sloan's. I got the man to take the tractor into the yard, load the trailer, and face us for home. Along the way I started to change gears again, and my dangerous confidence returned. From Ardcarne there is a steep hill past the old parsonage down to Moroney's gate. In the car, my father often switched the engine off on steep hills to save on fuel. I decided to do likewise. On the hill it quickly gathered silent speed and all I could do was to hold on for life. I bounced off the high grass margins a number of times but didn't climb the low stone walls. Miraculously, neither tractor nor trailer overturned. I went at speed past Moroney's gates. When it slowed and stopped I was shaking. If anybody had been on the road I would have mowed them down. After a long time I got the tractor turned and drove back slowly. "I told you there was nothing to it," Andy said when I drove into the yard. It was amazing that neither tractor nor trailer was damaged. "Still, you have to be careful," I said, and was silent about everything else.

He took to breeding pure-bred Cheviots imported from England. When the time came to sell the lambs, he felt he wouldn't get their true price locally. I helped him pack them into the back of the old Ford transit van, and we set off together for the Dublin market. It was a journey of four or five hours then, through Longford, Edgeworthstown, Mullingar, Kinnegad, Enfield, Kilcock, Maynooth, the lambs bleating for their mothers the whole length of the journey. The market was off the North Circular Road. We got there around six o'clock in the evening. The lambs were penned. We cleaned out the van and replaced the straw. Andy had brought hay for the lambs and left them water. The market would start in the early morning. I was already hungry but was too shy to ask where we'd eat or sleep. We then drove to a house on the far side of the city. An elderly lady welcomed us—she was a cousin of Andy's—and gave us tea and thin slices of toast. By the time we left I was ready to eat the chairs.

Outside, it was a clear cold night. Andy told me we were driving to the top of the Sugar Loaf Mountain. The market was starting so early that it wasn't worth our while getting a bed for the night, he said. He had brought his telescope along to watch the stars for a few hours. There would be a great clear view from the top of the Sugar Loaf and I could watch with him if I wished. We climbed high into the Dublin Mountains. There was no other car or van on the Sugar Loaf that night, and all the stars in the sky sparkled. Andy set up the telescope. We could see across the whole city, the lights strung all around the bay. The night was bitterly cold. I pretended interest in the skies, and Andy was an enthusiastic guide, but I took nothing in. To this day, I know little of the skies, other than the Plough and the North Star and Orion, and often wish I had availed of Andy's knowledge when it was there for me, but not that night. I was weak with hunger and shaking with the cold. I said I'd try the van for shelter, but it was as cold in the van as out under the stars. I drifted into a state in which I was no longer hungry. After I don't know how long, Andy and his telescope joined me on the straw. Neither of us slept. We lay side by side in frozen silence. Not long after the first light entered the van, Andy checked his watch and we rose. Outside, it was a white world. The stars were still clear but not as bright. We had to drive slowly down the mountain because of the icy road, and then across the empty city to the market.

Andy combed and brushed the lambs, but I was no help. Several times I thought I was about to faint and had to lean on the bars of the pen. Men passed around me like shadows. I must have asked Andy for money to get tea and something to eat because I was afraid of passing out. He looked at me in alarm: he couldn't move from the pen as the lambs could be sold at any minute and I might get lost on my own in the market; as soon as the lambs were sold, we'd go to the big lighted hotel he pointed out on the other end of the market. We would not have long to wait. After what seemed an age, the auctioneer and his clerk and the buyer gathered round the pen. They gathered as suddenly and silently as a school of fish. Men entered the pen to feel the lambs. The auctioneer called out the details of their breeding, and the bidding began.

Andy was delighted by the price and told me that the journey had been well worthwhile. He was handed a docket by the clerk as the auctioneer and buyers moved on to the next pen.

We exchanged the docket for cash at a small window and crossed the road to the great lighted hotel. The white lamps guarded the long stone steps up to the heavy mahogany doors. The hotel was for the big dealers, merchants and auctioneers, and we must have looked very much out of place, except for Andy's accent and bearing. The tables were covered with heavy linen and we were given linen napkins. A waitress in a black and white uniform brought us a silver teapot and a plate of bread, then a great mixed grill. "It was worth the wait," Andy smiled. I waited until I saw what use Andy made of his napkin, and then followed him with knife and fork. I was so weak and the big dining room so strange that I ate slowly, gradually eating everything in sight until I could hardly move. In the glow of warmth and repletion, I felt like sleeping. I had no fear or consciousness of the loud prosperous men all around us. I was too tired and by now too full and happy. When we walked through the bustle and noise of the closing market to the van, I was intrigued by the new yet remote solidity of my tread.

Andy drew up for petrol at the first filling station. I noticed then how low the gauge was, but not until years later did it occur to me that Andy hadn't the money for either a boarding house or a meal until the lambs were sold. Once he had the money, a Mr. Moroney in Dublin couldn't go anywhere else but to the grand hotel.

When Andy returned me to the barracks, he praised me to my father, who was delighted. Soon after, my father was mainly responsible for arranging Andy's marriage to a young local girl, Annie Beirne, who was nursing in Belfast. In order to marry her Andy converted to Catholicism. At his baptism my father was one of his sponsors. Now Andy was able to lead his men up to the high altar during sung Masses and to bark out commands as the men presented arms before and after the consecration. Before his conversion he had to remain outside the church door while his men presented arms. Annie Beirne was intelligent and practical. After a few years they decided to sell off the beautiful rundown house and lands. The debts were paid and they bought a smaller place in Kildare. The house and lands were bought by the Leydens, who had made their wealth from the Arigna coal pits and were not interested in bees or libraries or the stars. By then I too was on the move and no longer had need of that dear, blessed library.

I have often wondered why no curb was put on my reading, as it was out of character for my father to allow me to read unhindered. I can only put it down to his involvement with the Moroneys, which was close to infatuation. Even his voice changed when he spoke about them. They approved and encouraged my reading. By allowing it, he saw himself reflected to his advantage in their eyes. While he was harsh and ungiving with most people, when he found someone who impressed him, he fell into a kind of thraldom. Seeing me sitting and reading for hours must often have put a great strain on his natural impatience and need of attention, but it was held in check by the greater need of the Moroneys' approval.

There are no days more full in childhood than those days that are not lived at all, the days lost in a book. I remember waking out of one such book beside the sewing-machine beneath the window on the river in the barrack living room to find my sisters all around me. They had unlaced and removed one of my shoes and placed a straw hat on my head. Only when they began to move the wooden chair on which I sat away from the window light did I wake out of the book, to their great merriment. Now this happens only when I am writing, and happens so rarely it is barely worth remarking on, perhaps once in every two or three years. It's a strange and complete happiness when all sense of time is lost, of looking up from the pages and thinking it is still nine or ten in the morning, to discover it is well past lunchtime, but there is no longer anyone around to test the quality of the absence by unlacing and removing a shoe. I have often wondered too if it would have made any difference if my reading had been more structured or guided, but there is no telling such things in an only life. I read voraciously at first, for nothing but pleasure; that changed imperceptibly with the years to a different order of pleasure that was both recognition and discovery and sometimes a pure, unfathomable joy.

My sisters did not seem to need or want this luck of school and books and the river. They had a different kind of luck. The life under our father forced us into a close band for our own protection. This closeness remained with them and grew after its initial need had disappeared. Instinctively, they learned to act together with more cohesion and solidarity than was possible for any single person. This bond was to last and grow throughout their long lives. Individually, they could be very sharp about one another but without that sharpness ever threatening the deep strength and affection they had for one another, and they seemed able to flower individually within that closeness instead of each submerging herself within the group in order to preserve their togetherness. Much self-discipline and good manners were necessary as well for such a constant to have endured so many vicissitudes for so long, but I suspect it was all made possible by need and habit and love, allowing them to adventure further into what they already knew. I had been separated from them by maleness and age, and that separateness was further sharpened to a moonlit edge by the suffering surrounding my mother's death, which they seemed to escape. On the other side of this divide, my baby brother was their doll or plaything. He was both confused and spoiled, and eventually all the natural advantages of good looks and intellect that came to him so easily were thrown away, as if life itself meant nothing.

After I had been moved to Master Kelly, Breedge and Rosaleen remained with Mrs. Watson, and during that harsh year I often envied them their peace. When the time came for them to leave national school, my father, surprisingly, sent them as boarders to the Mercy Convent in Longford—surprising because he would have been loath to part with the money for the boarding and tuition fees and uniforms. It turned out that he had a rich cousin in Longford, a midwife, who owned a successful maternity home, and some months before he sent them to the Mercy Convent he began courting Mrs. Maguire. On Sundays we would be all scrubbed and dressed in our best clothes and packed into the Ford and driven to Mrs. Maguire's for afternoon tea. She lived in a large bungalow in its own grounds in a fashionable outskirt of the town. This continued while the twins were boarders in the convent. Every Sunday we'd drive to the convent. In their dark uniforms the twins looked waif-like. Breedge, the stronger and better looking but the less intelligent, was having the easier time and was the more forthcoming of the two about their life there. Our father was a great favourite of the nuns. We'd then all drive the short distance out the Dublin Road to the maternity home. I remember it vaguely, the heavy carpets and armchairs and sofas, a heavily pregnant woman in a nightdress smoking in a corridor, tea wheeled into the large sitting room on a trolley, my father's gravity, his slowness of speech and movement.

Naturally, those visits seemed long to me, but I think they lasted only a couple of hours. Then we'd leave the twins back to the convent for another week and head for the barracks, our father giving out the Rosary as he drove. I had always assumed that Mrs. Maguire paid the convent fees that year, but my sisters tell me that it wasn't so. He paid them, hoping to involve Mrs. Maguire in his motherless family. When no offer of help with their education was forthcoming, he took them out of the convent at the end of the school year, and we never visited Mrs. Maguire again. It has always intrigued me that people like my father no longer feel any need to keep up even a semblance of continuity and politeness when they do not get what they want. This does not require much effort and softens the brutal obviousness and keeps doors partially open. On a very basic level it might even be in their own self-interest. In an endlessly changing world circumstances may come round when they have no choice but to deal with that person again.

All this time he was sporadically trying to get himself married, and we were drawn into some of these adventures because of his insistence that he was marrying for our good. It took him several years. Much of what took place was both sad and funny. The closest he came to marrying at this time was to a Miss McCabe, a small, gentle woman, a principal of a school. She was probably in her early fifties. We all liked her and were hoping they would marry.

Every year my father took a bungalow for two weeks beside the ocean in Strandhill. In his obsession with money and in order to defray the expense of the bungalow, in our first year he brought a lorry load of turf to the ocean and had us sell it in bags door to door. We found this humiliating and would have much preferred to have remained hidden in the barracks. The rain never lifted during those first two weeks, and we sold all the turf and he made money. He was full of plans to take even more turf to the sea the following summer. Fortunately, the weather came dry and hot and he had to take most of the turf home. While this ended his taking of turf to the sea, we continued to come to the rented bungalow for the same two weeks every year. We met Miss McCabe a number of times that year, and she planned to spend the holidays with us at Strandhill. We had the usual rented bungalow. She stayed in one of the big hotels on the sea front, but spent a great part of each day with us, even to saying the Rosary at night. As he gave out the Decades, our father was as sanctimonious as he had been charming throughout the day. The belief was that they would get engaged at the end of the holiday. Then late one morning a porter came from the hotel with the message that Miss McCabe had a "turn" in the seaweed salt baths that morning. She had been seen by a doctor and was resting in her bedroom. My father assumed that the turn was a heart attack. The effect was startling. Within an hour he had gathered up the pots and pans we'd brought, written a letter to Miss McCabe, and packed the whole family except myself into the small blue Ford. I was left behind to deliver the letter to the hotel, lock up the bungalow, leave the keys with the landlord and travel home on the next day's bus. I was joyful to be left alone, and waved vigorously to the blue Ford as I watched it drive away.

With less joy, I headed for the Golf Links Hotel and was shown to Miss McCabe's room. It was very large and she was in bed at the far end of the room. "I'm sorry you got sick," I said as I handed her the letter. She became oblivious of me as she read. After she'd finished the letter she started to read it again.

"I'm sorry," I blurted out. "We were all hoping you'd marry him."

"It wasn't your fault. Where is your father now?"

"He's gone home with all the others."

"Why were you left behind?"

"To close up the bungalow."

She asked me to bring her the handbag which was in the armchair, and she gave me a pound note, a king's ransom, the fee each of the ten priests would have to be given for a High Mass. "Spend that for me this evening. Tell your father I'll write him. There are some things I want to return."

I bought a raft of comics, ice-creams and chocolate éclairs, and spent a most wonderful evening moving between the bungalow and the roaring Atlantic on the sea front, but each time I passed the Golf Links Hotel I had a strange, uncomfortable feeling that I recognize now as both unease and shame.

This was to be my last summer at the ocean. The following year I refused to go, saying I had too much to do around the barracks. Either this suited him or he felt that excessive force would be needed to get me to go, and I was allowed to remain behind, to my relief and joy, and to watch them all drive away.

About this time, whether he felt there wasn't sufficient drama in his life or that he was determined not to be outdone by Miss McCabe, he decided that he was dying. His hypochondria had always led him towards all kinds of medical books, and in the curtained medicine press he kept thermometers, senna leaves, sulphur, cascara, various powders, measuring scales and glasses which he used to make cleansing prescriptions. These he administered to himself and us. We hated the concoctions. They had a bitter taste and most were violent purges. We were used to seeing him take to his bed regularly with named and unnamed illnesses. We'd then bring him food and medicines to his room. When he wanted attention he pounded the floorboards with a walking stick or boot, and would grow angry if it wasn't immediately forthcoming. Even with the tensions emanating from the upstairs room, the house was a much more pleasant place without him. Vesey, the police doctor, would come in his car and climb the stairs to the room, and usually they spent a long time in conversation. In the mornings and evenings the barrack orderly took him various ledgers and papers to sign. Then, without warning or obvious signs of recovery, he would rise one morning in a flurry of activity, shave, dress, sit to his meal in front of the big sideboard mirror, and issue many instructions before marching down to the dayroom for the morning inspection. Then everything would resume more or less as normal until the next time he took to his bed and the same process was repeated.

This time he was many more days in bed. His voice was weaker except when he forgot himself in irritation or anger. His movements were limping and slow when he rose, and I had to help him the few times he needed to come down the stairs and climb back up. Dr. Vesey came every day to the barracks. The three guards looked grave-faced and worried. At the end of the

Rosary each night, we prayed solemnly with him for his recovery. We were told he was being sent to the Depot Hospital in Dublin. I had to search out and bring him many papers and documents and a metal box with two keys. The box wasn't large and was the colour of grass and mud, army surplus he had bought at an auction. A solicitor from Boyle, Forbes or Wynn, came to the barracks and spent a long time with him in the bedroom. That evening he rose, dressed slowly in his uniform, and came slowly down the stairs, pausing every few steps to rest on the banister. He ordered the girls what to pack for the hospital and gave the barrack orderly the evening off. When he called me down to the day-room he told me to shut the door. He was sitting by the turf fire. The metal box stood open among the ledgers and inkstands on the trestle table.

He explained that it was unlikely he would return alive from hospital, but I was not to worry: he had made all necessary provisions. He opened the box. The wad of money in the rubber band was for the immediate expenses of the funeral. The large envelope contained all his instructions, together with bank and post office accounts, government bonds and insurance policies. He was to be buried with our mother in the plot in Aughawillan. Immediately after the funeral I was to open the big envelope and read his instructions, and then take it to the solicitor in Boyle. He would give me all necessary help. The other larger package was of no immediate concern: it contained mementoes and things of sentimental value that might be of interest as we got older—our mother's rings and jewellery, medals and certificates, old photos, old letters. Another envelope contained a copy of his will. We could not stay on in the barracks. A new sergeant would soon be replacing him. If we dallied and remained on, we would all be carted off to the orphanage. I was to buy a house and small farm—there was more than sufficient money—and I was to bring all the others up on the farm in his place. One such farm and house for sale was Paddy Mullaney's. It was going cheap. He almost bought it himself. I shouldn't fool around looking at other places. In his view, I wouldn't do any better.

I knew Paddy Mullaney's farm and the slated herdsman's house well. I had hunted hares in those stonewalled fields on the edge of Oakport with Nellie the fawn greyhound and Tom Gleeson. We would all gather in that small house and I would have to bring them up. What had seemed unreal at first was now becoming all too real. Life without him suddenly seemed infinitely worse than the life we had with him in the barracks, and I broke down and begged him not to die.

He counselled me gently: we can control neither the day nor the hour. He spoke of our mother and how he would be joining her, and that the two of them would watch over us and pray for us together. He gave me the key. I was to open the metal box with the key when the news came. I was still sobbing when I took the metal box upstairs and placed it beneath the wardrobe in our bedroom. He tousled my hair affectionately and said he had great confidence in me and that we'd all manage.

Even looking back, I find the scene incredible. I was fifteen years of age and legally a minor. There was no way even then that a boy my age would be allowed to take charge of such monies, purchase a house and farm, and bring up a large young family on his own. Uncle Pat, Uncle Jimmy, Aunt Maggie, Aunt Katie were our nearest of kin: they would have taken charge. He was seeing Pat regularly about engines; he was counselling Katie about her family and seeking her advice about his own; and he was still fighting with Maggie. Jimmy alone would have nothing to do with him, but none of the four was ever mentioned. I knew nothing of this and believed him completely. He knew the law but was determined to indulge his fantasy. The strict enforcer of the law was himself lawless. When I told the others, they started to cry, but then Frankie and Dympna changed to laughter and were shouted at by the rest of us, very much in our father's own manner.

He left for the Depot Hospital the next day. Within a week he was home; they found him in perfect health. We were overjoyed to see him return, released from the silent anxiety and tension of waiting for the news of his death. For a day, he shut himself away upstairs. Dr. Vesey came and we heard angry words from the room. The next morning he rose in a loud flurry of activity, tramped down the stairs, shouted for hot water, sharpened his razor and shaved, polished his silver stripes and buttons, his boots, and sat facing the big sideboard mirror. That morning he ate very little. On the stroke of nine, he placed his white handker-chief inside his cuff and tramped loudly down to the dayroom for the morning inspection, banging the door.

For some days I didn't know what to do with the key to the metal box. Instinct told me not to hand it back. Eventually, I left it on a small table by his side of the bed, and was relieved when next I looked to see that it had disappeared. Not a word was said.

Breedge was apprenticed to a dressmaker, Mrs. Daly, who lived in one of the Rockingham gatehouses, a beautiful circu-lar stone house. Mrs. Daly's family was reared. She was hard-working and kind. Breedge was well liked by the Dalys and became a skilled clothes-cutter and seamstress. As she was my father's favourite, he might have chosen dressmaking for her because of his own mother's trade; but in the narrow, emerging world of the people who belonged to the lower echelons of the new infant State it was seen as a come-down in the world for the daughter of a teacher and sergeant. I remember a man con-gratulating him ambiguously, "People will always need clothes anyhow."

Rosaleen he sent as a trainee assistant to a family drapery in Cootehill in his own county of Cavan. They were a large prosper-ous family, the elder children away at university, the others at boarding schools. The father and mother ran the successful business, a mixture of fashion and serviceable clothes and footwear for people from the country, and they were both pillars of the church and town. Rosaleen was given her board and a minute weekly wage. She did serve in the shop from time to time, but most of what she did was housework. Except when she was in hospital, this was the first time the twins had ever been separated, and Rosaleen was miserable. From the start, the draper made sexual advances. "He could not keep his hands to himself." She preferred housework because she was in the comparative safety of the wife's domain. For a long time she suffered in silence. I was closer to Rosaleen than to any of the other girls, and she wrote me at the school in Carrick where the letter couldn't be intercepted. I didn't tell my father, got away for the day with money on some excuse or other, and took the morning bus to Cootehill. I found the shop. She got leave to come out with me for the day, and when she told me all that was happening I saw that we had no choice but to leave together on the evening bus.

"What will he say when we turn up?" was her only fear. "Will he not go crazy?"

"He'll say nothing," I reassured her. "He better not say anything."

Rosaleen may have had Breedge in mind. Earlier, Breedge had run foul of his blind rage. She had twisted and fallen on her ankle carrying spring water from the priest's well. She managed to limp home, but her foot started to swell quickly. It was a Friday evening in Lent, and we all had to attend the Stations of the Cross in the church. He demanded that she go. She showed him the swollen ankle, spoke of the pain, and showed him that she could no longer get her foot into her shoe; but there was no way of reasoning with him in this mood.

If she could not wear her own shoes, she could go in his boots. She had many admirers and the thought of tramping up the village to the church in her father's boots was more horrifying than the swelling and pain. She refused. He took her upstairs and started to beat her into submission. Hearing his shouts and her cries, Guard Walshe opened the dayroom door, as if he was considering going upstairs, and paced about and rattled the doorknob before going back into the dayroom. I was studying at the table in the living room.

"Why don't you go up and see if you can help her?" Monica begged me.

"He'd just beat me up as well. What good would that do her?" I answered. I was inured to such beatings. Hardly a day went by without one or more. I had not yet reached that time when I'd be forced to meet him and take him on.

"Maybe Guard Walshe will go up?"

Guard Walshe came out and rattled the doorknob again, but he did not go upstairs.

He failed to get her to go to church in his boots. Her vanity was stronger than his brutality, but even if she had been willing to wear his boots she would not have been able to walk. It was a bad break. During the night the pain worsened so much that she cried out and continued crying. No one in the house slept. In the morning he took her to Donoghue, the bonesetter in Cloone who set the ankle but botched the setting. In certain weathers the whole leg swelled. Veins had been set into the break. The ankle had to be rebroken, the veins taken out and sewed back together and the bone reset when she went to nurse in England. Donoghue set a number of our bones before he had to leave for America, pursued by litigants, but my father always defended him, blaming the litigants for their greed: Donoghue was cheap.

Since my mother's death I slept with my father in the big iron bed with the broken brass bells, at the head of the stairs, directly across from the large room where the barrack orderly's bedclothes and the office supplies and the one typewriter were stored. In the next room along the landing, my five sisters and brother slept. At the end of the landing was the maid's small room. The windows of these rooms looked out on the barrack entrance, Coote's Archway, Lenihan's long orchard wall and most of the village. Outside the window in my father's room the big sycamore tree and the river and navigation signs at the entrance to Oakport. When there was a clear moon over Oakport, it lit the whole row of brass bells along the iron railing at the foot of the bed. Many times I counted in different lights the thirty-two tongued-and-grooved boards of the ceiling when I couldn't sleep. There was a fireplace that was seldom lit and a small, white enamelled pot with a penis-shaped spout for urine, which was kept on his side of the bed and which I emptied in the mornings. When my father came late to bed and enquired as he took off his clothes if I was awake, I nearly always feigned sleep. He never interfered with me in an obviously sexual way, but he frequently massaged my belly and thighs. As in all other things connected with the family, he asserted that he was doing this for my good: it relaxed taut muscles, eased wind and helped bring on sleep. In these years, despite my increasing doctrinal knowledge of what was sinful, I had only the vaguest knowledge of sex or sexual functions, and took him at his word; but as soon as it was safe to do so, I turned away on some pretext or other, such as sudden sleepiness. Looking back, and remembering his tone of voice and the rhythmic movement of his hand, I suspect he was masturbating. During the beatings there was sometimes the same sexual undertow, but louder, coarser.

At the time I got free of his bed, we had the last of his disastrous maids. Anybody vaguely normal never stayed. Mary Kate was her name, in her late fifties, a blacksmith's daughter from close to Ballymote in Sligo. She never washed, and lines of dirt showed in the folds of her neck. All her early life had been spent keeping house for her father and brother, also a blacksmith, and when her father died and her brother wanted to marry, she was driven out like many women in her situation at the time. She had a rich fantasy life around her father and her nephews and nieces, about whom she was always boasting. Her brother or her brother's wife she never mentioned. I'm sure my father paid her a pittance, but she was forever trying to curry his favour. One of her ways of doing this was to bring to his attention anything that put us in an unfavourable light. She must have been very obvious. He never took any action. All we received were warnings. Our closeness in the protection of one another had become so efficient that her opportunities for carrying further stories were soon cut off. She identified me as the ringleader, and all her energies went into unmasking me and reporting my perfidy to my father.

I had managed to acquire the small room off the living room for study in warm weather. This was the room where the sides of bacon were cured in salt before being hung from the ceiling. Mary Kate resented the privacy I enjoyed there and suspected me of reading for pleasure instead of studying. One evening she entered the room silently and jumped me from behind. She was heavy and strong, but I was angry enough to unseat her from my back, but not before she had seized a *Hotspur* from among my books and papers. This was a weekly comic that ran serial stories. There were many such at the time. *Champion, Wizard, Rover.* They were mildly addictive, and we traded them at school. Mary Kate took the *Hotspur* in triumph to my father, but to her intense disappointment he took no action, though I think he enjoyed seeing me at a disadvantage.

"If reading that rubbish is all the use you can make of your studies, I'm afraid your friend Brother Placid will find that he has backed a dud. Anyhow neither of you can accuse me of having stood in your way."

This had the effect of making me even more determined to study and do well, and I only read for pleasure when all schoolwork was done. Mary Kate continued to try to catch me out, but was never again successful. I had only to place a few objects against the door to warn me of her approach, and there was seldom anything incriminating for her to find.

Soon afterwards she fell ill. Her family were contacted. When they did not respond, my father arranged for her to be moved by ambulance to the small hospital in Carrick where our grandmother had died. We never heard from her again. When we came to clear out the little room at the end of the landing, it was found to be dirty beyond belief. The room had to be completely cleared out and scrubbed. My father wore a towel over his nose and mouth as he rushed theatrically in and out. Many things that had mysteriously gone missing from the house were found beneath the bed—fishing baits of mine, tennis balls, a doll belonging to Dympna, a packet of raisins, an unopened half-bottle of Redbreast, a child's sewing kit and many other unlikely things.

Now that the room was no longer needed for a maid, I made a determined effort to get it for myself. I would be able to study there as well as sleep and would no longer need the downstairs room. I was given my way. My young brother was then moved to my place in our father's bed. He was six then, going on seven, and was delighted by the move, as my father presented it as a promotion within the ranks of the troops. That I was free of his bed almost certainly hastened open confrontation, but such was the level of his violence and my growing strength that it could not have been long delayed.

When it did eventually happen, there was a worn inevitability about it. Mentally and physically I was growing stronger by the day. The house was becoming dangerous for everybody. I could use the twenty-two and knew where the bullets were kept. I loaded it a number of times in preparation. Fortunately, nothing happened while it was leaning in the corner, loaded, the safety catch freed. Then late one evening he hit me hard without warning. There did not have to be a reason. The blows could come out of a moment of irritation or misunderstanding. As I have intimated, I suspect there was something sexual in his violence, because the blows could flare up on nothing, and afterwards it was hard to trace them to a cause. I remember feeling a wild sense of unfairness and a cold rage as I fell. I rose and went straight up to him, my hands at my sides, laughing. He hit me. I fell a number of times and each time rose laughing. I had passed beyond the point of pain and felt a strange cold elation. He was growing uncertain. I had passed beyond fear. My sisters told me much later how terrible it was to watch as I got to my feet again and again, laughing. He broke and turned away. "God, O God, O God. What did I do to deserve such a life, to get saddled with such a pack! A son that would raise a hand to his father."

He and I knew that an extraordinary change had taken place. My face was so bruised and swollen that I could not move out for days. He was anxious that I should not be seen in the shape I was in, even solicitous. I could have moved out if I had wanted to, and there was nothing he could have done, but in this concealment we were agreed. I would have had to admit that he had given me this beating, and I would have been ashamed to admit that I possessed such a father.

Some weeks afterwards I found him beating one of the girls and shouted at him to leave her alone. Without thinking, he turned and struck me violently across the face. His fingers left tracks across my face, but I hardly felt the blow.

"Do that again and you're finished," I said. I felt there was no end to what I could do if he moved. I would tear him apart, limb by limb, his nose and the sides of his mouth first. He fell back, crying. "I reared a son. I reared a son that would lift a hand to his father. I reared a son."

When I took Rosaleen home, I was able to reassure her that nothing would happen to her, and she trusted my certainty: there would never be uncontested violence in my presence in the house again. He made a show of welcoming Rosaleen home, but quickly sought me out alone.

"What's she doing?"

"She's come home."

"What's she going to live on here? Fresh air?"

"She was being abused." I saw by his face that I couldn't have said anything more damaging, and he didn't want to hear.

"Have you proof?"

"I have her word."

"That'd go a long way in court."

"It's enough for me."

"Of course I'm told nothing. I don't count," he began. "I'm not consulted about anything that goes on. I don't exist. Pay no attention to me. This old fool has to carry the can for everybody so that they all can sit back. God, O God, O God, what did I do to deserve such a cross." That night he recited the Rosary in a rage.

Rosaleen stayed at home to housekeep in the barracks. Many young girls were going to England to train as nurses. With their broken education, nothing but the most menial jobs was open to Rosaleen and Breedge in Ireland. We decided together that if they went to England they would have some of the security that training and a profession give. In Ireland the training hospitals demanded fees, while in England the nurses were paid while they trained.

We got application forms and applied to a number of hospitals in London. The applications were in the post before my father got wind of the plan. Naturally, he opposed it, complaining that he was never consulted about anything, but gradually he was won round: there were local girls from respectable families already training in England; they'd have a profession for the rest of their lives; they'd get paid while they trained; it would cost him nothing. Then he heard of a daughter of Harrington, the saddlemaker in Boyle, who had risen to the position of assistant matron in Whipps Cross Hospital in East London. He went to Boyle, saw Harrington, got his daughter's address, and wrote to her. He kept up this correspondence for years.

The two girls were accepted for training at a number of hospitals, but chose Whipps Cross. This took away our father's opposition. Before they left for London he got a list of all the religious services available to Catholic girls training at Whipps from Matron Harrington.

Aunt Maggie took over Margaret's and Monica's first year of secondary schooling, keeping them at her own expense with difficulty to herself. She had recently married Michael Breen, a boilermaker who worked in the railway sheds. He'd grown up on the edge of a links golf course near Dundalk, had been a caddie as a boy, and was a scratch golfer who played in some of the big amateur championships. In another time and place he might have made a living as a small-time professional. He was even more impressed by rich and powerful people than my father, and many were attracted to him because of his golfing prowess. With a few drinks in him, he sometimes tried to talk like them. After a day's golf and a pleasant evening in the golf-club bar, it was gall for him to have to change into his boilermaker's suit in the morning. When he married Maggie, he believed she was younger and had much more money than she had. The sideboard in the living room became a silver altar to his golfing triumphs. He resented the lodgers and Pat, and soon the house was cleared. Michael Breen was tipsy one evening when he said something insulting to Pat. Pat rose, slowly took out his key, and without a word threw it on the floor. He collected his clothes from upstairs and left by the hall door to live on his own in a house he had already purchased beside his garage. He had a boy who did odd jobs around the garage collect the rest of his belongings from the shop. When next he saw Michael Breen, he spoke to him as if nothing had happened, but he wasn't to set foot in the house again for years. It tells much of Maggie's character that in spite of her infatuation with her husband, she kept Margaret and Monica for a year, and sent them to secondary school against his opposition. It was my father who took them away after making additional demands that Maggie refused to meet.

Monica and Margaret were naturally bright, but I think it was touch and go for a time whether or not they would ever get any further education. I believe my father was shamed into sending them to the convent in Boyle.

The other guards who had less money than he had and the more ambitious local parents were by this time all trying to send their children to secondary school. Monica and Margaret cycled; sometimes they got lifts. My young brother, who had finally escaped from the name of Jude, after the patron saint of hopeless cases, into the safety of the more ordinary "Frankie," was then at national school in Cootehall with Dympna.

My father's fascination with anything mechanical continued. The windmill he erected beside the big sycamore tree—after his visit to the dumb parents in Aughavas—never provided electricity for the barracks. Eventually, he lost all interest, and after years of turning idly in different winds it was blown down in a storm. The windmill was replaced by a small two-stroke engine which he kept in a workshop across the small yard from the scullery door. He spent hours on end in this workshop. As well as benches and tools and old car tyres and tubes, the workshop contained an extraordinary display of old batteries bought cheaply at auctions. Some of them were large and of glass and looked beautiful. There were also tall glass jars for holding acid and distilled water. He had strung up a small lighting system, and when it was working and the running engine was flickering in the light bulbs, he was excited and happy. The lighting plant was also used to charge the wet batteries for the radio instead of sending them into Stewart's in Boyle. We were relieved and happy for him, and proud when the lights were working, though we preferred the calm of the oil lamps.

The engine never worked for long. He was forever taking it apart and reassembling it again. Eventually, he'd have to gather the small parts into an apron and in frustration take them and the engine to a garage. On one such occasion I helped him gather the small parts into a brown apron, and we went off with the engine to Pat's garage in Ballinamore. He must have been boiling with frustration. When we were no more than a mile out of Cootehall, he suddenly stopped the car and decided to check the parts again. As soon as we opened the apron, he found that a small, essential part was missing. He accused me of losing it, though I knew nothing about the part, and beat me up on the side of the road. He turned the car and headed back for the barracks. We found the part on the workshop bench where he had left it. That the unfairness was proven gave me steel. I refused to go to Ballinamore and would have nothing to do with him for weeks, though he tried all kinds of blandishments. Why my father was never able to master engines given his intense interest and fascination has always puzzled me. These small engines were not complicated.

Though Pat knew about engines and was one of the few people other than the Moroneys to continue a long relationship with my father, it was difficult to get him to speak about my father. He could be forthcoming on many subjects, but getting any information from him about my father was like extracting teeth.

"Why do you think the sergeant was never able to learn anything about engines?"

"O Frank. O Frank. O the Sergeant," he shook with silent laughter.

"But why? He is in some ways intelligent. That we can't take away from him."

"No confidence," he answered gnomically.

"You mean he didn't feel he could learn? That he never had the confidence or patience?"

"Something in that line. No point in coming in second." He shook even more with laughter, and it was useless to press him further.

This brought back one of the stranger episodes of our lives in the barracks in a different light. My father was a devoted listener of a programme on the Athlone station, *Making and Mending,* with Peadar O'Connor. Peadar's voice and presentation was so doleful and plodding that we used to make fun of it in secret: "You get the hammer, and you take the nail, and place the nail on the wood. Then you strike the nail with the hammer . . ."

When a sister educational programme was announced, my father became excited. *Listen and Learn* was aimed at people who had missed out at school and wanted to further their education and also to help those still at school. He wrote away at once for the accompanying booklets. He bought boxes of white and coloured chalks and made a small blackboard, which he painted a shining black, and hung it in the space between the sideboard mirror and the scullery door. He also cut and peeled a long light sally from the hedges, which he playfully whistled through the air.

I had read through the booklets soon after they arrived and felt I would have little difficulty following the programmes. On the evening of the opening programme, the air of expectancy and tension was great. In his blue uniform, my father was as polished and shining as on court day. Well before the time, we all gathered about the radio as if for the Rosary. Such was the restlessness of my father's excitement, that once the programme began it was not easy to concentrate on what was being explained. Then it was over, and we moved from the radio to the new blackboard, which was neat and well made, but the wrong paint had been applied. When he tried to write with a flourish of his cuffed sleeve, the chalk skidded on the hard surface without leaving any recognizable mark on the board, and he was reduced to making writing patterns in the air with the stick of chalk as he proceeded to lecture and demonstrate and question. Among the notes in the booklets was a set of questions designed to test the listener's understanding. I had always assumed he knew a great deal more about everything than I, but soon, with dismay, I saw that he was getting many things wrong. I became intent on keeping my head low and sliding through, attracting as little attention as possible, but when he began haranguing and shaking one of the girls after she had given the right answer, I said, "She's right," as deferentially as it was possible to say such a thing.

He looked at me in pure amazement. "Prove it!"

Though I stumbled, the error or misunderstanding was so basic that it was not difficult to prove. The booklet was consulted. He was wrong. We were all silent. We didn't know what he'd do next. Very slowly he handed me the stick of chalk and moved back behind the table and sat down as a member of a class.

"If you're that smart *you* go ahead and teach."

"I'm not able. I don't want to teach."

"Teach!" he roared.

I stumbled through a few lines before saying again, "I'm not able to teach."

"Teach. Now you're finding out how easy it is."

"It's not easy. I never said it was. I don't know how."

The best that can be said of such scenes is that they end, and I am not sure how this proceeded further or how it ended. He probably reached for his peaked cap and stalked down to the dayroom to be signed out on a patrol of the village, muttering about the impossible, ungrateful pack he had the deep misfortune to be saddled with. On one such patrol and in a similar mood, he came on Jimmy Kelly cycling home from the village without a light on his bicycle and launched into a long punishing lecture. "For Christ's sake, Sergeant, will you either leave off or give me a summons, but quit the sermon," Jimmy was driven to say. He was given a summons.

Before the next broadcast my father scraped the hard paint off the blackboard and replaced it with paint that received the chalk, but the lesson went no better. Long before the end of the series, they were abandoned as completely as the windmill turning idly alongside the big sycamore into whose high branches the aerial from the radio disappeared. He never threw out anything for which he had paid money, and whenever he happened on the *Listen and Learn* booklets he would tell himself and us that he had been a great fool to think that he could ever learn us anything, and that he might as well have been wasting breath on the desert air.

The beatings, the cries, the shouts, the anger, lingered like shame in the house, but the time when he could do as he wanted was finished. Did he know that what he was doing was wrong, or care? He knew it didn't look well from the outside, but he kept the outside as far as possible at the same iron distance as he kept the past. Whenever he got wind of a visit from any of our mother's relatives who had any position, like the priest Charlie Friel, he rounded us up immediately from Gloria or wherever he had us working and made us wash and dress up to be presented as the big happy family. He seemed to have an uncanny instinct for how far he could safely go, but on at least three occasions he sailed very close to danger: once, when he hit me on the head with the blade of a shovel at the potato pit; and when he gave Margaret such a terrible beating that she went into a cataleptic fit. She escaped into the darkness of the lavatory. We found her sitting there in silence. When we lifted her from the seat, she was frozen into the sitting position and had turned blue. We carried her into the house. After an earlier beating had the same result, he rang for Dr. Vesey, who came and gave her an injection. As far as we knew the doctor did not question how it happened. But he may have, as this time he did not telephone for Vesey. He had us bathe her with warm water until her limbs and circulation returned to normal. Until they did so, he paced anxiously and silently about, entering and leaving the room several times without uttering a word.

Another time Breedge came at speed from the village on her bicycle. The brakes failed when she tried to turn in the short avenue. She crashed against the low wall between the sycamores and was catapulted into the barrack garden, almost hitting her father who was digging potatoes inside the wall. When she got to her feet to find him standing over her, she said, "Howya!" She must have been in a state of shock, as it was unthinkable for her or any of us to address him so familiarly. He had been frightened by the crash and the sudden landing and outraged by the casual familiarity. "Such disrespect," he roared. "I'll teach you *Howya*," and he set about her with the spade in full view of the barracks and the road. Amazingly, she had escaped unhurt from the crash, but was bruised and limping for days from the blows of the spade. It never occurred to him that it was a near-miracle that she came safe from the crash.

All of this was taking place in or around the barracks which was never without a guard, day or night, but he was their superior at a time when any authority went unquestioned. It speaks of how bad it became that a number of times over the years the three guards came to him in a deputation to say that if the cries and beatings didn't stop they'd be forced to report him or take some action. Then there was always a cessation for a time before the violence resumed again. He was never reported.

The school, the library, the river, they all became a refuge and a strength and an escape, but stronger than all three stood the Catholic Church. The church dominated the little village. It was larger and richer than the church in Aughawillan, with a stained-glass window above the altar that had been donated by the King-Harmons, and was more of a presence in our lives. This was partly because of its nearness—we could drop in to pray on our way to the shop or the well. The church was an extension of the house and the barracks, but with different laws and a higher authority, and it opened outwards.

My father was head of the Pioneer Association and one of the sodalities. We attended all the ceremonies, those that weren't obligatory as well as those that were. Soon after moving from Aughawillan, I was serving on the altar in my old white surplice and a new red soutane, as the colour had also changed with the diocese. Old Father Glynn was our parish priest. He lived with his brother Danny in the blue-and-white presbytery at the end of the long avenue of limes.

Father Glynn was gentle and old before his time. The rumour was that he and Danny drank in the evenings, and if you came late to the presbytery on any business, Danny would answer the door and "you could get run." Scattered among the yew and cypress trees in the small church grounds were the graves of former priests of the parish. Hedges of laurel bordered the paths to the church doors and ran all the way round to the sacristy. Here we prepared for Mass while the priest robed. We had our different tasks—to light the candles on the altar, to pour the wine and water into the small cruets, arrange the finger bowl and fresh linen. Then we'd wait in silence for the second bell to ring. As soon as the first strokes rang out, at a signal from the priest we'd bow to the cross and go in twos out on the altar, separating to left and right at the steps, followed by the priest bearing the covered chalice. After Mass, Father Glynn would chat pleasantly to us as he unrobed, and we'd wait and walk with him along the laurel hedges out of the churchyard.

That first winter and spring in the barracks after my mother's death, when I was ten, I was prepared for confirmation. All the doctrinal instruction took place in school, but on certain evenings Father Glynn conducted ineffectual classes in the church. On good evenings these classes always started late. We'd gather at the appointed time and watch Father Glynn walking up and down the avenue of limes reading his breviary while we amused ourselves among the cypresses and headstones. A Mikey Flanagan was in our class. At the time, many farms reared guinea fowl for export to England, and Mikey learned to imitate their cry. When he climbed high into the big cypress by the gate, so perfect was the imitation that he was answered by guinea fowl from houses all around the village. The shriek was terrible but didn't disturb the old priest at his prayers. During the course of those evenings Mikey gained the name that clung to him for the rest of his life, the Guinea Flanagan. I remember the smallness of the class and the old, overcoated priest in the vast emptiness of the church and nothing of his instruction; the cries of the guinea fowl I remember with piercing vividness.

There were three churches in the parish: Cootehall was the parish church, Crossna and Drumboylan were served by curates, the churches roughly three miles apart. Confirmation was held that year in Crossna. When I was cycling with my father in my new blue suit to Crossna, I saw a boy my own age, black-haired and pale, with his mother outside the post office at Knockvicar. Paddy Morahan was his name. The mother was holding the two bicycles. She had sent Paddy in, and when he came out they shared chocolates or sweets. Like us, they were on their way to Crossna for Paddy's confirmation. I was almost physically sick with grief and envy as we cycled past, and whenever I remember that scene, I think what a poor, short-sighted emotion human envy is. Within a year Paddy's mother was also dead. Afterwards he and I spent five years together in the same class in Carrick and became close friends and remained friends all our lives.

The church ceremonies always gave me pleasure, and I miss them even now. In an impoverished time they were my first introduction to an indoor beauty, of luxury and ornament, ceremony and sacrament and mystery. I remember still the texture of the plain, brown, flat cardboard boxes in which the red and white and yellow tulips for the altar came on the bus when there were no flowers anywhere. I think not of the great ceremonies of Christmas and Easter in that small church facing Henry's but of the Stations of the Cross in Lent and the feast of Corpus Christi. There were never more than a handful of people gathered around the organ loft for the Lenten Devotions—my father, his children, a teacher or two with their children, a guard's wife, her children, a few religiously disturbed people.

I see the dimly lit church, rain and wind beating at the windows, the stirring of the great trees outside, the smell of damp, three altar boys in scarlet and white, one with a cross, two bearing lighted candles, moving from Station to Station, the priest genuflecting as he names each Station, the name echoing in the near empty church, the chanting, *O Jesus who for love of me didst bear Thy cross to Calvary in Thy sweet mercy grant to me to suffer and to die with Thee.*

Corpus Christi was the feast of summer. Rhododendron branches were cut from the Oakport Woods and taken by cart and tractor to decorate the grass margins of the triangular road round the village. Coloured banners and streamers were strung across the road on poles. Altars with flowers and a cross and white linen were erected at Gilligan's and the post office and Mrs. Mullaney's. There was always an enormous crowd, everybody in the parish who was able to walk, the different sodalities, like ragged Roman legions, walking beneath their banners. The Host was taken from the tabernacle and carried by the priests beneath a gold canopy, pausing for ceremonies at each wayside altar. Solemn benediction was always given at the post office. Hymns were sung all along the way, and I remember the coughing and the slow shuffle of feet in the dramatic silences, girls in their white First Communion veils and dresses scattering rose petals in the path of the slowly moving canopy. A uniformed guard stood at each of the three entrances to the village, at the bridge, at Lavin's, and at Cassidy's Cross. For that one hour of the year, the Divine Presence left the tabernacle and travelled our ordinary roads for one mortal-immortal hour beneath the sky.

The missions attracted as large a crowd, and packed the church each evening for a whole week. Every few years Redemptorists came to the village like a small band of strolling players and thundered hell and damnation from the pulpit. There was a distinct air of carnival. Stalls selling rosaries, medals, scapulars, prayer books, holy pictures and other religious objects were set up outside the church wall. There was a blessing of holy objects on the closing night. The Redemptorists were brought in to purify through terror, and were appreciated like horror movies. "He'd raise the hair on your head!" Lesser performances were described as "watery." Some of the local priests were able to match the Redemptorists with their own thunder, and they too were appreciated.

A young man replaced Father Glynn for a few months when the old priest fell ill. His sermons were short and delivered quietly in plain language. They related Christianity to the lives of people and stated that reflection on the mystery of life was itself a form of prayer, superior to the mouthing of empty formulas: he touched on character assassination, backbiting, marital violence, child beating, dishonesty, hypocrisy; he claimed a primary place for personal humility and love of others and charity of mind. Many were furious. My father in the front seat was incensed. He lifted up the heavy kneeler, letting it down with a crash on the flagstones to show his disapproval. He did this three times. The young priest refused to be intimidated; he paused and looked directly at him before continuing. My father did not lack support. The criticism took the form of a deep and troubled censoriousness at what the modern church was coming to. They rejoiced when Father Glynn returned. What they wanted was hell and damnation, which they could apply, like death, to other people. I suspect it is no accident that funerals remain our most frequent and important carnivals.

The truth that the priest represented, I believed then, stood outside and beyond human manipulation and bullying. I was able to follow it intimately Sunday by Sunday at the priest's side on the altar, through the great feasts of Christmas, when the church stood like a lighted ship moored in a sea of darkness, to Ash Wednesday, through Lent to the glory of Easter, Whit of the gift of tongues, when it was dangerous to go on water, to Ascension Thursday, to All Souls of the living and the dead. Before the printed word, the churches were the Bibles of the poor, and the Church was my first book. The story of Christ as I followed it through these ceremonies gave meaning and depth to both the year and our lives. The way was travelled not only in suffering but in ecstasy. I was introduced to all I have come to know of prayer and sacrament, ceremony and mystery, grace and ornament and the equality of all women and men underneath the sun of heaven. This was a greater authority than my father's rule in the barracks and one to which he also had to subscribe. He could not go against it and remain within the law in the front seat of the church every succeeding Sunday. My father's world went inwards to darkness and violence, lies and suppression: the school, the library, the river, the Church, all went outwards, to light and understanding, freedom and joy.

In the beginning was my mother. The only way that life could be continued with her was through prayer. When I slipped into the empty church to pray for her, images of our life together kept returning to displace the words of prayer, and I would try to shut out all those things of the world as I willed the mind on God. God in those prayers, I realize now, was blankness. Many times I imagined my mother in heaven, close to the throne of God, meeting Mary, walking in the heavenly gardens with the angels and saints. There she would wait for me under the cloudless sky in that one eternal day, but if she was already in heaven, she had no need of prayer. I knew from the casuistry of the catechism. It was I who needed prayer, and if I did not keep my soul free, I would never join her there. I thought of her, too, in purgatory, but she of all people was hardly deserving of fire, and I was not able to imagine her in the flames, even with ecstasy on her face at the prospect of the joy of God.

In the evenings, after wheeling barrows of sods from Langan's slane out on the spread, or facing the black banks of turf that had to be scattered, footed, wind-rowed, clamped and dragged out in small loads to the road with the jennet, she often came to me as if in a dream. We were gathering sticks again from the hedges, or sitting in front of the blazing fire, or going again past Brady's pool and Brady's house and the street where the old Mahon brothers lived, past the dark deep quarry and across the railway bridge and up the hill past Mahon's shop to the school. All that seemed paradise now. Time had healed that first pain of loss. My sense of her had been weakened by all the new experiences crowding in with each new day, but the promise still remained that one day I would say Mass for her. But for that I would never have been able to resist my father when he tried to take me out of school and put me into the store in the small town near Dublin. If I had left school then, I would have had to abandon all hope of ever becoming a priest. To keep this promise, I would have gone to any lengths. If my father had persisted, I would have left the house and gone to Pat or Maggie or anybody for help.

At this time he lost the contract for the convent laundry and we were given back our summers. We had still to save the turf for the house and for a small government contract he had to supply the dayroom, but these were nothing compared to what was needed for the laundry, and we had become quick and skilled at the work. I think it was always a sore trial for him to see us idling in the sun, and if given time he would invent work for us.

I was now the only one who used the barrack boat, and on these days I went on the river. If I didn't want to fish, I rowed into an inlet, and among the reeds and drowning leaves I read. When I woke out of the book, I would come into the drone of flies, the sudden splash of a fish, the whine of the saws deep in Oakport and the far, far distant noises of the farms. Over many days and months, gradually, a fantastical idea formed. Why take on any single life—a priest, a soldier, teacher, doctor, airman—if a writer could create all these people far more vividly? In that one life of the mind, the writer could live many lives and all of life. I had not even the vaguest idea how books came into being, but the dream took hold, and held.

The examinations were fast approaching. I knew I would do well but not how well. If I won a scholarship, I could go on to Maynooth in spite of not coming from a diocesan seminary.

Either way, I knew I would have little difficulty in entering the colleges that served the foreign missions, and a priest was a priest for ever. The place of ordination was only of consequence in the eyes of the world. All the days of his life the priest would celebrate Mass. In substituting the dream of becoming a writer for that first long-held dream, was I not replacing that old dream with an impossible dream that would allow me to go towards the world dressed up in this new ideal? I would no longer have to die in life in order to circumvent death and the judgment and to keep the promise to her I loved. Instead of being a priest of God, I would be the god of a small, vivid world. I must have had some sense of how outrageous and laughable this would appear to the world, because I told no one, but it did serve its first purpose—it set me free.

After many years of trying to find a wife, my father was now proceeding cautiously again towards marriage. Agnes McShera came from a large family in Drumboylan, where the rich short grass of Roscommon gave way to the rushes of Leitrim and its shallow soils. An older sister was married to Larry O'Hara, a quiet, gentle, small farmer on the outskirts of the village. Two sisters were nuns, a younger sister a nurse. A brother Pat lived on the small family farm with his mother. Another brother, Michael Joe, was a bus driver in Dublin. The youngest, Tommy, was a respected local tradesman and small building contractor. An older brother was in America. Agnes was the plainest of a handsome family, but she was intelligent, strong-willed, and had great charm. When very young, she joined the household of a stock-broker in Manchester, and made herself indispensable, travelling with the family everywhere—to the Bahamas, the West Indies, South Africa. She got her brother installed as a gardener in the Manchester house, but he did not remain long. "I learned at the Exchange today that war is about to be declared," the stock-broker told him on the eve of war. "I expect you to do your duty,

Pat, and join up. The garden will have to manage." "That night I was on the boat out of Liverpool," Pat said.

Agnes stayed and came home on holidays in the 1950s, when she met and fell in love with my father. She was more than ten years the younger, and was able to make the most of her appearance with a stylish, understated sense of dress. Though opposite in temperament, they shared some similarities. In different ways, they both were wilful, and they identified strongly with the Church and looked down on the world from which they had come and which was all around them. Tom Leddy, when he called out of the blue, could not have committed a worse offence than to mistake Agnes for the housekeeper. After so many failures, now that this attractive person was within his grasp and there were no obstacles of any kind in the way, my father started to procrastinate and had, I think, to be given an ultimatum. Around this time he called me down to the dayroom where he was alone covering for the barrack orderly.

"There's something that concerns the whole family that I want to discuss," he began.

I knew at once what it was and waited.

"Were I to decide to replace your mother—may heaven be her dwelling place—with someone else, how would you view it? Would you have any objection?"

His tone and the words brought back in all its rawness the scene when he said, "You miss your mother very much," soon after her death, and went on to say that if she had recovered, even if she remained an invalid he would have been happy to carry her every day up and down the stairs and to take her outside to sit in a chair in the sun.

"This has nothing to do with my mother. She's dead," I said angrily.

"I didn't ask you that," he said, as if imploring the On High for patience. "I asked if you'd have any objection."

"Of course not. It's none of my business."

"It affects the whole family. Whether you like it or not you're still a member of the family, and you're the eldest."

"The family isn't marrying the woman. You are marrying her, or she is marrying you."

"It still affects the family. This is just more of your regrettable attitudes. Bringing somebody new into the family affects everybody. The family will be there in the years ahead for everybody to come back to whether they choose to or not." He was censoriously angry. I was just able to contain my anger.

"Breedge and Rosaleen are in London. I'll be gone out of here in a couple of months. Margaret and Monica will be gone in a year or two. The only person it affects is yourself and maybe Dympna and Frankie."

"Whether the family are here or away, they are still members of the family and it affects everybody."

"Look," I could control myself no longer, and rose. "I told you I have no objection. I think you are very lucky to find anybody. Marry the woman but don't bring me into the business." I got up and left.

I don't know how he presented this scene to Agnes McShera, or if he told her at all, but she disliked and distrusted me from the beginning, and we came gradually to see one another as enemies.

Their engagement took place in Sligo. Not only was a ring given but, by special permission, they exchanged vows before a priest, which was highly unusual even for that time, since those vows were as indissoluble as marriage vows, without conferring any rights.

Later that summer the results of the Leaving justified Brother Placid's faith when he cycled out to the potato field in Coxhill. I could now go on to university, but in the first year or two I would have needed some financial help in addition to the scholarships. I knew that it would be forthcoming from my father only if it wasn't requested, and I was too practical and too proud to ask. I had also a number of other choices, and for a time kept all the doors open. In this aftermath, my father insisted on driving me everywhere for interviews and orals. He who couldn't get leave when my mother was dying or for anything that didn't interest him could now get away any time he wanted. There were times when he abandoned his usual taciturnity on these journeys and betrayed all the intense pride and excitement of the owner of a prize greyhound.

When I got a call to the teachers' training college I accepted it at once. That it was described as a "call" tells of the vocational origins of the profession within the Church in Ireland. The State paid full board and tuition and guaranteed employment at a time when jobs were like gold dust.

When I told my father, he was plainly relieved. "I'd have given you any help I could if you went on to the university, and Miss McShera has savings she said she'd be willing to give, but I'm glad to see you so responsible and that you take the others into account. I still have a large family to support and have a duty to each of them," he said heavily.

As soon as I heard the words I knew I had decided well. I would have been given no help if I had needed it, or it would have been given so grudgingly that it would have been impossible to accept. The real reason I was going I told no one. The teaching hours were short. There were long holidays. I would not have to think about money. These were all the means I needed to follow my dream. The guilt I felt at turning my back half-heartedly—on the death in life that was the priest's choice and on that dear promise to say Mass—I was able to partially resolve by telling myself that teaching was my mother's profession and was sometimes called the second priesthood. In all this there was much confusion and ignorance as well as long suppressed adolescent emotions, but the idea that first took shape in the tarred boat among the reeds and drowning leaves under the dark Oakport woods that I would write was now as clear as a single star. That I had not even the vaguest notion as to how on earth it might be achieved or realized did not seem to trouble me for a moment.

The year was 1953. In the 1950s a half-a-million people emigrated from this small country, nearly all of them to Britain, far more than in any other decade in the entire century. These emigrants were young and poorly educated, for the most part, and ill prepared. Names like Holyhead, Chester, Crewe were burned into the national consciousness, but mine was a silent generation, and it disappeared in silence. The boat trains were full and the boats were not much better than cattle boats, and the boat to Liverpool did carry cattle in its hold.

"How far are you going, Pat?" ran the joke of the time about the men on the train who had no ticket and had to make for the lavatory every time the ticket inspector came round.

"To America if my arse sticks it!"

The men sold their physical strength, the women their willingness to work long hours. They came home in summer, the men blowing in the bars about the never-ending overtime they were earning, the women sometimes appearing with their English husbands in tow. "Cheers! Pa," the English son-in-law raised his glass to his father-in-law when they went down to the pub for a pint, ran another joke. "Lord, son, don't cheer in here or we'll get put out!" These emigrants were looked down on by the new class closely connected with the Church which had done well out of itself after Independence: it was somehow all their fault that they had to go to unholy Britain to look for work. In 1953, when I entered St. Patrick's, teachers were paid far better in this impoverished country than in Britain, almost certainly because of the profession's close links with the Church, and St. Patrick's attracted some of the best minds in the country. I had become one of the privileged few who had escaped the trains and the cattle boats and was allowed to work in my own country.

In that country, individual thought and speech were discouraged. Its moral climate can be glimpsed in the warning catch phrases: *a shut mouth catches no flies; think what you say but don't say what you think; the less you say, the more you'll hear.* By 1950, against the whole spirit of the 1916 Proclamation, the State had become a theocracy in all but name. The Church controlled nearly all of education, the hospitals, the orphanages, the juvenile prison systems, the parish halls. Church and State worked hand in hand. Women and single men were in a lower scale on the public services, a higher scale was in place for married men. The breaking of pelvic bones took place during difficult births in hospitals because it was thought to be more in conformity with Catholic teaching than Caesarean section, presumably because it was considered more "natural." Minorities were deprived of the right to divorce. All artificial forms of contraception were outlawed. Learning Irish was seen as a means of keeping much foreign corrupting influence out, but the catechism was taught in English.

People did not live in Ireland then. They lived in small, intense communities which often varied greatly in spirit and character over the course of even a few miles. Part of the pain of emigration was that the small communities they had left were more real to the emigrants than the places where their lives were happening and where their children were growing up with alien accents. There was a hidden bitterness, but sometimes it was not so hidden.

I heard it expressed clearly on a London building site in 1954. Many of the men were sent their *Roscommon Herald*s or *Western People*s from home every week. They read them greedily and often exchanged them at work. During a break from work a man was reading aloud from one of these newspapers. Another wet summer in Ireland was turning into a disaster and prayers were being offered in all the churches for the rains to cease. A young Clare man was in our gang. "May it never stop," he said without a trace of humour when the reading finished. "May they all have to climb trees. May it rise higher than it did for fukken Noah!" One night as I emerged from the tube, I was surprised by a round, orange moon above Whitechapel. For a moment, it seemed as if the moons of Gloria, of Oakport and Ollarton's had joined me in London. "Hello, moon," the same boy from Clare who had wished floods on the whole of Ireland laughed out. The two of us were returning from a dance. "I see you, moon, have come over to do a spot of labouring as well!" I was going home at the end of the summer; he wasn't.

In the communities, the local and the individual were more powerful than any national identity, and much of what was postulated was given no more than lip service, as shown by the success of Patsy Conboy and his ballroom. Most people went about their sensible pagan lives as they had done for centuries, seeing this conformity as just another veneer they had to pretend to wear like all the others they had worn since the time of the Druids. Most affected was the new class closely connected with Church and State, and St. Patrick's Training College was one of the institutions at its very core.

Again, my father had no difficulty getting time off from the barracks, and drove me to the door of the college. He would have liked to have been able to inspect the place and to meet the dean and the president, but fortunately that wasn't allowed. St. Patrick's was run by the Vincentians and was a very strange institution then, mirroring the official country. We were all between seventeen and twenty, except for a few university graduates who were older. A percentage of places was reserved for native Irish speakers from the Gaeltacht areas. They had entered through preparatory colleges where everything was taught through Irish, but nearly all of us who had come in through open competition would have won university scholarships at a time when only two scholarships were on offer in most counties.

For a third-level institution it was extraordinary. We were allowed outside the walls on the afternoons of Wednesdays and Saturdays and all day on Sundays, but we had to return for meals and Evening Devotions and be back within the walls before the gates closed at ten. Anybody late had to enter through the president's house and provide a plausible explanation. For this to happen more than once or twice meant expulsion. A year or two before, a boy returning late from a dance, and leaving his girl home, decided to scale the high wall rather than enter through the president's house. He was loath to risk his good trousers on the curved barbed wire, and threw them over the wall and followed, to be met by the dean's flashlamp. "I'm sorry but it won't happen again, Father," he said contritely as he picked up his trousers. "No. It won't happen again," Father Johnston, a sinister priest who was known as The Bat smiled grimly. In the morning, the boy was gone.

Attendance at daily Mass and evening Devotions was compulsory. There wasn't a historical, literary, philosophical, or even a Gaelic society within the college. But there were a number of religious societies. Not to belong to at least one of them was dangerous. They gave us hardly any education, which, considering what was likely to be on offer, was no bad thing. *Ni beidh sibh arais* (ye won't be back) was the constant threat, and at the end of every year there were four or six who were not *arais*. Used to the freedom and the open ways of Carrick-on-Shannon, I found the place barbaric, but those students who had come through the diocesan seminaries found St. Patrick's blissful by comparison.

What was under scrutiny at all times was not our education or aesthetic or moral development but our willingness to conform. We were to be sent out as non-commissioned officers to the priests in the running of the parishes, secondary to the priest in all things including education, cogs in an organizational wheel. As it happened, the place was perfect for my secret vocation. The courses the college provided could be safely disregarded until a few weeks before the exams: up to 90 per cent was required to gain admission, and only 40 was needed to pass out, and you were neither more nor less a national teacher whether you got 90 or 40. What education I picked up was from other students.

Books were discussed secretly and passed around, and I continued to read for pleasure, a pleasure that was subtly changing all the time from those first adventures in Moroney's library.

The huge waves of organized devotion that marked the Marian Year of 1954 were thought a greater triumph of Irish Catholic and national solidarity than the Eucharistic Congress of 1932. No factory, no football pitch, no fishing boat was launched without the blessing of a priest or bishop. All new housing estates built in the major towns and cities had a shrine or Marian grotto at their centre.

In 1932, when she was waiting to marry my father, my mother listened to the excitement generated by the Eucharistic Congress on the convent radio in Ballinamore. In the summer of 1954 my father remarried. When St. Patrick's closed for the summer, I took the boat for England to look for work on the buildings. Religious feeling does not die easily. When I walked off the boat at Holyhead to the waiting London train—and thought of Shakespeare, Milton, Dickens, all the great English writers I had read and studied—I felt awe, as if I was stepping on to sacred ground.

The work I found on a building site off the Commercial Road was rough but well paid. On Sundays I went out to Leytonstone to see Rosaleen. My father had persuaded Breedge to delay her departure for England and attend his wedding. Most of the trainee nurses were Irish. Rosaleen had already made many friends and seemed happy. She had a natural aptitude for study and was enjoying the courses. When I asked how she had adjusted to life in England, she smiled sadly: "Life in the barracks was a great preparation. Everything here is a cakewalk by comparison." We hired a boat and went for a row on the artificial lake, with all the other boats racing and splashing around us, and spoke of the empty river and Oakport. My father was writing regularly to Rosaleen demanding my address. I told her not to give it, but when next I saw her a letter with the familiar handwriting was waiting. This was full of recrimination and complaint, mostly about my ingratitude after all he had done for me, and asserting that since his marriage the house was even more open to the whole family than ever before, and to make it so was also one of Agnes's chief aims. I replied that I had no quarrel of any kind with him or Agnes. I wished them both happiness. I had come to London for the practical reason of earning independent spending money and to see Rosaleen, and I looked forward to seeing them in the barracks when I returned.

Other letters followed in quick succession—some with new complaints, others with vague references to how mistakes are made from time to time within all families and they should never be taken too much to heart; and a new theme was taken up that he was never to let go of in the next few years: alone and separate he and I might not amount to much but together we could take on the world. A few of these letters I answered politely, but I had said all I intended to say.

When I returned to Ireland I went straight into the training college. That year four students had not been called back for their second and final year. They were not *arais*, and as we walked round the path that circled the football field under the lime trees in the breaks between classes and meals and study, all the talk was of them and the reasons why they had not been brought back. We were now the senior students and could watch coolly the excitement and uncertainty of the new class.

A letter from my father awaited me to say that he and Agnes were driving to Dublin the following Sunday in order to meet me. I was dismayed when I met them. They were like supplicants seeking my approval. I found the situation farcical. I was nineteen years of age and nobody needed my approval. He had plainly told Agnes how much the family meant to him and how much he suffered on our behalf. She made a hesitant little speech saying how much she wanted to make the house hospitable and welcoming to the whole family, whether they were at home or away. I was hardly able to stay seated with the acute discomfort I felt, and rushed to assure her that I wished them nothing but happiness and that I'd spend the whole Christmas with them in the barracks as soon as the college closed. Having gained that assurance, my father could not leave well enough alone and started to complain about how much worry I had caused him by going off without leaving an address and not answering his letter.

"I did answer your letter. I answered two or three."

"How long did it take you? I suppose we have to be thankful for small mercies."

I'm afraid I watched him coldly.

"Daddy was so worried that there were nights when he couldn't sleep," Agnes said.

At Christmas I went home to the grey stone bridge, the triangular field, the river, the navigation signs into Oakport, Coote's Archway, the villagers, the three guards, the barracks. Without making any new purchases or much rearranging, Agnes had transformed the big living room. Everything was neater, cleaner, warmer, and here and there touches of colour lightened the room. She could not have been more welcoming or more charming. The meals she cooked were delicious. My father still dined alone, facing the big sideboard mirror, and he was flourishing. He was at his most charming, as if he was playing a new person or part, and only in odd flashes was there a hint or threat of violence. As before, when we were in Aughawillan, he was courting me. In some months I would be a teacher, in the same social class, on a slightly higher rung, and he had a vision of me becoming the principal of a local school. I'd have much free time; he'd be retired; he saw the two of us working happily hand in hand, making money together as we had done once before. I neither encouraged nor disabused him of this fantasy, but listened in fascinated disbelief.

He had already bought "The Nurseries," a beautiful stone house on twelve acres at Grevisk outside the Rockingham walls. The land had been the nursery gardens for the Nash house above

Lough Key. In its heyday fourteen gardeners worked the fields, and the head gardener lived in the stone house. There were great trees on the land, exotic plants and flowers brought back from India and China, grass-grown walks. The soil was rich. There had been nothing casual about the purchase: he bought it after long negotiations with his retirement in view. There was a gate in the high Rockingham wall across the road from the house to a bridle path that led through woods and pastures all the way to Rockingham House. Along this bridle path the various ladies of Rockingham used to ride to discuss with the head gardener which plants or shrubs should be transferred from the nurseries to the house gardens.

I thought the place was beautiful and enjoyed helping him about the fields and the wild gardens. "Alone we are nothing," he would recite like a mantra as we worked, cutting up fallen trees or dosing the few black cattle or cutting back growth in the orchard: "Together we can take on the world."

Agnes was clever and she was well read and had the rare quality of being able to give her undivided attention to whomever she was with, so that time flew and very ordinary things I said appeared original and interesting in her company. In this atmosphere it was easy for her to elicit confidences until I saw that everything I said was being carried to my father. At the same time I noticed that Dympna and Frankie were confused and unhappy. They were both good-looking and clever, Frankie unusually so. He could pick up knowledge so easily that he was often bored, and sometimes difficult. They had been shielded by their youth and the rest of us from the worst excesses of the house, and in the last years my father's instinct to do as he pleased had been so curbed that they had enjoyed normal freedoms. As my father flourished in Agnes's infatuation, he was devouring all the attention, and Dympna and Frankie were starving. In very subtle ways, Agnes had restored all my father's old power and dominance so that in a very different manner the whole house revolved around him once again. Through praise and flattery she was orchestrating Dympna's and Frankie's reactions around my father. When they refused to perform as she wanted, she withdrew that support and praise. They had been used to much attention from Breedge and Rosaleen. Now the twins were in London. For years they had been the only parents they had known.

This did not affect Margaret and Monica. They were both charmed by Agnes's company but had been through fire. The experience made them naturally withdrawn and watchful, and they were studying hard to make their own way out of the house and into the world.

I could see vaguely what was happening, but there was nothing I could do, and in a few days was back in the training college. I came home to the barracks at Easter and again in summer when I graduated. I did not get a school immediately. I wasn't worried because I knew the State trained no more teachers than it could employ. The Bat had a long list of positions to fill for priests who wanted young teachers, but I hadn't gone to him. The best schools and positions he gave to his favourites. He would probably have given me a school had I asked. I was in neither his good nor his bad graces, and I would have been paid during the long holidays. *"Bhfuil scoil agat go foill, Mac Eachrain?"* He asked me once as he walked in his black soutane among the tables in the refectory. *"Nil, a Athair,"* I replied, and there it was let rest. He wasn't prepared to offer me a school, and I wouldn't ask. If I went to him I would have to take whatever school he gave, and it could have been anywhere in the entire country. The life of a teacher was permanently on view in the small parishes, and only in Dublin could I disappear into my own and my secret life without being noticed, but a great number of the other students, for different reasons, also wanted schools in the university towns and cities. I was even thinking of returning to England.

Eventually, I went back to the barracks and helped Agnes's

brother, Tommy McShera, put a new roof on the stone house in Grevisk. Tommy was a skilled tradesman and was pleasant and easygoing. My father was delighted with the free labour. His plan that we would join up and work together had now taken a firmer root. Each day he scrutinized the ads for teachers in the *Irish Independent*. There is the possibility that he was afraid I wouldn't go to work at all, but it was only the vacancies close by that excited him.

In September I got an appointment in the town of Athboy. I soon moved from there to Drogheda. Within a year I was in Dublin.

The years that followed were slow and full and sometimes difficult: it is only in the looking back that they seem to have gone quickly. I was never to spend as long again in the barracks as the summer I helped Tommy McShera re-roof the house in Grevisk, but I continued to go back regularly enough. In England, Breedge joined Rosaleen late that summer, and they both went on to qualify as nurses.

When Rosaleen was fourteen she was in an accident with Lenihan's van as she was turning in the short avenue to the barracks on a bicycle with a can of water from the priest's well. Frank Lenihan was driving from the avenue out on to the main road. In the collision she was thrown into the air. Her arm was broken. She was badly bruised and had severe headaches for weeks. They were both found to be negligent: Rosaleen hadn't full control of the bicycle and hadn't given a hand signal before turning in the avenue; Frank Lenihan hadn't stopped before driving out on to the main road, and was the more seriously negligent. Rosaleen was awarded £350 (a considerable sum then), and it was left in trust for her with her father until she reached twenty-one. We thought we would have difficulty getting the money, but as soon as I mentioned that it must be due, he attacked me as if I was impugning his integrity. He paid out the sum immediately but kept whatever interest had accrued over the six to seven years. I was prepared to question him about the interest, but Rosaleen was happy with what she had received and didn't want the unpleasantness that would have certainly ensued.

Margaret and Monica passed easily into Dublin Corporation and the Civil Service as clerical officers. They would have preferred teaching, but neither could sing, and music was an obligatory subject for women. Agnes's brother Michael Joe, the bus driver, had bought a Victorian house off the South Circular Road, and Agnes arranged that they lodge with him and his wife when they went to Dublin to take up work. When Dympna followed them into the Civil Service, room was also found for her in the same house. Because there was constant news and commerce between the two houses, through this move Agnes ensured that all three girls remained within the orbit of the family and Daddy. There were certain times in those years, like Christmas and parts of the summer, when all the girls were at home together. They were good-looking, attractive girls in their flower. Agnes enjoyed their presence, as if she was again part of a gang of girls at the outset of her life. Their father also enjoyed himself wonderfully, though what he was plainly enjoying was himself in the reflected light of their youth and beauty.

I returned now only on short visits, but saw that he had already tired of the pre-eminence Agnes had so artfully created around him. She often looked harassed and nervous, but was fierce in his defence against all criticism and sided openly with him whenever Dympna and Frankie ran foul of his moods. I often thought of her in those years as his terrier. The two younger children seemed to belong to a different family. Because they had been cushioned by their youth from the worst brutalities, they were more open and trusting, and expected life to come easily. Now they were changing. Dympna became more hidden as she went about her chores and school and study, but was fostering a slow, smouldering anger that she would never cast. Frankie was a wonderfully open, affectionate, intelligent child, but was by now disturbed and beginning to cause trouble at every turn.

My father, in the meantime, was courting me as assiduously as he had once courted when trying to draw me away from my mother. He was now writing to me regularly. Hardly a week went by that he didn't have news of upcoming vacancies in local schools and houses and lands for sale. It was clear that he thought I would eventually tire of life in Dublin and come home. He had a sharp sense of what might draw me home. Among the places was a beautiful ivy-covered house beside the bridge on the riverbank at Knockvicar. Attached to it were thirty-five acres of pasture and rough timber. Beside a wooden bridge that crossed a stream going down to the river in front of the house was a tree covered with climbing roses. My father offered a guarantee to the bank as well as a personal loan, but I knew these offers would not remain uncomplicated if they were ever taken up:

> *You are probably correct about the land at Knockvicar. Surely you are correct when you are not enthusiastic. The price asked was not too high, £2000, and while I might be only able to give a guarantee to a bank for half this amount I have a shrewd idea a bank would accept a deed or mortgage on the place for the other half. It might well be bought for £1000. If you intend to stay all your life in Dublin etc. etc. you may be sure I know nothing except that individually we might accomplish little but as a team nothing might daunt us. I am not as young as I used to be and etc. etc. But I have written too much.*

For my part, I was content to answer non-committally. Outright rejection of these endeavours would bring aggression and recrimination. This way a truce of sorts was maintained. At the same time, he was trying to draw me over to his side in his ongoing war with Agnes, while presenting me to Agnes as the difficult son who had always misunderstood his efforts on behalf of the family. Dympna and Frankie were the undeserving pawns and buffers in these machinations.

In 1956 Rockingham House burned down. The 365 windows shattered, the roof collapsed, and that night the whole country-side was lit for miles around as far as the dark slopes of the Curlews. All that remained were the underground tunnels, the wine cellars, the basement, the sunken tennis courts and a shell of the walls. My father suspected arson, though Sir Cecil and Lady Stafford King-Harmon were photographed several times that week at the Newmarket Yearling sales, and he started investigations. The great walled estate was acquired by the Land Commission and split into 65-acre farms. "Could you think up a bit of influence for yourself and me?" my father wrote sarcastically about the politics of the divide.

Attractive and sexually the most confident of the girls, Breedge was the first to marry. She met Con O'Brien in an Irish dancehall in London. He was from the town of Kanturk in Cork, where his father was a baker. At fourteen he left school to enter the bakery. Good-looking and musical, he played the saxophone and sang in a small-town dance band while working in the bakery, and when the band folded he joined the tides leaving for England. There he found work on the buildings and had hopes of starring in another band. Breedge was bowled over by his good looks and confidence and knowledge of trendy clothes and fashions and musical hits. They became engaged almost immediately. He in his turn was taken by her beauty and confidence, but even more impressed that she was a trained nurse and the daughter of a sergeant of the guards. So besotted was Breedge that she expected universal approval of Con when she took him home, and was hurt by anything less than a rapturous endorsement.

In the staid, conservative world of the barracks, with his jewellery and trendy outfits, he appeared like a figure out of pantomime, which his heavy drinking and talkativeness did nothing to dispel. All that Breedge could extract from her father was the grudging, "If he does you, Breedge, I'm sure he'll do me." This brought tears, but such was her capacity for self-deception within the deep emotional ties to her father that after a few weeks back in London she had converted this into a ringing endorsement. When her wedding took place in London, she begged him to come to London to give her away—she had postponed her entrance to the nursing school in order to attend his wedding—but all he did was send a small cheque to cover part of the expenses.

The Garda regulations required that all guards be transferred within twelve months of their marriage to a local woman. My father managed to have this move put off for a number of years, probably through various pleas and representations—his age, his record, the young children he had still at school. When the transfer could be postponed no longer, he was given Leitrim village, where the white bullock had lain down in the middle of the road all those years before. The transfer could not have been friendlier: Leitrim was only four miles from Cootehall; the living quarters were spacious and comfortable; neither Dympna nor Frankie would have to change schools; he would be able to continue to work his new farm and prepare the house for his eventual retirement. At a function in the parochial hall, he and Agnes were given a going-away present. A few weeks before he was due to move, he changed his mind again and decided to retire, and went to live permanently in The Nurseries. No sooner had he done this than he regretted it, and began to resent his own decision.

By this time, I had drifted from the Church. So imperceptibly did it happen that it was not clear even to me whether I had left the Church or the Church had left me. I still enjoyed the ceremonies, and went to Mass or didn't go, depending on whether it was politic and on what I felt. In school I taught the catechism and led the children in the obligatory prayers with the same ease as when I believed. I had affection still and gratitude for my upbringing in the Church: it was the sacred weather of my early life, and I could no more turn against it than I could turn on any deep part of my own life. Through work and reading and reflection I had come to separate morals and religion, to see morals as simply our relationship with other people and the creatures of the earth and air, and religion as our relationship with our total environment, the all that surrounds our little lives. I had come to see the story of Jesus as a story among other sacred stories that sought to explain and make palatable the inexplicable. Given my lack of any strong feeling and easy attitude to superficial observances, I am not sure why I would no longer kneel for the nightly Rosary on those visits home. I must have seen it as both an empty charade that had become an instrument of domination and a step too far to take any longer. I tried to make my withdrawal as discreet as possible by going outside or to my room when the time came to kneel. My father was furious and deplored especially the example I was setting for the younger members of the family. He must have continued the quarrel by letter. I don't remember the exchange, but a letter of his on the subject survives. In the exchange I must have stated my beliefs, or lack of them, bluntly, and may have attacked the hypocritical posturings that passed for religion:

> *Grevisk*
> *Trinity Sunday*

> *My dear Sean*
>   *Your letter was unworthy of you, hence my failure to reply so I might impress that on you.*
>   *Your religion or lack of it is to be deplored and my vows won't cause you unhappiness either in this life or the* log *state.*
>   *I must insist on your filial co-operation so that you won't make other members of the family as unhappy as*

yourself. I must for myself claim the same privileges for myself. In all other respects you can accept me or leave me alone as a loving father.

Your Daddy

P. S. In case you have any doubt about my ambiguous statements, with the little provisos, you shall always be welcome in sickness *or* health.

Daddy

When that difference eventually died down and he was faced with the choice of not seeing me, he had no difficulty in abandoning his insistence that all members of his family subscribe to his unswerving religious beliefs. Now he used my lack of religion in his ongoing war with Agnes, looking to her for sympathy at the same time as he was undermining her at every turn, and she grew increasingly hostile. News of local farms coming on the market and vacancies in nearby schools stopped. With my lack of belief, he saw that I could not take up such positions. Unorthodoxy of any kind would not be possible in the small parishes, where the teacher was expected to be one of the pillars of the Church, and he understood this instantly.

When I came back at Christmas with Monica and Margaret—Breedge had a daughter now, and she and Rosaleen remained in London—the initial gaiety could not conceal for long how poisoned the house was. Between my father's aggression and Agnes's more subtle control, Dympna had lapsed into a state of sullen submissiveness, broken by fits of high spirits so unnatural as to seem unreal. Frankie was very disturbed, openly confrontational, and everything was being done by my father—threats, scolding, abuse, sarcasm—to make the situation worse. Agnes was being forced to defend herself against my father with a passive aggression of her own, and was proving the stronger. When his more extreme threats were called, they emerged as bluff. She was also drawing in her own local family, who were more often about the house, but she was fiercer than ever in her defence of her husband against all outside criticism. I helped him much about the land that Christmas: and the great temperamental differences between us could be hidden in the work. For his part, he could not have been friendlier, in a bluff, jocose, forced fashion. Instead of trying to draw me back into his own life in the country he was now talking of selling the place and moving to Dublin. As he had always some plan or other—elsewhere for him was nearly always more attractive than where he was—I listened sympathetically, but in private dismissed it as impractical. Here he had a beautiful place. His wife was from here. Her own mother and family were close. She would hardly welcome the move to a Dublin neither of them knew. Usually, he turned against his own plans the moment they became feasible. This time I was wrong.

I was only a couple of weeks back in Dublin when I received this letter. The enclosure was a For Sale advertisement for a large, rundown property above a greengrocer's on the North Strand:

Grevisk
8/1/60

Dear Sean

    I meant to give you enclosed and ask you to look into the matter for me but I forgot.

    It is imperative that I get out of here and as soon as possible not in my interest as I have a way or means of getting out but in the interest of the family. Therefore, I request that without delay you take Monica, Margt., into your confidence, get a house or flat for us in Dublin to which we can move without delay. I am sick, sore, tired

*of hearing such as I fell out with this one, that one, the
latest being Tommy, need I say I had no dispute with
him. The sum total of it is I am an X Police Sergeant and
they are having their satisfaction.*

*Hope the blood is circulating briskly and keeping the
terrific cold out.*

*Love
Daddy*

As a sergeant, he was unnecessarily strict, many of his
exactions petty. An entry in his Garda notebook for the
"10th/16/1958," shortly before his retirement, reads: "While
driving my car across the bridge of Cootehall Pat Moore was
standing with his bicycle. He was talking to Mr. and Mrs.
McCabe. I blew the horn and he would not leave. I stopped and
blew the horn and he moved to his own side of the road."

Any of the other guards would have waved or stopped for a
chat or passed on. I'm sure they didn't move in the first place
because they didn't know why he was blowing. There was no danger to anybody. Another car would be heard coming a mile away.
If Pat Moore wanted to be as pedantic as the sergeant, all he had
to do was to turn his bicycle round in the direction of Boyle to be
on his correct side of the road. He moved simply because it was
easier and kept the peace. Now my father could blow at nobody.
He was no longer protected by his uniform, and stood as just
another man among men.

I knew him better by then than I knew any living person, and
yet I had never felt I understood him, so changeable was he, so
violent, so self-absorbed, so many-faced. If it is impossible to
know oneself, since we cannot see ourselves as we are seen, then it
may be almost as difficult to understand those close to us,
whether that closeness be of enmity or love or their fluctuating
tides. We may have an enormous store of experience and knowl-

edge, psychological and otherwise, but we cannot see fully because we are too close, still too involved. There was also something dark or forbidding in his personality that made people reluctant to speak about him, and he himself never offered any explanation for anything he ever did.

"Your father is an actor," I heard some people say over the years, and it had a ring of truth, without that truth becoming clear.

"You mean he doesn't know who he is and acts out his life in parts?"

"He's an actor." They would say nothing further. "Which of us knows who we are?"

I had lived some years apart from him, and had some distance now as well as knowledge. As I reread the letter stating his immediate need to move to Dublin, the truth I had glimpsed intuitively in the description of him as an actor began to grow clear. He was a man who acted out his life in parts and who lived his life, as far as it was possible, in roles, nearly all of which he had abused while remaining protected within the role. He had set out as a gifted, difficult only child, both over-protected and spoiled, while remaining exposed to his mother's violent corrections.

I suspect his happiest role was in the IRA, where his propensity for violence was tempered by cold calculation and a keen sense of self-preservation. From the beginning, he was and remained a devoted member of the Catholic Church. From the IRA he went straight into the first intake of recruits for the new Garda Force. Quickly promoted, he was the head of police in rural districts where he was the law, from his early twenties until practically the time of the last letter. Having secured the hand of my mother, the teacher with the salary, he was able to play the handsome, charming sergeant throughout the country for years to many girls and women, while remaining the sergeant who was dangerous to cross. His attention to duty and his keeping of records were such that on his retirement his career was described as "exemplary." While my mother remained his "loving wife Sue," as soon as I was born he became "Daddy." When she was dying, he chose to write to her instead of going to see her and was the "devout member of the Catholic Church," interceding for her through prayer and fasting and enrolling her in Novenas of Perpetual Adoration. As stern, authoritative Daddy, he criticized and reprimanded her while she was on her deathbed; but he was unwilling to visit or bring any kindness or comfort to the living person.

Now that he had lost the role of sergeant, all that remained was "Daddy." This remained his most permanent role, changing subtly with his declining powers and increasing dependence. With extraordinary assistance from Agnes, he never stopped trying to draw us back within the orbit of Daddy.

I had dismissed his idea of moving to Dublin when he brought it up. Now I saw how deadly earnest he was and how much of a piece with his general thinking and psychology it all was. Nothing was ever done without calculation—even his unpredictable violences never took place other than in an environment in which he was protected.

He would move to Dublin, away from where he was no longer protected by his position of sergeant, away from where he had accumulated enemies and much dislike. Once he acquired a Dublin property, we would all move in with him and pay him the rent we were now paying landlords. I began gradually to see how attractive it would be from his point of view. In this one move he'd discomfort and uproot his wife, rid himself of her relatives and the people he had antagonized as sergeant, and establish himself as Dublin Daddy. He might even rent other rooms in the house to lodgers, and, given his resentment of his wife, he might easily have plans for putting Agnes to work running a boarding house, as he once had us working the bog.

I went to Margaret and Monica, but not in the way he intended. Their reading of the letter was the same as mine. We agreed that I write a letter saying we would give him every possible help in finding a flat or house in Dublin but that we wouldn't leave our own rooms or lodgings to live with him. We thought it necessary to state this at the very outset, as we didn't want him uprooting himself for our sakes. He would be moving to Dublin in his own interests, not ours, and all three of us signed the letter.

He never answered the letter.

When Margaret and Monica visited him a short time afterwards, they found he had taken to his bed, and he refused to see them. Agnes was kindness itself, but his room remained closed to them for the weekend of their visit, and he never once appeared.

"Daddy takes these notions and then it's all forgotten about," Agnes told them cheerfully.

No sooner had he been rebuffed on one front than he was conducting war on another. Probably resenting the money he had to pay Rosaleen from the settlement of the accident with Lenihan's van, he demanded that she pay him a part of her salary every month. She had a room and board in the nurses' home, but what was left was little enough for any young woman's needs. He had done so much for her, for all of us, receiving scant gratitude, and now that he was retired and out on pension, with the additional responsibility of a wife, it was Rosaleen's duty to contribute to the upkeep and education of the remaining members of the family.

His letters grew so demanding that she contacted me. As she found the letters too distressing to read, it was agreed that she'd send them to me unopened. I'd write the reply, which she would then copy out in her hand and post. I'm afraid the task delighted me: the masks set me free. I pointed out the amount of money he had even at the time he went away to die, his present pension and property, and how, in addition, he had pocketed the money from the sale of our mother's Aughawillan farm. He brought us up in near starvation and violence and slavery, and we owed him nothing. I had an excess of material and was intent on expressing it in a light so clear that it would be difficult for him to dismiss or ignore, while at the same time retaining Rosaleen's reasonableness. The effect was instantaneous:

Grevisk
22 May '60

Dear Rosaleen,

    Oh! Dear! Such a letter.

    I think you misunderstand your mother, R.I.P., did not will or wish you any money when she died & for an obvious reason. With that I completely and emphatically close that.

    When you demanded your post office book (by your tone, general attitude etc. you insulted me and I was on the alert for a cause. I believe yet I found it). . . . If you or anyone else thinks money can buy me, well you have another guess coming. Both of you came, I should say all three came & went last year without question and went back without time for any of us including Margaret so if I expect little I shall not be disappointed.

    From Hell's Hole at Malin Head to a wee village called Tullaghan is over 100 miles. From Tory to St. Johnstons is 90. From Teelin to Barnes Gap must be 90. So?

    Mrs. Cannon was at the Pioneer dance,

Daddy

Nothing was faced or answered directly. The sudden obscure rhetoric at the end obviously covers his time as a sergeant in Donegal and is both a threat and a statement of his independence, if it makes any sense at all. There were many such letters, until

Agnes wrote to Rosaleen asking her to close the correspondence, as poor Daddy was close to breakdown. She also accused Rosaleen of being unduly influenced by me against her father. I answered this letter as well, which Rosaleen copied, and it closed the correspondence. Almost immediately it became the past.

At this time, Breedge had been staying in Grevisk for three months, to her father's increasing irritation. In the year 1960, events occurred with such rapidity that they seemed sometimes to overlap and merge. In a London bedsit, with a wife and baby and another on the way, Breedge's husband, Con O'Brien, was finding the reality of labouring on the buildings intolerable after his dreams of stardom. The shape this took was a determination to get out of England and go home. Breedge was almost as careful as her father with money and had saved enough for a deposit on a house. Con's plan was to buy a fish-and-chip van with the deposit and operate it out of his hometown, travelling to wherever there were crowds, football and hurling matches, race meetings, markets, shows, dances. With his training in the bakery, simple cooking posed no difficulty. They bought the van with the house deposit. Con was convinced he had a travelling goldmine on his hands. Breedge and his family peeled and sliced the potatoes while he and the van went from town to town. For its time the idea was good and someone with a business instinct could have made serious money and expanded. Con had no such instinct. Whenever he made a killing he celebrated. The small council house was already overcrowded and everybody was on edge. When Breedge wasn't peeling potatoes, she kept to the small room Con's family had given them, though they needed it for themselves. She seldom saw her husband, and when she did he was mostly tipsy. For his part, he was happy. When he wasn't on the road with the chipper he was running about with his old pals of the town. Then one night after a hurling match, when he had sold out everything in the chipper, he celebrated with friends. On the way home he fell asleep at the wheel. He was unhurt, but the chipper and the whole enterprise was a write-off. Breedge was distraught and turned to her father. He drove all the way to Kanturk and took her home. She left her daughter with her husband and parents-in-law.

While my father was fond of declaring that "my house is open to every member of my family without exception, whether they choose to include or exclude themselves," it was never to be taken at face value. On short visits, our presence in the house gave him back his role in an undemanding form and relieved his increasing boredom and sense of being hard done by, but this changed once any demands were made on him.

Breedge would have been a light burden. She adored him all her life and would have been happy to become a child of the house again while recovering from what she had been through. All she would have needed was her meals, and she would have done anything to please, helping in the house and even out in the fields. Though he had driven a long journey in answer to her call for help, he was soon using every psychological ploy to drive her away, writing complainingly to the rest of us: "It is easy to cause me pain. It would appear all is not well with Brigid. Why would she wish to stay here for three months? Owing to her condition [her pregnancy], I evaded the issue and shall give no answer to anyone but Con. I don't like it."

Whatever he wrote Con, or whatever methods he used to make Breedge's stay intolerable, he reported to me with satisfaction, "The house was thronged for Whit. Con came in a car with his mother. They took Brigid home Sunday!"

There was some discussion as to whether they would return to England, as Breedge wanted, or try to stay on in Kanturk, which was Con's wish. In a letter to Rosaleen, my father came down firmly on Con's side. Con, like himself, was head of the household and should be deferred to in all things:

Now for Brigid. I am very glad to have your assurance that she is happy. Do you think she should risk it by

showing a preference [for returning to London]? I think
she should carry out Con's wishes in the matter and,
apart altogether from the bad job I am continually being
reminded of doing for my family. I think it is Con should
make the decisions and I further think that Brigid's place
is helping him.

At this time, Frankie dislocated his elbow. I could not prevent my father from taking him to Michael Donoghue, the Cloone bonesetter. I warned Frankie about what had happened to Breedge's ankle and gave him money to come to me in Dublin where I would have him X-rayed if his father refused.

The very same week Margaret was diagnosed with TB in Dublin. The drugs that mastered the disease were by now more than a decade in use, but the stigma, like leprosy, was still in many minds. When I was growing up in the barracks I heard talk of a large family—Collins was their name—all of whom were exceptionally good-looking. One of them got TB, and when the five sisters, all beautiful, went to a dance, no man asked them to dance because word had gone round that the disease was in the house. Margaret was still lodging with Agnes's brother, and his wife became afraid that she would infect their two young children while waiting for a place to be found for her in hospital, and she went home to Grevisk:

Grevisk
(Saturday)

Dear Sean
I hate to bother you but it is in family interest so I
can only hope you appreciate & co-operate.
Had Frankie's arm X-rayed. Indeed, when you were
finished with the boy I had no alternative. On my return

*from the bonesetter last night I got an awful shock to
meet Mgt. As I understood she was going back to work
and so this letter is about her. Why won't she go into a
San. and get cured of her TB? It is all very well to say you
have no responsibility and I have no doubt you would
like to think it is so but if the bits I gather up are any
indication, you are influencing her and here I must ask
you to use that influence to have her got into a San. If it
doesn't happen shortly I know we are faced with a
nervous breakdown if not worse.*

*As I said Sean I had F. arm X-rayed. It showed up
nothing. I knew that, but it just left me poorer.*

*Try & use any influence you have with Mrgt. It is a
grave risk to Dymp. to have her here apart from the
seriousness to herself.*

Love
Daddy

P. S. If I am wrong forgive me I pray

I knew him well enough by now to understand the letter at a
glance. Dympna was the cover for the danger he felt himself to be
in and the stigma that might be attached to him and his house. I
contacted Maggie. She and Pat drove to Grevisk and took Margaret to Ballinamore. She remained happily in the shop facing the
closed railway line and station until a place became available for
her treatment in Blanchardstown Hospital. While she waited
there, my father never once visited, though Ballinamore was less
than an hour away. She spent six months in Blanchardstown and
left completely cured. Neither did he ever visit her in the months
she was in the hospital.

While she was there, the conflict between him and my brother was coming to a head. When I went in to teach one morning, I found Frankie standing among the children playing on the concrete yard. He had hitchhiked to Dublin during the night and early morning and hadn't been able to find my address. I introduced him in the teachers' room, and he was welcomed and given tea and sandwiches. I showed him how to get to my digs, and by the time I came from school he had made friends with my landlady and was rested.

My father had attacked him and he had fought back. In the struggle, he knocked my father to the floor and was holding him by the arms while Agnes shouted and beat him about the head with a brush. He was hardly fazed at all by what had happened, and laughed uproariously as he imitated Agnes's efforts with the brush and our father's groans and shouts; it was the stuff of domestic farce. Only later, when my father started making dark hints and threats, did he grow afraid.

He stayed with me two days, and on Friday evening I took him home. He was sixteen and would be seventeen in November, and he was almost fully grown. What was agreed between us was that he'd give home and school another try. He was able to absorb information far more quickly than I could at his age. I knew he'd have no difficulty with exams and there wasn't much more than a year to go to his Leaving. "I've been thinking of going to England," he said.

"You can still go to England and you're intelligent enough to know that you'd be better off there with the Leaving. Why don't we see if you can get it first? It's not all that far to go now," I said, though I knew that a year and a few months must have seemed an age to him.

My father was full of the drama of it all when I took him home. Agnes was hostile. "Frankie let us all down," she said. "He needs encouragement and praise not cutting down to size," I argued, but I might as well have been speaking a foreign tongue. My father walked from the room. I had hoped without much hope that he would settle and in some way stagger to the end of his schooling. A few weeks later a surprising offer arrived. My father wanted my help to beat up my brother:

Grevisk
16th

Dear Sean

The "Traveller" continued going to school until Friday. On return he informed everyone he was not going to school any more. Questions elicited the fact he did not attend school until 11 a.m. owing to a "toothache." He was discovered by Brother Placid who administered eight slaps. The suspicions are he gave old guff to Brother Placid.

I know a way with that gentleman but at least I'd have to have your approval as I would not have the approval of any of the girls. Indeed it might be well if you were present as there is always a danger of collapse owing to age and weight. It may be as well to allow him to hang about for a year or so. Indeed he might go off of his own accord and attend school, but I cannot see it happen.

There is a danger of serious nervous breakdown in my case as I have all the time being worrying. I considered entering a mental hospital and it might be the best place in all my circumstances.

Love
Daddy

I went immediately. There was a horrible atmosphere in the house. Dympna especially had shrivelled into an unhappy shell of herself. Everybody except my father appeared afraid to stir, and he moved with a ponderous, self-enclosed deliberateness. "Surely you realize it's a serious offence to beat up somebody?" I said to him when we were alone. "You mean I haven't the right to defend myself?" he countered. The beating up that both of us would have administered would also have been presented as self-defence, with me coming to his aid. I saw that to express what I felt would be mere wasted self-expression. "We have to get him to go back to school," I said. "You're a better man than me if you can, or he'll go until your back is turned, and then this old fool will have to carry the can. Of course I don't count. I don't count. I don't count at all."

"He needs encouragement," I said stubbornly.

I went to the monastery and asked for Brother Placid. The mute girl was as beautiful as I remembered her, and she struck the flat brass gong on the wall a single blow. After a long time, Placid came slowly down the wide stairs, polishing his spectacles with a white handkerchief as he came. For a moment, it was as if I had never been away.

His clear features expressed surprise and then pleasure when he saw me. We liked one another. In the big dining room we sat and talked. He told me that he had been forced to punish Frankie a number of times. The boy had missed days without explanation but, more disturbingly, he had become a disruptive force within the school, influencing younger and weaker boys. He was smoking and drinking. Naturally, Frankie had kept all this from me. "The pity is that he has loads of ability, but there's something wrong or missing," Placid said.

"Things are not great at home."

"How is the good sergeant?" he asked, his eyes twinkling behind the shining spectacles.

"He is just the same. He'll not change."

Before I left it was agreed that if Frankie returned to school he could do so with a clear slate, but this time he would have to keep it clean.

I told Frankie all that I had learned. He was both sheepish and defiant. "All I care about is what you do from here on in," I told him sharply. He agreed to return to school the next day, but with a distinct lack of enthusiasm. When I told my father of the arrangement, he called me a fool: the boy would come to nothing and I was wasting the school's time and my own time, and when I came around again I would find him in the mental hospital.

Not much time was won by my intervention. He and his father remained at war within the house; at school he was again in trouble, skirting expulsion. One morning he set out for school and again hitched all the way to Dublin. It was evening by the time he reached the city, and he went straight to where Monica and Margaret lived. He had already written to Rosaleen and was determined to go to London. The girls contacted me. I offered to take a flat where the two of us could live and to send him to school in Dublin: "It's going to be no holiday. If I find that you are not studying you'll be out on your ear before you know," I warned him. He looked at me for a moment as if considering the offer seriously, and then broke down in tears. "I'm sick of school and studying. I can't bear it any more. I'm going to go to London." I saw he was too disturbed and restless to settle down under my, or anyone else's, tutelage. We rang Rosaleen. She had received his letter and had room for him and would meet him off the early morning train at Euston. Margaret, Monica and I took him out to the boat at Dún Laoghaire the next evening. The girls were in tears when we bought his ticket. I talked my way on to the boat and saw the purser, a middle-aged, kindly man, and explained how he'd never been away from home before. The purser could not have been more helpful, and gave him a small room beside his office and promised to see that he got on the London train when the boat reached Holyhead. Rosaleen met him at Euston. Within a week he found work in a big office block in the city.

He had the height and strength of a man, great mental quickness, a natural sunny amiability, and was charming when he wanted to be; but he was also insecure and angry. He had received little praise or nurture, and in many ways he was still a child:

> 6 King Edward Rd.
> Leyton
> London E.10

Dear Sean

You must be wondering what the devil has become of this nit-wit of a brother that he did not write, but knowing my irregular habits I am sure you will understand. I was thinking of getting a job in the evenings but have decided against it having worked out that I can live economically on my earnings—with £19.18s10d net wages per month x £2 for my keep & £2.2.0 for bus fares & dinners, I will have £4.16s10d for clothes & cheap entertainment—how boring! I am beginning to make arrangements for booking up for night school in Sept. & I intend to take out my GCE which is equivalent to the Leaving Cert. I was glad to find out that I could take Irish as a subject as it would be a great help to me if I decided to go home to live, I mean afterwards. I am quite happy at my work although the first week nearly drove me crackers as I was sorting out receipts which had not been sorted for several months. But now having got them in order I will only have to do a few hours of it once a fortnight. I got on to more interesting work last week, paying dividends to stockholders or I should say drawing up lists of stockholders & the amounts of stock. I found it very amusing as I came across the most peculiar names. I am sure my co-workers thought I was a little bit gone from the silent mirth which my countenance betrayed. After several fruitless attempts at pronouncing Mr. McGahern

*they decided to call me "Mac" by which I am known
even to the manager now. It is a huge block of offices & I
am the only Irish person except for one or two porters.
They are very nice people & never refer to my nationality
or even call me "Paddy." One "smart alec" thought he
would have a joke at my expense by calling me Paddy on
the second day at lunch, but was almost exterminated by
the looks of disgust he got from the others. I had a
wonderful joy ride today down from Aldgate to
Kingsway to deliver some kind of papers for checking or
something. Of course I did not rush myself in getting
back & even helped myself to a cup of coffee in
preparation for the return journey . . . I can get a good
dinner & sweet in the canteen for 1s&3d which is very
reasonable. I can't think of anything more to write for
the present & could you blame me because with neither
law or order on this letter plus the awful spelling I cannot
bear to read over it to see what I have left out. Rosaleen
will be writing soon. I will be looking forward to seeing
you in July & if you have time in the meantime you can
drop me a line. I nearly forgot to thank you for your
letter & also I wish to thank you for the money you gave
me. After you left the room in which you left me on the
boat I just walked slap-bang into Martin Carthy & a
nephew of his wife who was the same age as myself so I
had company the whole way to Euston. Hoping to hear
from you if you have time to write.*

*With best wishes
Frankie*

Given his inner restlessness, it was too much to expect his life
to go as smoothly as the letter indicates, and he spent a few rocky
years around London before he went back to night school. His

father wasn't either hopeful or encouraging: "I heard Francis was coming on holidays about Christmas, that he was returning to school to get his 'Leaving' all of which I am sceptical. He is 18 and I daresay due for N.S. now. I cannot see him making a success of anything poor lad. I wish I was wrong and I hope I am."

He was wrong. Frankie went to night school, got his GCE, and then easily passed the exams to get a degree in accountancy. He had a natural talent for mathematics and went on to gain difficult higher qualifications. From Accounts he changed to Management. He ran a number of factories and small businesses around London before rising to become Financial Controller of BBC Radio.

Dympna was miserable after Frankie left. She was the most like her father in appearance, and seemed to grate on him more than the rest of us. Her dogged passivity made it difficult for him to attack her physically now that he was, to some extent, being checked and watched, but he did all he could to unnerve her. Without much hope, she did the Civil Service exam a year early, hoping to get away. Her father's reaction was predictable: "Dympna starts her exam Tuesday in Dublin. She may try to get away with Rosaleen [to London]. To my grief I know the 'get up' [Dympna] has not the atmosphere of work an exam entails etc. etc."

She did not get a high position in the exam, but that year, luckily, it was sufficient, and she left for Dublin without waiting to sit for her Leaving. She wasn't happy in the Civil Service and, like Frankie, went back to night school, eventually winning a place at the University of Reading, where she got a good degree, and began teaching near where Breedge and Rosaleen lived and worked in London.

Now that we were gone and he had finally got rid of us all, our father renewed with increased vigour the campaign to draw all of us around him again. This did not extend to going towards us in any way. The only wedding he attended was Monica's, as she was married from Agnes's brother's house, and since Agnes was determined to attend he had little choice. His reluctance was expressed through a comical sense of the great burden and responsibility he was being forced to bear. Breedge and Con eventually returned to London to start again at rock bottom—with two daughters now, and the house deposit gone. Rosaleen was a great help to them, as she had been to Frankie. She too was getting married. Her father refused her invitation as he had refused Breedge's. Every one of us attended Rosaleen's wedding, and I acted in my father's place. There was great gaiety and lightness all through the day of celebration, but I felt that Rosaleen was more than a little disappointed, in spite of all her reservations about him, that he had made not the slightest effort to be present.

My life in the Dublin of the time would not have been much different to the lives of many young men. We worked. We went to dancehalls and cinemas and theatres; the big hurling and football matches in Croke Park, race meetings in the Phoenix Park or Baldoyle or Leopardstown; we met and talked and drank and argued in bars. In hot summers we swam in the seas around Dublin or went on excursions into the Dublin Mountains. The girls we picked up in dancehalls we courted in doorways and back alleys, and on dates took them to cinemas or out to places like Howth by the sea. Oysters were cheap then, as were the plates of fresh prawns sprinkled with parsley. They were served in small bars by the sea, with plates of buttered brown bread and slices of lemon and pints of stout. The girls didn't drink stout or beer; the more adventurous had wine or gins-and-tonics and even brandies; most of them didn't drink alcohol.

Much has been written about the collusion of Church and State to bring about an Irish society that was childish, repressive and sectarian, and this narrative hardly suggests otherwise. People, especially young people, will find ways around a foolish system, and difficulty can often serve to sharpen desire, but many who could not were damaged or were driven into damaged lives.

In the world of the young who were interested in reading and writing and ideas, the strictures of both Church and State were secretly laughed at. I still had the dream that I would write. This replaced the call to God, and it was as untempered as that first call by experience of the world. No doubt, many young men and women had that same dream, and none of us knew or cared that there was so little room. I read now out of curiosity as well as pleasure. I could pick and choose, and the pleasure was changing. The story was still important, but I had read so many stories that I knew now that all true stories are essentially the same story in the same way as they are different: they reflect the laws of life in both its sameness and its endless variations. I now searched out those books that acted like mirrors. What they reflected was dangerously close to my own life and the society that brought me up, as well as asserting their own differences and uniqueness.

There were many good secondhand bookshops, especially along the quays. One book barrow on a corner of Henry Street was extraordinary. Most of the books the barrow carried would now be described as modern classics. How the unusual Mr. Kelly acquired them we never asked. We assumed he stole them. Books were discussed and argued about around the barrow; intellectual women could be met there, and there was no man more alert to the sexual possibilities of these encounters than Mr. Kelly. Though he had a wife and a large family in the suburbs, was a devout Catholic, a Republican and a racist, he observed no contradiction once his self-interest or pleasure came into play. At weekends, dressed as an officer of the Republican Army, complete with leggings and a cocked hat, he collected money in the bars for the youth wing of *Oglaigh na hEireann*. Eventually, he was seized by the IRA, stripped naked, tarred and feathered and tied to a tractor in a field in the outer South Dublin suburbs. The incident was in all the newspapers. When he was released from hospital and was back at his barrow on Henry Street, when asked if anybody had been arrested or if a prosecution was imminent, he replied stiffly,

"The matter is being handled internally." He considered it a sign of the woeful degeneracy of his captors that they used car oil instead of real tar as a foundation for the feathering.

In more reliable surroundings, it was easy to get a desk in the National Library. The staff were kind and brought rare books on request. There were inexpensive seats at the back of the Gate Theatre and there were many pocket theatres, often in Georgian basements. Out in Dún Laoghaire there was the Gas Company Theatre where we had to walk through the sentinels of gas cookers to get to see Pirandello or Chekhov or Lorca or Tennessee Williams. The city was full of cinemas. I remember seeing *Julius Caesar* with Gielgud and Brando playing to full houses in the Metropole. At weekends, cinema tickets were sold on the black market. One black marketeer, a pretty girl I knew, showed me a fistful of unsold tickets one wet Sunday night and said, "If I don't get rid of these soon—and at bloody cost at that—I'll have to let down me drawers before the night is out." And there was the tiny Astor on the quays where I first saw *Casque d'Or, Rules of the Game,* and *Children of Paradise.* The pleasure that found its first expression in the books of Moroney's library was becoming wider and more various even as it deepened.

The school I was teaching in was well run. The teachers got on well with one another, and most of the children came from homes where learning was valued. Teaching is always hard work, to bend young minds from their animal instincts and interest them in combinations of words and numbers and histories; but it has its pleasures—seeing the work take root and grow, encouraging the weaker children so that they grow in trust and confidence, seeing them all emerge as individuals. I liked the eight-year-old boys I taught, and I believe most of them grew to trust and like me. Once the children ran free from the school at two fifteen in the afternoon, the rest of the day was my own.

For the first two years, I attended evening classes at University College, and the degree added a small increment to my salary.

Some of the teachers who attended these classes with me went on to further studies and different careers, but I saw that the university could not give me what I wanted. Neither could the bohemian bars around Grafton Street. The violence and megalomania and darkness of these bars were as familiar to me as the air around my father. A single visit to McDaid's was enough to cure me of any desire for literary company for a month. Like all closed, self-protective societies, they believed that everything of importance took place within their circle, while all of them were constantly looking outwards without seeing in this any contradiction; but by this time, I also had good friends within the city, individuals like myself. We were always glad to see one another and to meet, and were untroubled when time went by without a meeting.

Among those friends was a family of brothers, the Swifts. All but one of the seven brothers worked together in an advertising display business they owned. I first met the youngest of the Swifts, Tony, who had attended the College of Art and was a talented painter, in a bar of a dancehall, and through him came to know the others. Another brother, Patrick Swift, was by then an established painter in London. An older brother, Jimmy Swift, was quietly brilliant and deeply read. All the seven brothers had enormous charm. Sometimes I would call at their factory near Connolly Station as it was closing, and if they were free we'd go for a drink together.

All this time I was writing. Nearly everything I wrote was discarded, but eventually enough work survived to be able to be shaped into a first novel. I showed it to Jimmy Swift. He liked it enough to send to his brother Patrick in London, who was editing with David Wright a magazine devoted to painting and writing called X. David Wright liked the prose and published extracts in the spring of 1960 that attracted the attention of a number of publishers. Again, I believe I had extraordinary luck. Without knowing hardly anything of the business or politics of literature,

I was published almost immediately when I was still young, and without encountering the usual barriers of rejection.

Among the publishers who had contacted me was Faber and Faber. By this time, I saw that the novel was too flawed and refused to show it to them, but told them I'd be glad to write a second novel. On the strength of a first chapter, Faber gave me a contract to write *The Barracks*, and while it was still in manuscript they persuaded me to enter it for an important prize that I felt I had no hope of winning. I entered and won. With that, the long secret life of reading and writing came to an end. The teachers in the school were glad, though some looked at me and my teaching a little suspiciously, as if I was no longer one of them; but this did not last long in the face of the daily life and grind of teaching. My photograph was in most of the newspapers, and there were a few articles. Maggie wrote how delighted she and Jimmy and Pat were and how everybody was asking to see the newspapers and the photos. My father's reaction was not as uncomplicated:

All last week you were the topic in Cootehall but I think they would prefer if you were born in the parish or shown to have some connection with it. Mrs. Henry saw your photo in the Irish Press *and brought it to Jim in bed. She hid the name. It was a very bad photo. Jim is as excited as if he got a prize. I had a few congratulations and put it off as an everyday occurrence. Brother Placid will no doubt be looking for some cheap publicity.*

I feel I am getting relapsed in the cold. I hope not. All I wish to say, Sean, is if it was adversity I'd be with you just the same. I'm glad it is other.

Love
Daddy

The cut at Brother Placid went back to the time I won the scholarships and Placid put my photo in the local newspapers as an advertisement for the school. He disliked Placid and saw it as a form of gloating and self-congratulation.

I sent my father a prepublication copy of *The Barracks*. I had no expectation that he would read or like it, but as I intended sending copies to Maggie and Pat and Jimmy I didn't want him feeling excluded or that I had anything to hide. The setting and the rituals of barrack life are replicated in the novel, but the characters are all imagined. The sergeant in the novel bears hardly any resemblance to my father. He is relatively uncomplicated and far more attractive. The novel begins and ends with the ceremony of the children lighting the lamps. He seems to have read the first page: "Dear Sean, Thanks for book received. An old etc. garda sergeant sits here in the dark hoping that the lamp will show light or at least flicker. Daddy." He never spoke about it again. The novel was published in 1963 and was widely praised. In his own newspaper, the *Irish Independent*, it was reviewed glowingly by John D. Sheridan, whose humorous articles were particular favourites of my father. When he first discovered I was trying to write, in his fondness for doling out advice he used to recommend that I copy John D. Sheridan. After his review, "Classical Tragedy in the Barracks," John D. Sheridan's name was never mentioned in the house again.

Against this small but general tide of approval, the library committee ordered that the novel be removed from the shelves of the Ballinamore Public Library. Directly and indirectly the Church controlled the libraries through these committees in much the same way as they controlled the schools. The spirited county librarian, Vera McCarthy, fought those removals, and when she was forced to take the books from the shelves placed them beneath the counter and loaned them to anybody who asked. Maggie, it seemed, was equally unafraid. She was furious when the novel was removed. A young priest who was a customer in her shop was told to take his custom elsewhere until *The Barracks* was put back on the shelves.

Maggie fell ill with the same cancer that killed my mother and was treated in St. Luke's in Dublin. I was very fond of Maggie and went in to see her often. My father retained all his old resentment of her, and on hearing that she was terminally ill dressed up in his most sombre clothes to go all the way to Dublin to stand at the foot of her hospital bed to say, "Margaret, not my will but thine be done." He had left by the time I came in to see her. I found her distraught. I had to wait several minutes for her to grow calm enough to tell me what had occurred.

"Your father was up," she said. "He stood at the foot of the bed like a priest or an undertaker and said, 'Margaret, not my will but thine be done.' I must have told him to buzz off or something like that, God forgive me, and he turned on his heel and left."

I had to assure her against everything I knew that she wasn't going to die, and I did not leave her till she was calm and able to laugh a little. We began to mimic him as we often did together. "God, O God, O God, what did I do to deserve being born into such a crowd." In her last years the life around her had begun to acquire an incredible sweetness. The last thing she needed to be told was, "Margaret, not my will but thine be done." He who would not go to see his own wife when she was dying or attend his children's weddings or visit my sister Margaret in the long months she spent in Blanchardstown could now dress up and travel all the way to Dublin to deliver himself of this poison.

I was so angry that I went directly to him and told him in rough language what I thought. I was wasting breath. He saw it as another example of ingratitude and lack of respect and that I'd always side with my mother's relatives against him.

She did not live long after being discharged from hospital, and died above the shop. When news of her death came, I hired a car and drove with Margaret and Dympna to Ballinamore. All that concerned my father while the body was being removed from the house to the church was that I'd be seen to go back with him to Grevisk instead of remaining in the town with my mother's relatives. This pressure was brought to bear through my sisters and stepmother. I would have preferred to stay in the town, but I didn't greatly care, and I went back to please my sisters.

I was still angry about his visit to Maggie in the hospital and was coldly polite when we met at Maggie's house and around the ceremonies in the church. As soon as we were back in the Grevisk house, he began a violent tirade, attacking me, attacking Maggie, attacking us all. He was the victim. I listened and watched the violence once again feed on its own flames, grow more wounding and hurtful, but I was inured to it by now or thought I was, and soon I had enough. "Shut up," I told him harshly.

"Are you talking to a dog, sir?"

"No," I said, but I was unyielding.

Agnes went to comfort him and was brushed aside as he went to his room. As soon as he was gone, she started to complain: that I should know better, Daddy was like that and meant no harm, it would all pass as if it had never happened, and don't you think for one minute that you can change Daddy at this stage. I hope I stayed silent.

One trait she and my father did share was that neither could accept a compliment. Agnes was a consummate flatterer, but even when it was genuine she would turn a compliment aside dismissively or retaliate with further compliments until they lay strewn about like wilted flowers or devalued currencies. They also shared a certain darkness. Once I heard Agnes remark casually as she smoked a cigarette, "I don't think you'd be able to stand people if you didn't know they have to die."

Some contrary passion possessed me that evening. I began to flatter her coldly and refused to be thwarted by her retaliation until she was driven to join my father. "We better wash up," my sister Margaret said as soon as she was gone. In the morning my father was in great form, charming everybody around him. The previous evening had ceased to exist.

In the years that followed, my reputation drew people to the house—journalists, the curious, others—even writers. They were not welcomed:

Grevisk

Dear Sean
A Mr. Kiley [the distinguished writer and critic, Benedict Kiely] blew in one day last week. I think he was on the razzle. Should you see him tell him I heard he was a decent fellow and that I'll attend his funeral if I hear of it.

Regards,
Daddy

Kiely could be loquacious. Whatever he said must have rankled. From the little I could glean, it seems he was threatened with whatever tool my father was using around the house when he called—a scythe, a spade—if he didn't desist and leave.

A race memory of the function of the old Gaelic poets was proving to be alive and active. A butcher from Drumshambo arrived at the house in bad need of my services. There were people who were making his life a misery in the town. If I'd go to live with him for a few months he'd pay me handsomely and give me the low-down on his tormentors. I would then use this information to put them in a novel so that they'd never be able to show their face in public again. He wanted my father, who didn't find any of this funny, to drive with him there and then to Dublin to put his case to me. My father had great difficulty in getting rid of him. He couldn't threaten the butcher with a scythe or spade.

A similar visitor came by soon after the publication of *The Dark*. As well as being banned and sacked at this stage, I must have acquired some underground reputation as a poet of domestic violence. This subject may have been too close to home. My father's tone is uncharacteristically circumlocutive:

> *Grevisk,*
> *Boyle,*
> *Roscommon,*
> *Ireland*

Dear Sean

> *I am often reminded (unfortunately) when people are not courteous to me that I am at fault or that perhaps their idea of courtesy isn't mine. Indeed we have such a variety of visitors from time to time it would be foolish of either Agnes or I to worry whether or what they thought.*

> *On my last visit to Pat his first question was did you meet Paddy Heslin. I told him no so he said he's gone over looking. When I arrived Agnes had a laughing story of gross insult for me. I laughed too and said that is not Paddy's usual form so he must [be] under a terrible strain.*

> *To cut it short he returned about 8 p.m. most excited & insulting. He wanted you in the worst way possible. If I put it to him we'd fly out & take you back to write a story, a book, what have you?*

> *It appears a sister of his in Donegal has a politician for a husband who has mistresses and one "tidy." The sister is the mother of eight, got abused, assaulted etc. and you should write about it. In any case I gave him all classes of excuses & finally I got rid of him telling him I'll write. Recently I saw Montague, Plunket etc. in a series on T. E. Hope not you because he'd be sure you were in*

*Dublin. He claims relationship to McManus. So much for
courtesy!*

   *Brigid tore the ligaments of her leg and is in
plaster & walks with a stick or crutch.*

   *Of course Agnes sends her regards. She went visiting
this p.m. to her Auntie (Molloy) as Uncle Pat had a turn.
By the same token I had one last night. I have in mind to
book a plot in Ardcarne [the local graveyard]. The family
can decide what's best in due course.*

   *Poor Shep gets more hungry each day passes but the
cats appear to [be] contemplating perpetuating the
species as I counted five or six cats about lately.*

*Love & regards
Daddy*

In Dublin in the winter of 1963–64 I wrote *The Dark,* too
quickly. I also won the Macauley, a prize of £1000, which stipu-
lated that the winner travel abroad for a year. It was a large award
for the time, as £1000 could purchase a small house in Dublin. In
the summer I met the Finnish theatre director Annikki Laaksi in
Paris. That October I was given a year's leave of absence without
pay by the school to avail of the Macauley. I went to Helsinki and
later in the year married Annikki Laaksi. Finland was not a country I felt I could ever live in, and after Christmas we moved to
London and then to Spain, where we had been given the loan of a
house on the Almeria coast.

While we were there *The Dark* was published in London in
May of 1965 but seized by the Customs and banned in Ireland.
This gave rise to violent controversy, and I was glad to be in Spain
and out of the storm. In Dublin, we had looked on the Censorship
Board as a joke. Most banned books weren't worth reading and
those that were could easily be come by. I somehow never thought
that it could have anything to do with me or my life. Now that I

was in the middle of it I found it childish and unpleasant, and I was a little ashamed that our own independent country was making a fool of itself yet again. I wondered privately if the novel had been written less quickly and with more care that they might not have noticed. I refused to take part in any protest on the grounds that it would do the whole sorry business too much honour. Back in London I wrote to the school stating my intention to return at the end of the year's leave of absence. The headmaster replied that there would be difficulty if I tried to return to the school. He advised me to obtain a position in London, and would be only too happy to write references. While I wanted no part of the censorship row, I was determined, as the school had been my work and livelihood for many years, not to go quietly. In awkward situations in Ireland, great pressure is brought to bear to do the so-called decent thing and go quietly away. I was not prepared to go quietly.

I crossed to Dublin and turned up at the school on the day I was due to return. I informed nobody and there were no journalists at the school. All the staff were on edge but everybody welcomed me back with great friendliness. When the bell rang for classes, a deeply embarrassed Mr. Kelleher, the headmaster, read out a legal letter from the manager saying I was barred from entering the classroom. He read this out in the corridor with his back to my old classroom door. Father Carton, the parish priest of Clontarf and the school manager, had gone on holiday to avoid the unpleasantness. I spent the rest of the day in the school. Now that our ordeal was over, the headmaster did his best to make me comfortable. He gave me a newspaper to read. "Hardly a day goes by but there's something about you in the paper, *A Mhaistir,*" he said pityingly. I drank endless cups of tea. I had a pleasant lunch with all my old colleagues, and at 2:15 we all left together as if it had been just another school day.

I still had the school manager to see when he returned from his holidays. Father Carton saw me reluctantly. In a roundabout way he told me that he wasn't to blame, as the order for my dismissal had come from the Archbishop. "You have gone and ruined your life," the old priest told me. "And you have made my life a misery as well. I can't put my head out the door these days but I'm beset by bowsies of journalists." When pressed by the Teachers' Union for a reason for my dismissal, he replied in writing: "Mr. McGahern is well aware of the reason for his dismissal."

I met the full board of the national Irish Teachers' Union in the late middle of an afternoon. They were careful and hostile. Some of the men had taken whiskey to brace themselves for the meeting. Word had leaked out through the newspapers that I had married a Finnish woman in a register office. The General Secretary, another Kelleher, who had also braced himself with whiskey, allowed his irritation with me to overcome his caution. "If it was just the auld book, maybe—maybe—we might have been able to do something for you, but with marrying this foreign woman you have turned yourself into a hopeless case entirely," he said. "And what anyhow entered your head to go and marry this foreign woman when there are hundreds of thousands of Irish girls going around with their tongues out for a husband?" he added memorably, especially since not many of them had been pointed in my direction.

My father was writing to me all the time. He never ceased. I went to Grevisk to see him and Agnes. Now that I had lost my job he was on my side and wanted to attack people on my behalf. With allies like my father, I would have no need of enemies.

There were letters for and against me in the newspapers, debates on television and radio, and I was glad to get back to London. The protest against my dismissal that mattered most to me came from the parents of children I had taught. Outside of that I didn't greatly care. In the Dáil, the Minister of Education was asked by the Leader of the Labour Party, Brendan Corish, about what had become known as the "McGahern Case." How is it, the question ran, that while the State pays for the training of teachers, their salaries and the running of the schools, it has no say when it comes either to the hiring or firing of teachers, irrespective of their rights as citizens; and could he give a satisfactory reason to the House for Mr. McGahern's recent dismissal. The question was crafted carefully. While it was a statutory offence to sell a banned book, it was not an offence to have written that book. "When the Church decides on a course of action, it generally has a good reason for that action," the Minister replied. It turned out that my case was far from unique. Following a BBC television programme, I received letters from men who, like me, had been trained in St. Patrick's but were now teaching in Birmingham and Glasgow and Newcastle. According to their letters, they had been sacked because they had run foul of a bishop or a priest, or had infringed some article of Catholic dogma and had no recourse but to disappear silently into Britain, a later version of *Ni beidh sibh arais*.

The following summer I returned with Annikki on a visit. She took instantly against the country, seeing it as paternalistic, duplicitous, priest-ridden, and she was particularly incensed by the position of women. I knew this not to be the whole truth, but also saw that there was no way she would have agreed to live in Ireland had I been able to keep my job. In that way, my sacking became matterless. She also disliked my father and refused to stay more than one night in the house. He disliked her too, but once he saw that she wasn't in the least afraid of him grew intrigued by her foreignness and beauty. By then it was too late.

In a letter to us both, this surprising reflection on roses must have been intended for her eyes: "I gave a doz. rose bushes to someone as a present once upon a time. I love roses. They so very well represent life. The thorns are there to prick but still the beautiful bloom comes again and again—if you have patience." In all my time with him I had never noticed this love of roses and thought the passage hilarious: "They so very well represent life! . . . *if* you have patience."

In London we stayed in the big house Breedge and Rosaleen shared with their husbands and daughters while searching for our own place. Our early situations were reversed; I was now turning to them for help. I got work as a supply teacher without difficulty. Often Rosaleen and I had breakfast together. She would be coming in off night duty. I would be going out to the schools. "They were dying off like flies last night," she said one morning of the work in the emergency theatre she ran. Whenever the operating theatres were quiet, she read, but the nights went by more quickly when they were busy. Rosaleen had a sharp, comic talent for description, and we were both very fond of one another, and often left those breakfasts reluctantly, I to catch the bus to school, she to bed. Annikki liked my sisters and was happy in the house, as long as we weren't going to be there for ever. At weekends we'd often all go for drinks to the Three Blackbirds together.

After a month, we found a flat to rent in Notting Hill, and later moved to an apartment overlooking Victoria Park in Bethnal Green. During those years we spent in London, my sisters, my brother and I met regularly, visiting each other, and sometimes we met to shop in markets or for casual drinks in bars. While I went in and out of school Annikki was translating Ostrovsky's plays. She had lived and worked in Russia and spoke the language fluently. At weekends we were often invited to dinners or parties in London and Oxford and the English countryside. Often there were people from the theatre at these gatherings as well as writers and journalists, editors and academics, and while she was sought out and admired, she was never happy. Though she could speak a number of languages and her English was now fluent, she felt she could never belong in England. In a different way I felt the same, but didn't care enough whether I belonged or not for it to make any difference. When I would express regret at not knowing other languages, she would say, "What do we do but learn to express less well in another language what we can already say far better in our own." In the summer she returned to Helsinki to work for Finnish Radio and I remained in London, and this became a pattern. While she was there she received an offer to work in television over the following summer. That winter we translated together a Finnish novel, *The Manilla Rope* by Veijo Meri, for my American publisher, Knopf. She translated the original text into rough English, which I then turned into Irish/English speech. The final version we worked out together, checking the translation against the original Finnish.

She continued to translate from the Russian. I went in and out of school. In the evenings I wrote sentences, but they never seemed to grow into work or anything interesting. I suspected I had been exhausted by those Dublin years of work, and I was content to wait until the need to write came back; but even in this silence I had no doubt that I was still serving the idea that had first come to me in the tarred boat hidden in reeds under the dark woods of Oakport. For now, we had the normal life of a young couple in London. We went to cinemas and theatres and galleries, to restaurants and bars and the great London parks.

In the early summer Annikki went back to Helsinki to work in television, and I joined her when the schools closed. I enjoyed the beauty of the seas around the city and the long, white nights, meeting the friends we used to see when we were first together here; but before I left I was even more certain than before that I could never live in Finland. She was earning a good deal of money working in television and was happy. Between us there was a deep unease that neither of us was willing to articulate: in Finland she was famous and I was her appendage; in London, in a much lesser way, the situation was reversed. This weighed on her more heavily. By the time she returned from Helsinki I was beginning to write again and was immersed in the new work. There was now a further complication: she was offered permanent work in television as well as the possibility of doing freelance theatre productions of her own, something she had always wanted. She would earn far more than the two of us were earning in London, and she wanted me to return with her to Helsinki. We would get a comfortable apartment overlooking the sea in the middle of the city, and I would be able to write without having to go to work.

This, I told her, I could not do, but if she wanted the job badly enough she should take it and we'd see if there was any way we could manage. She said that the marriage was under enough strain as it was and wouldn't survive. She turned the television offer down, but the unhappiness continued to grow all through that London winter. In the early summer, we split up unhappily. Those who believe the availability of divorce makes it too easy to end marriages have no understanding of divorce. A divorce is like a death, but instead of that inevitable end, the person that we have loved stands there as a living reproach of deep failure. I told Annikki to take what she wanted from the apartment, but she took little, and I gave away most of what remained. As the apartment emptied, those hours in the poor rose garden when the furniture was taken from the rooms in Aughawillan and stacked with the brown hens in the crates of the red lorry while my mother was dying came back with such vividness that I started to shiver in the summer's heat.

My days as a supply teacher in London had also come to an end. I was given a research fellowship at Reading University that entailed a little teaching but in fact was designed to allow me to write. "What will I teach?" I asked deferentially after I'd been given the job. "Teach them anything you like, my dear," the brilliant Donald Gordon, the Professor of English, told me gaily as he poured us both another gin-and-tonic. "I've been teaching them for the last twenty-eight years, and they have never understood one word *I* have taught them; and you can take my word, my dear, that they will not understand one word *you* say to them either: so teach them anything you like, my dear."

I had met Madeline Green, and we began to live together. The following spring I was offered a visiting professorship in America, and we travelled there together. When we came back, we lived in Paris, where she had a small apartment. A first book of stories, *Nightlines,* was published. It was more than well received and I was awarded a substantial prize. For the first time in years I had some money. One evening in Paris I asked Madeline if she would be interested in living in Ireland for a year: if she didn't like it we could leave at any time. Through a friend we found a house to rent by the sea near Clifden. We made friends, we had drinks with our neighbours in the local bars, we walked or cycled everywhere, and it was easy to get lifts. On more ambitious outings, we took the bus to Galway. I was given the use of a boat and started to fish on the ocean.

One night at the Pier Bar we were greeted with unusual excitement. Everybody was reading a Dublin newspaper. I was dismayed as soon as I saw the headline: "McGahern Takes Cottage in Connemara." The locals were pleased with the write-up because it praised the beauty of the place and mentioned some notables who were living close by.

"Are you afraid they're going to come looking for you?" Patrick O'Malley, who owned the post office and was also a postman and farmer, punched me playfully awake. He was humorous and very sharp and we were friends. Often in the evenings we worked the fishing boat together.

"No, it's not that bad, but it's bad enough," I told Patrick. "We came here without telling anybody—my sisters, father, nobody. The first time they'll know I'm back is from the newspaper."

"You're in a fix, then," Patrick grinned, understanding the situation perfectly.

"In a fix but we'll manage."

I wrote my sisters explaining why we had returned without telling anybody and invited them to visit. I wrote my father that I was back in the country and that we'd call on him. He knew my marriage had ended but would not have known of Madeline. I knew he'd meet the new situation censoriously, but did not care. I'd go through with the outward observances.

There was a young priest on Inishboffin with a beautiful singing voice. We had met at late-night sessions in the Renvyle Hotel. Patrick O'Malley and I had a small contract to supply the Renvyle whenever we had a surplus of fresh mackerel. No money ever changed hands, but we had a small account in the bar and restaurant. As I had become friendly with the priest, I asked him if he would drive us to Roscommon to visit my father for an hour or two. He was glad to drive us and had plenty of time. Father Gibbons generally dressed in casual clothes, but for this occasion I asked him to wear black and the Roman collar.

When he heard the car, my father came to the front door, which was open, but as we advanced up the avenue, he withdrew back into the darkness of the hallway. I saw him standing in the shadows as I walked to the door. I would have knocked had he not come forward. I introduced Madeline and the priest. As a counterweight to my father's silence within the house, Agnes started talking incessantly. I answered all her questions but was otherwise silent. She talked about my sisters and brother and their children and everything that was happening in their lives. She made tea. A plate of biscuits and freshly baked bread was passed around. My father sat immobile in his big chair. Over tea, he began to question the priest, and Father Gibbons answered all the questions openly and directly. Not since we arrived had he addressed a word to me or to Madeline. After tea, I must have wandered outside with the priest and Agnes, leaving Madeline in the house. My father had gone to the bathroom, and when he returned she became aware of him glaring at her. Here, she was a guest in his house, at a disadvantage, and he was glaring at her, not offering even a word of welcome. In her anger, she felt rooted to the chair. She would not give an inch. Perversely, he was charmed by the aggression his own aggression had created, and turned gallant. She responded coolly to his overtures, and this increased his interest. When we left, he walked us all the way out to the gate. This was a local custom of courtesy, but one which he seldom observed. "Madeline can call on us again any time she wants," he said. "This blackguard will call any time it suits him, but *you,* Father, better not come back unless they make you a bishop!"

I thanked Agnes, thanked him. "It's a poor day when a son has to thank his father," he said heartily.

"I thank everybody." Then we were gone.

We hired a car some time after that and visited both my uncles. Pat was still living alone in the house next to the garage. Maggie's shop was now a small supermarket, and the new secondary school had grown up all around the old railway buildings. Jimmy also lived alone in a cottage on a couple of good fields on the outskirts of the town. His gentle wife, Bridie Keegan, died a few years before Maggie. His three children were all in England. He had the pension now and felt too old and isolated on the mountain. He brought his bees with him into the town, and the hives stood in a white row at the head of one of his new fields. He also kept a small cow. While Pat's house was comfortable and ramshackle, the neatness and spareness of Jimmy's cottage was breathtaking: it too was like a perfectly run boat or small ship; nothing was there that didn't have some use. He was suspicious of Madeline at first, but slowly warmed to her, and I knew that would not change. He had kept the home place and drove with us into the mountains.

We walked up the narrow lane my mother loved. Weeds sprouted from the thatch on the house, but none of it had yet fallen. The coats of whitewash no longer shone, the arch of whitethorns still stood at the entrance to the rose garden, but the garden itself had gone riotously wild. The fields too looked like a wilderness. "It does not take long," Jimmy smiled ruefully at the appearance of the place. "Paddy [his son] can do anything he wants with it. I doubt if anybody will ever live here again. It's too backward and too poor." We stayed with Pat that night and he took us on a tour of the countryside around the town. Madeline liked the place and the people she met.

In Cleggan, that summer by the sea was hot and dry. The Army pitched tents above the strand for military exercises. We danced at a marquee that was erected in the middle of the village for a whole week. Patrick and I had pots and nets as well as lines. We caught lobsters and crayfish and plenty of crab, some salmon and sea trout as well as the usual pollock and mackerel, mullet and rock fish. Patrick sold the salmon but we kept the sea trout. Madeline seldom came when Patrick and I were fishing but often was with me when I was lifting or setting pots. We took visitors out in the boat, and a few times we went on our own to Inishbof-fin. This was hazardous except in calm weather. When the boat engine overheated, it stopped and all that could be done was to let it drift until the engine cooled.

Once I had done my own work for the day, I often went and helped Patrick on the bog. Patrick was intelligent and proud, quick and generous, but also extremely competitive. When he saw how quickly I was getting through the turf, he thought I was cheating. He could not have imagined the hours I had spent in Gloria, scattering, footing, windrowing, clamping all those lorry loads of turf my father sold to the "auld Rev." Even when we worked side by side, he was still suspicious for a time. During one of those evenings I told him we were thinking of buying land and settling in Ireland. Immediately he wanted us to settle here. With his quick curiosity, he knew everything that was stirring for miles around. Very soon he found a house and land for us close to the village, twenty acres, most of them along the ocean. The house by the side of the road, solid and slated, was no beauty. The plans had been read wrong. The back was to the road and the ocean, and the front faced inland. Patrick had been to the solicitor and learned that four thousand would buy the lot. We would not get a better buy. For some reason, the place could not be auctioned. Madeline did not like the house, and faced with Patrick's high enthusiasm and my obvious willingness to go along with it, grew troubled. Patrick was all for going into the solicitor there and then to conclude the deal. "The house is solid as a rock. You'd have to pay far more if it faced the road. They were always eejits. Done up, it'd look fine bit, but if you still didn't like it you could sell it to some fool of a tourist and build your own house. There are several sites. The land alone is worth far more than the price. There's bog attached as well," he laughed, knowing Madeline's dislike of work on the bog. He looked downcast when I told him we'd have to talk it over and tell him in the morning.

It turned out that Madeline hadn't anything against the house—she saw how easily it could be made habitable—and she loved the setting and the fields along the ocean, but she didn't want to live there. She thought the place would become too fashionable. She was more attracted to the countryside she had seen inland and where I had grown up. If she had liked it, I would have been happy to stay in Cleggan, and would have made my way. I was as drawn to the ocean as I was once drawn to the river and Oakport, but in most other ways her preference suited me better. The people and the language and landscape where I had grown up were like my breathing: it would take years to gain that knowledge in a new place.

When I told Patrick that we had decided against buying the house and fields, he was not surprised. "I could see it in her face," he said. He was already thinking of other places for us. I had not the heart to tell him that it was not the house but the place. He thought it the most desirable in the whole wide world. When he visited us some years afterwards in Leitrim, he could not wait to get back to the sea and where everything was happening.

We drove to Leitrim and looked at the many small farms for sale, until we found the low hill with small fields and tall thick hedges in behind the Ivy Leaf Ballroom. The stone cottage was restored and added to. We bought a few cows for the fields, and set out from there. To make a living from my work turned out to be easier than I had imagined, and we didn't have to disappear into England or America, other than by choice, and we were never away very long.

———————

This is the story of my upbringing, the people who brought me up, my parents and those around them, in their time and landscape. My own separate life, in so far as any life is separate, I detailed only to show how the journey out of that landscape became the return to those lanes and small fields and hedges and lakes under the Iron Mountains.

Jimmy died shortly before we came back, but Pat remained, and we saw him often. The people around us were spirited and independent and kind and full of a mocking fun. They helped us and we helped them. Though they went to Mass every Sunday and voted at elections, beyond these outward observances they had little regard for either Church or State. Though not as aggressively independent as Patsy Conboy, they approved of Patsy and gave him every help with his dancehall and swimming pool and motorcycle track. They were their own women and men, and they knew that if they could not wrest a living from the fields, neither Church nor State would come to their aid. "Is there much money in this writing business?" I was sometimes asked. "Not much but enough," I reassured them, and they nodded comprehendingly: it was like most trades.

Through the long powerful influence of the Church, the spoken language was full of religious imagery, sacred and profane—receiving took place at both the altar rail and in bed—and everybody had grounding from their compulsory schooling in Catholic dogma and doctrine. After Mass on Sunday, a parliament of men gathered in Bonesetter Woods to discuss the world. He was in the same tradition as my father's friend from Cloone, Donoghue, who had long since fled to America, but Mikey Woods set only the broken bones of horses and cattle: he had given up on the two-leggéds, as he couldn't stand the roars. "There's nothing more educated than an animal. They haven't to be told what to do," he'd declare. Mikey was the president of this parliament. Many of the men had worked in England. A speech demanded of everybody and was then discussed. Much of what went on was facetious, but there was a simple man, John Logan, who had a stammer and was full of religious scruples.

"I was going to the r-rails to r-receive, when I b-bumped into this f-fat woman and I g-got an almighty horn. Was it a s-sin, Mikey, to r-receive with a h-horn?"

"Did you receive?"

"I d-did, Mikey."

"Gentlemen, discuss," Mikey roared. "Was it a sin or was it a sign of health?"

Men and women were generally separated by the worlds of work. The women ran the houses and the children; the men worked the fields and went to markets and met one another in bars. On Saturday nights whole families, men and women and children, went to town to do a big shopping. There they split up as well, the women to do their shopping, the men to do their own. There was an air of great festivity and friendliness, of meetings and greeting all through the town. When the shopping was done, they would all meet up in bars, each locality to its own bar, and the news of the week was discussed. Once news ceased to be local, it was no longer of any interest. Eyes that a moment before were wild with curiosity would glaze as soon as the news crossed a certain boundary line.

In those first few years, we still had no car. We walked and cycled and took the bus to town, and these too were festive outings. Sometimes in the evenings and on Sundays Pat would drive out to the house. Occasionally he would ask, "Would you think of driving up to see that man in Roscommon? He's been complaining that ye haven't been up in a long time."

Sometimes we would go with him. Those visits were always tense, though my father continued to meet Madeline with excessive friendliness. I was watchful. I had seen for too long that he was interested in thought or discussion only as a means of domination and of wrong-footing the other person, and I was careful not to be drawn. When he could find no other purchase, sometimes he would try to attack me more openly. He would mention writers he had seen on television and praise them highly.

This both angered and amused me, angered by what I saw as his intent and amused because I knew he had never read the writers or knew anything about them.

"They seem to be doing much better than yourself."

"That wouldn't be hard."

"You don't mind being left behind, then?"

"I don't feel left behind. You do your own work and take what comes."

"You could be forgotten about."

"We'll all be forgotten, some sooner, some later. Anyhow success is not our aim."

"What is your aim?" he asked slowly, sensing he had the advantage, as if conducting a cross-examination in court.

By this time I had enough. "To write well, to write truly and well about fellows like yourself," I said.

"Now, Frank, you'll have to look out. You'll have to watch yourself." Pat, who couldn't read or write, started to shake with laughter.

"That wasn't fair, Sean. You should let those things go with your father," Agnes said when he had gone outside with Pat.

"It seemed like war to me, Agnes. Sometimes, unfortunately, you have no choice but to meet fire with fire."

Agnes usually talked agreeably if incessantly, often to Madeline about my sisters' families, as if talk itself could paper over all that was going on. Eventually, Madeline found the visits too tense, and usually stayed behind when I went with Pat.

Pat's amiableness and humour and his easygoing nature concealed wells of stubbornness. He and my father had a patter about engines and business that had been honed over years. Even on this ground my father could not refrain from attacking Pat from time to time. When it happened, an implacable wall went up. Pat would give not an inch. Then my father would march outside in a rage and complain about my uncle's thickness and the McManus stubbornness which all his unfortunate children had inherited and which he had been forced to know and to suffer all his life.

For years he had been threatening to leave Agnes and to live with his daughters, and she was eventually forced to call this bluff. Once she did, she established her place and dominance within the house with a ruthless efficiency. Once this was done, she allowed him to undermine and demean her at every turn within her dominance, and was even fiercer than ever in his defence and protection. What she could not have known was that he was planning to disinherit her. An Act of Parliament had been brought in to prevent men like him from disinheriting their wives:

Dear Sean

Many things delayed my answering your letter.

Too bad you saw fit to introduce a discordant and controversial note into an otherwise excellent letter. I have no wish to enter a controversy.

When I bought here I knew & was told it was property and entailed having responsibilities. I did not wish to sadden you. I made a will. All my responsibilities will in 1964 reach full age. Since last year—an Act of Parliament made my will useless and on my death all my property goes to one person [Agnes]. Reasonable provisions are already in existence for that person by

*pension. Furthermore, I would much prefer spending my
days left to me far removed from certain people as I
suspect them rather expensive . . .*

If he had had his way, he would have left Agnes without a house of her own in old age. When he got short shrift from me and was told Agnes should get everything, he approached my brother with more success, saying he wanted to pass on the name McGahern with the inheritance. He made me the executor of this will, and it was to cause much trouble after his death.

On one of my visits with Pat he began to complain how little I visited the house and that Madeline didn't come any more. "I have come many times. Isn't it about time you and Agnes visited us?" "We hardly move out any more." "Well, you visit Pat here often enough, and he is only a few miles away. Madeline would be very glad to see you and Agnes."

They came in their small car by way of the narrow bridge into Cootehall—where he had blown his horn at Pat Moore for stopping to chat, with his bicycle turned the wrong way—and by way of Leitrim village to Keshcarrigan, the same route I took with the jennet and the white bullock on the second part of the journey to Cootehall, when the last ties with the Aughawillan farm were severed. At Keshcarrigan, they entered the lanes between the high banks and tall whitethorns and poor rushy hills that led to the house on another low hill between the two lakes.

Agnes drove. My father was recovering from a slight stroke, which he had handled admirably, regaining nearly all his movements, and he had taught himself to write again. It almost seemed to be a relief to have at last a real disability after all his imaginary illnesses.

They left the car out at the road and walked all the way in around the lake and up to the house. Everybody else drove to the house, but they obviously felt that the lane was too poor and rutted. The day was an unseasonal day in summer, dark and wet, with a driving bitter wind. Waves were beating against the lake wall and spattering the lane with blobs of foam. Above them leaned the tall hedge of sally, ash, oak, rowan, wild cherry, alder, hawthorn, heavy with rain. My father brought Madeline a half-bottle of Powers, and he presented it with great charm.

"It's very good for colds with sugar and hot water, a slice of lemon and a sprinkling of cloves," he said.

She thanked them both and made them welcome. I was all the more careful because now I was the host. Agnes was on edge, and I tried without any success to put her at ease: it was as if the visit had been accomplished as soon as she set foot in the house, and her single thought was to leave at the first possible opportunity. My father, in contrast, was relaxed in the white rocking chair, and took obvious pleasure in prolonging the visit. Most of the time he talked to Madeline. Tea was made and passed around with a plate of buttered bread and cake and biscuits.

"We better be going, Daddy. We won't find night coming on," Agnes said a number of times, until eventually he rose, fixing her with a sharp look.

We got coats and walked them all the way out to the car. The image of Agnes walking ahead with Madeline was more like the image of an escaping bird than a terrier. I kept pace behind with my father's slow, halting walk. The wind and rain showed no sign of slackening. Occasionally, we were spattered by the waves breaking against the wall.

"What do you think of the place?" I made the mistake of asking. I should have known not to ask through long experience, and it was as if some atavistic, perverse craving for his approval triumphed over all my knowledge.

"It'd do for an old pair like Agnes and myself who just need to get our heads in," he said dismissively, meaning it was no place for a couple in the middle of their lives.

Agnes had the car turned for home by the time we reached the road, the engine running, talking animatedly to Madeline through the rolled-down window. When he shouted at her for wasting petrol, she turned the engine off. He delayed a long time saying goodbye to Madeline, and when he got into the car, Agnes had difficulty restarting the engine. Eventually, she got it going, and drove inexpertly away.

His trouble with all things mechanical followed him on this visit. Close to Keshcarrigan the engine stopped. I can hear too well, "O God, O God, O God, woman, can you tell me this, is there anything you can ever do right?" He lifted up the bonnet and spent a long time working at the engine. He got her to use the starter a number of times, but each time the engine was dead. By now, the rain was very heavy, and he sat back into the car in a rage.

As good or bad luck would have it, a cousin of ours came along on a tractor. Liam Kelly was a student in Maynooth at the time, and was working on his father's farm during the long summer holidays. He was a grandson of the house in which my father's Crombie overcoat was stolen from the porch when he was courting my mother. The family had been given a larger farm close to Keshcarrigan by the Land Commission in return for their Aughawillan farm, which was then split up among their poorer neighbours. Liam Kelly would have stopped for anybody in trouble, and he thought he recognized my father.

"Is there anything I can do to help?"

"Ring Pat McManus in Ballinamore for him to come out or for him to send Billy Keegan out," my father demanded angrily.

"I'll have a look at it first." Liam was used to working with tractors and machinery on his father's farm.

"I have looked at it and it won't go. There's no use looking."

"I'll have a quick look," Liam said.

"I have told you once that I have looked at it and it won't go. How many times do I have to tell you? Ring Pat McManus."

Despite my father's opposition, he lifted up the bonnet and started to examine the engine. The distributor cap had been removed and not replaced properly. Having put it back in place, he asked Agnes to try the starter.

"I have told you time in time out that it won't go. Go in the name of God and ring Pat McManus," my father roared, having by this time left the car and joined Liam over the engine.

As the engine was turning, Liam saw the simple fault: the choke connection had jammed. He released the choke, made a few minor adjustments and asked Agnes to try the starter again. The engine started up almost immediately. My father's reaction was to pound the bonnet with his fists. Liam felt that if he had been behind the wheel he would have driven the car at him. When he exhausted his rage, my father sat back into the car, banged the door without a word, and glared out like a violent, unappeasable child. Agnes thanked Liam profusely before they drove away. My father never spoke.

Within a circle of ten miles from the house were all the places we had known in Leitrim—Ballinamore, the bungalow beside the forge on the outskirts of the town, Lisacarn and the lane to Lisacarn, Beaghmore, the stark house above the bog at Cloone, Aughawillan and the Aughawillan farm. Outside the circle, in the direction of Swanlinbar and the North, lived Katie McManus, our maid and our last human link with the Aughawillan farm. Her husband was a customer of Pat's garage, and he told Pat that Katie would like to see me again. About ten years earlier, when I was still teaching in Dublin, my father wrote me:

I went to see Katie McManus. I thought they had gone to the USA. The son won a scholarship £84 & is in St. Patrick's. He does his Leaving this year. She is worried about him. Do you remember her? The school isn't, never was, much good. She is now a little wizened white-haired woman. She has two girls & a boy as well from

8 or 9 to 16 years. The husband is a road ganger & they have a nice cottage if not too much worldly goods. I did not see her since the boy was a baby 20 years or more.

My father never willingly let go of any relationship, no matter how bad it was. In this he was aided by the gentle country manners that were loath to turn anybody away. Of all my mother's people, only Jimmy would have nothing whatsoever to do with my father, and even he was polite when they met by accident.

I knew his dislike of Katie, and there were enough obvious distortions in the letter to make me suspicious of its objectivity. Katie's son had to be very bright to win a county scholarship. St. Patrick's was the diocesan seminary in Cavan, an old and established school. When my father attended the Latin school in Moyne, the sons of prosperous families, the future diocesan priests, lawyers, doctors, teachers, merchants, were all going through St. Patrick's. The seminarians Moyne produced were set for America and Africa. This might have rankled. And my father loved to see people worried: it opened the way for his advice.

I went to see her one Sunday afternoon, bringing chocolates and whiskey. The house was in a long lane, whitewashed and traditional, with fowl and fruit trees and flowers and a vegetable garden. New rooms had been added to the house, the roof slated. The house was on a small farm very like our own. The animal houses and sheds stood a little way to the side and were similarly whitewashed and kept. They scolded me for bringing the chocolates and whiskey, and that too was traditional. Katie's husband was over six feet, slow and sure of movement, remarkably handsome and strong; he belonged to that generation of men who had no consciousness of their good looks other than as a form of strength.

If Katie hadn't the swing of girls like Bridgie McGovern, she had whatever it took to attract good-looking men. Katie was small and white haired but fresh and pleasant-looking. There were wrinkles, but they came from the anxieties of love and laughter. Only the younger son was present. He and the father ran cattle together, had bought extra land, and were renting outlying farms. There were photos of the parents attending graduation ceremonies, as well as wedding photos on the white walls.

The scholarship boy had gone on to university and was working in one of the professions—engineering or law—in Dublin. The older girl was a teacher. The youngest was still at college. Katie had three grandchildren. The husband insisted I drink a glass of whiskey with him. The son did not drink. Then we had tea and sandwiches.

"Your father paid us a surprise call a good few years back," Katie said.

"I know. He told me. Did you find him changed at all?"

"Older. Slower," Katie said. "I don't think people like the sergeant change. He was still a fine-looking man."

Neither of us was prepared to press the conversation. Katie was anxious to know what had happened to my brother and sisters.

"Jude eventually became Frank, like his father."

"Thank God. What a name to give a child."

"He was wild enough to begin with, fought with my father, and cleared out to England. He was wild there too for a while, but married young, went back to school, qualified as a cost accountant, entered management. Now a chauffeured car takes him to and from work. He and his wife live in a large house on the edge of a forest, and they have four children."

"Whoever would have thought it when he was lying in the cot," Katie said.

Katie's husband seemed to be as interested in these histories as she was, but their son rose and excused himself.

"The twins still nurse in Whipps Cross where they were trained. Breedge is a ward sister and is married to a Cork man. They have two daughters. Rosaleen is married to a man from

Donegal. They have three daughters. She is a theatre superintendent and works nights. The twins never separated. They live in a big old house with their two husbands and their five daughters, close to the hospital."

"People said you couldn't tell them apart but I could never see that. I thought they looked very different," Katie said.

"It wouldn't do if the husbands made that mistake," I said.

"It could be awkward," Katie's husband laughed.

"Margaret never married but has a good position in the Health Board in Dublin. Monica was in the Civil Service, married a teacher, and lives with their children in Drogheda."

"And wee Dympna?" Katie asked.

"Went into the Civil Service. She's tall and like my father in appearance. She never wanted to go into the Civil Service in the first place, and eventually left for England where she got into university. She teaches in London and lives close to the twins and isn't long married."

She did not seem surprised when I told her that I had been married and divorced and had remarried. "I was certain you'd become a priest. If I'd have sworn anything I'd have sworn that," Katie said.

"The pull of life was too great," I said. "I always wanted to go on the river."

"I wonder sometimes if there's all that much to it," Katie said.

"It goes by," we all agreed.

Before I left she spoke with great affection of my mother and how she never met anybody who gave so little thought to herself and so much to other people, and the conversation turned back to the frail house in the middle of the field in Aughawillan.

"There's not a stone left standing of that house now," her husband said. "Sometimes I do the roads over that way. You'd never think it was ever anything but a field."

When word of my father's death reached me, the intensity of the conflicting emotions—grief, loss, relief—took me unawares. I believe the reaction was as much for those years in which his life and mine were entangled in a relationship neither of us wanted as for the man who had just met the death each of us face. He made many demands but gave little and always had to dominate. A life from which the past was so rigorously shut out had to be a life of darkness. Though I have more knowledge and experience of him than I have of any other person, I cannot say I have fully understood him, and leave him now with God, or whatever truth or illusion or longing for meaning or comfort that word may represent.

It was to this same recourse my mother turned whenever he tried to force her beyond the human limits she was not willing to go: *God direct us. He knows all. He can do all. In Him I trust. And the children. What shall I say? I can only ask God to make them better children and give me His help to bring them up in His fear and love. So I must pray hard and that is all I can do while here. It is not fair though to blame them for my illness. I only did for them what any other mother would do, and I was happier doing so, never the less I must try and mend my ways and theirs, God helping us all.*

She never really left us. In the worst years, I believe we would have been broken but for the different life we had known with her and the love she gave that was there like hidden strength.

It must have been a long and alien journey from those three rooms on the mountain through the years she spent with the nuns and the girls from rich families in the Marist Convent and in the training schools of Trinity College. Along the way she lost an earthiness that both her sisters and brothers had in abundance, but she never lost their sense of humour. What replaced that solid earthiness was a deepening trust in God. Through the violent history of Catholicism run the two dividing movements: the fortress churches with their edicts, threats and punishments; and the churches of the spires and brilliant windows that go towards love and light: *God has given me near perfect health for forty years and now that He has taken that health away it is for some inscrutable reason of His own to try and test my faith. In Him and by Him and for Him I live and place my trust and to Him alone I pray, knowing He will bring me safely along.*

Without the promise that one day I'd say Mass for her I doubt if I would have been able to resist my father when he wanted to take me out of school. I did, in the end, answer to a different call than the one she wished for me, and followed it the whole of my life. When I reflect on those rare moments when I stumble without warning into that extraordinary sense of security, that deep peace, I know that consciously and unconsciously she has been with me all my life.

If we could walk together through those summer lanes, with their banks of wild flowers that "cast a spell," we probably would not be able to speak, though I would want to tell her all the local news.

We would leave the lanes and I would take her by the beaten path the otter takes under the thick hedges between the lakes. At the lake's edge I would show her the green lawns speckled with fish bones and blue crayfish shells where the otter feeds and trains her young. The otter whistles down the waters for the male when she wants to mate and chases him back again to his own waters when his work is done; unlike the dear swans that paddle side by side and take turns on their high nest deep within the reeds. Above the lake we would follow the enormous sky until it reaches the low mountains where her life began.

I would want no shadow to fall on her joy and deep trust in God. She would face no false reproaches. As we retraced our steps, I would pick for her the wild orchid and the windflower.

ALSO BY JOHN MCGAHERN

THE COLLECTED STORIES

These thirty-four funny, tragic, tender, and acerbic stories represent the complete short fiction of the finest writer since Joyce and Beckett. With fierce honesty and plainspoken lyricism, McGahern circumnavigates a world that seems to have stopped on Easter 1916. In this world, sons strive to gain the blessings of unyielding fathers, youngsters grapple with the mysteries of sex, and grown men and women are reduced to children as they try and fail to possess—or even understand—one another. *The Collected Stories* are as beautiful as the Irish landscape and as heartbreaking as Ireland's history.

Fiction/Literature/978-0-679-74401-6

BY THE LAKE

With this magnificently assured novel, John McGahern guides us into a village in rural Ireland and deftly, compassionately traces its natural rhythms and the inner lives of its people. Here are the Ruttledges, who have forsaken the glitter of London to raise sheep and cattle; gentle Jamesie Murphy, whose appetite for gossip both charms and intimidates his neighbors; handsome John Quinn, perennially on the lookout for a new wife; and the town's richest man, a gruff, self-made magnate known as the Shah. Following his characters through the course of a year, he lays bare their passions and regrets, their uneasy relationship with the modern world, and their ancient intimacy with death.

Fiction/Literature/978-0-679-74402-3

Printed in the United States
by Baker & Taylor Publisher Services